P9-EEN-578

INTERNATIONAL THEMES AND ISSUES

VOLUME 3

SHAPING THE NEW WORLD

INTERNATIONAL THEMES AND ISSUES
A joint series of the Canadian Historical Association
and the University of Toronto Press

SERIES EDITOR | Beverly Lemire

Canadian
Historical Association

Société historique
du Canada

UNIVERSITY OF TORONTO PRESS

INTERNATIONAL THEMES AND ISSUES

A joint series of the Canadian Historical Association
and the University of Toronto Press

SERIES EDITOR | Beverly Lemire

SHAPING THE NEW WORLD

African Slavery in the Americas, 1500–1888

ERIC NELLIS

UNIVERSITY OF TORONTO PRESS

Copyright © University of Toronto Press Incorporated 2013
Higher Education Division

www.utppublishing.com

Library and Archives Canada Cataloguing in Publication

Nellis, Eric Guest, 1938–
    Shaping the New World : African slavery in the Americas, 1500–1888 / Eric Nellis.

(International themes and issues ; v. 3)
Includes bibliographical references and index. Issued in print and electronic formats.
ISBN 978-1-4426-0555-8 (pbk.).—ISBN 978-1-4426-0764-4 (bound).—ISBN 978-1-4426-0556-5 (pdf).—ISBN 978-1-4426-0557-2 (epub)

    1. Slavery—Brazil—History.   2. Slavery—Caribbean Area—History.
3. Slavery—Latin America—History.   4. Slavery—United States—History.
5. Slaves—America—Social conditions.   6. Slave trade—Africa—History.
7. Antislavery movements—America—History.   I. Canadian Historical Association
II. Title.   III. Series: International themes and issues (Toronto, Ont.); v. 3

HT871.N45 2013   306.3'62097   C2013-903280-0   C2013-903281-9

We welcome comments and suggestions regarding any aspect of our publications—please feel free to contact us at news@utphighereducation.com or visit our Internet site at www.utppublishing.com.

North America
5201 Dufferin Street
North York, Ontario, Canada, M3H 5T8

2250 Military Road
Tonawanda, New York, USA, 14150

ORDERS PHONE: 1-800-565-9523
ORDERS FAX: 1-800-221-9985
ORDERS E-MAIL: utpbooks@utpress.utoronto.ca

UK, Ireland, and continental Europe
NBN International
Estover Road, Plymouth, PL6 7PY, UK
ORDERS PHONE: 44 (0) 1752 202301
ORDERS FAX: 44 (0) 1752 202333
ORDERS E-MAIL: enquiries@nbninternational.com

This book is printed on paper containing 100% post-consumer fibre.

The University of Toronto Press acknowledges the financial support for its publishing activities of the Government of Canada through the Canada Book Fund.

Printed in Canada

Contents

Maps and Tables

Acknowledgements

The author is in debt to the generations of scholars and political and civil rights activists who have illuminated the role of African slavery in the histories of the post-Columbian Americas to where it is now understood as fundamental to the shaping of modern American societies.

The approach taken in this book was in part shaped by a course in comparative slavery in the Americas that I taught for many years at the University of British Columbia. I thank the many students who took part in History 444 for their influence on the way the subject can be taught. I am grateful for the contribution of Professor Beverly Lemire of the University of Alberta who helped refine the original manuscript and speed its completion.

I thank Dr. Tatiana van Riemsdijk of the UBC History Department for her conversations and advice on the use of sources for slave women, Eric Leinberger for the maps, Betsy Struthers for her excellent copyediting, and Natalie Fingerhut and the editorial staff at UTP and the anonymous readers of the first draft for their encouragement and expertise.

My greatest thanks are to my wife Vicky McAulay who read the first draft. Her editorial talents greatly influenced the final composition.

Preface

Between 1500 and the middle of the nineteenth century, some 12.5 million slaves were sent as bonded labour from Africa to the European settlements in the Americas. This book is intended as a brief introduction to the origins, growth, and consolidation of African slavery in the Americas. It chronicles race-based slavery's impact on the economic, social, and cultural development of the societies in which it thrived and helped shape. While the book looks at the African slave as a tool for European ambition and a key participant in the formation of new American societies, it also expressly acknowledges the slave as a person and describes the pain, demoralization, and inevitable sadness of the slaves' experiences. More importantly, it stresses the slaves' humanity and self-worth, the tenacity of slave family values, and the formation of original social and cultural values.

Slavery differed from one European colonial enterprise to another, and a comparative theme shapes the organization of the book. For example, the differences between the United States, Jamaica, or Brazil are apparent and numerous, yet all three societies bear the imprint of African slavery. All jurisdictions specified the legal status of slaves as permanent property and narrowed the definition to Africans, people of African descent and occasionally native Americans. Any comparisons across a three-and-a-half-century span illustrate the range and complexity of slavery in a variety of settings. African slavery in the New World created bondage on a scale unknown since the Roman Empire. The European remaking of the Americas—from the near destruction of its indigenous peoples to its reconstitution by colonization, repopulation, and biological intrusion (flora and fauna)—took its ultimate shape in tandem with slavery.

The book's chapter outline and contents are organized by chronology, location, and theme. Chapter One offers an overview of the subject with a discussion of how race-based slavery differed from other forms of European servitude and how its definition in racial terms separates it from older as well as other contemporary legalized or customary slave systems. Chapter Two traces the scale and conditions of the slave trade. The traffic in human cargoes was a vital, integral, and disturbing part of this history and to early abolitionists was the most viscerally troubling aspect of the enterprise. In each of Chapters Three, Four, and Five, the theme of depopulation and repopulation sustains the narrative with reminders of the devastation of native populations. These chapters establish the comparative theme of the text: how slavery was established and functioned in Latin America (with an emphasis on Brazil), in the Caribbean, and in North America and how in each case its functions and effects differed. Chapter Three reviews the way Latin American slavery took root and flourished, drawing its models from practices underway in the Azores and other Atlantic islands before Columbus set sail. From the earliest Portuguese settlement, slavery defined Brazil's economic, political, and social development. In the Spanish American Empire, African slavery was limited to specific regions, in particular in the mines and cities of South America and Mexico and the sugar islands of the Greater Antilles of the Caribbean. Chapter Four discusses the way sugar and slavery transformed the Lesser Antilles of the Caribbean after the advent of French, British, and Dutch colonization and created the most remarkable density of African peoples in the Americas. Chapter Five deals with the coming of African slavery to the British North American mainland and how in the seventeenth and eighteenth centuries it laid down the lines for sectional divisions, the later southern slave and northern non-slave states of the United States. Chapter Six deals with the experiences and humanity of slave women, children, and families in the various slave societies, and with all slaves as subjects, that is as persons, rather than simply as objects in the larger view of the system. Chapter Seven examines abolitionist movements and the spread of the opposition to slavery that began in earnest in the late eighteenth century. The creation of the black republic of revolutionary Haiti and its unique place in an era of political revolutions is discussed. Finally, the persistence of slavery in the United States to 1865 and in Brazil and Cuba to the eve of the twentieth century underscores the durability of slavery and the difficulty of erasing centuries-old institutions and the racial attitudes that went with those institutions.

A Note on Usage

America, American, Americas. The use of "American" as an identifier or adjective along with "America" as a place has been appropriated by the United States of America so that a citizen of the United States is referred to as an American both at home and by the international community, while a citizen of Mexico is referred to as a Mexican. The usage took hold in the era of the American Revolution and was adopted in formal and everyday use from the Declaration of Independence to the Constitution of 1787. The term Latin America was coined by the French in the nineteenth century to refer to all Latin-based language societies in the Americas, a definition that would apply to Quebec. Latin America is used in the following chapters to collectively identify the former Portuguese and Spanish Empires, even as those republics drew their names from their colonial designation, as Brazil or Peru for example, or were renamed for native precedent, as Mexico for New Spain for example, or for revolutionary or historical figures such as Bolivia for Simon Bolivar or Colombia for Columbus.

Much of the material in this text deals with Europe's colonies in the Americas (the collective term for the Western Hemisphere) as well as the early histories of the independent nations that emerged in the late eighteenth and early nineteenth century. Thus, for the period before 1787, what became the United States will be identified as the British North American mainland colonies or simply North America. When the term "America" or "American" is used, it will be made clear from the context if it refers to the United States, as in the "American South" or to the continent as a whole as does the term "Americas."

Black and Coloured. These difficult terms remain in use. They will be used throughout this text much as they appeared in contemporary records. "Black" is usually synonymous with what was a more commonly used term, "negro," which is the root word for black in various languages, and in most cases refers to pure African or Creole ancestry. In the British North American colonies and the United States, however, "black" and "coloured" were often used interchangeably. There, "black" gave way to "negro" and "coloured" in the nineteenth and first part of the twentieth century, and then "black" was recovered as an assertive usage by African Americans in the 1960s. In all of the Americas "mulatto" (white and black mix) was used more often to identify appearance rather than status. An important difference exists between North American and Spanish and Portuguese usages. In the former, the practice began early of identifying any person with African ancestry as "black" or "coloured," the so-called doctrine of the single drop (that is, of African blood). In Spanish and Portuguese America, an extended range of racial categories resulted from high rates of racial mixing ("miscegenation") and the way large numbers of manumitted (freed) slaves mingled and produced a population that can be identified as "free coloured" or "mixed coloured" or "persons of colour." In Latin America, those terms were used often to distinguish the person from "black" and had implications for social status. The Portuguese, in particular, were especially creative in designating specific racial identities by a spectrum of colour.

Slave. Except where the term is qualified by "native" (that is "Indian") it is always applied to the only other people who fit the category—Africans or their progeny. The association with *race* is explained in Chapter One. Where the terms "slave" and "servant" are found to be interchangeable in the record, the text will specify the difference in status.

Britain, England, United States. The text will use "England" and "English" as they applied to the period up to the Union of the English and Scottish Crowns in 1707 when the formal usage became "Britain" (or "Great Britain") and "British." Most British colonies began as English colonies but it is acceptable to use British in a retroactive sense. There is no United States until the term appears formally in 1776 (the Declaration of Independence) and officially in 1787 (the Constitution). Until the 1770s, the colonies were British and cited as "British North America." When it appears, the use of "North America" refers broadly to colonial and post-colonial (the United States) periods.

Measurements. Where possible, the great variety of units of measurement that show up in the records and secondary sources for temperatures, weights, space, volume, distance, mass, and currencies will be explained. The range of usages in a variety of languages and systems from the sixteenth to the nineteenth centuries is vast and can be meaningless unless explained. For example, "arrobes" is a Portuguese weight measure used in the sugar economy, and "leagues" refer to distance in a number of vernacular usages. Obscure, archaic, or redundant terms will be avoided unless quoted from original sources when they will be explained and converted. For measurements that are still in use, the text will quote the measure cited in the source. For example, there are 2.2 pounds to the kilogram. One imperial ton (the long ton) is roughly equivalent to a metric ton (tonne), 1,000 kilograms or 2,240 pounds. An acre is .405 of a hectare; there are 1.61 kilometres to the mile; one imperial gallon of liquid equals 4.546 litres, and one current United States gallon equals 3.78 litres.

Language. Non-English usages will be retained for the sake of distinguishing particular Spanish, Portuguese, or French terms where English equivalents are not obvious. An example of where the text will use non-English terms for multiple usages is a word like the French *Creole* that becomes *criolo/a* (male/female) in Spanish and *crioulo/a* in Portuguese and might refer to someone of Caucasian European or pure African stock born in the Americas. There is no single word in English that describes the Portuguese *engenho* (engine), which combined an agricultural sugar plantation with a sugar refinery. The Portuguese term will be explained and used throughout the text.

Chronology

Curacao settled by the Dutch in 1636.

Other island colonies are established in this period.

Africans arrive in the Lesser Antilles in increasing numbers.

Legal codes defining Africans and their descendants as property are applied in all the islands and in England's mainland North American colonies.

1650s   The first slave codes to separate African slavery from white servitude are written in Virginia and Maryland. These would be the models for the codes that followed in other English American jurisdictions.

The Dutch are driven out of Brazil after decades of control of Pernambuco.

1685   The French Crown writes the *Code Noir*, the most comprehensive body of slavery laws written as a national code by any imperial nation.

1690s   Gold discovered in Minas Gerais, expanding the reach of African slavery in Brazil.

1694   Destruction of the Palmares *quilombo* in Pernambuco (this was the largest community of free and escaped slaves in Brazil).

1700   The number of African slaves landed in the Americas since 1500 passes the 2 million mark. It will reach 10 million by 1850.

1707   Union of the Scottish and English Parliaments, creating Great Britain.

1713   The *Asiento* (the Spanish contract to transport slaves) is won by English interests.

1739   Stono Rebellion in South Carolina.

1741   Slave uprising in New York City.

1754   John Woolman, Pennsylvania Quaker and abolitionist, publishes *Some Considerations on Keeping Negroes*.

1767   French sugar exports from the Caribbean exceed British exports.

1776   Declaration of Independence announces "all men are created equal," but slavery is retained by the independent United States.

1787   Slavery is confirmed as a legal right in the Constitution of the United States.

	Society for Effecting the Abolition of the Slave Trade is founded in Britain.
1788	*Société des Amis des Noirs* is founded in France.
1789	French Revolution.
1791–1804	The slave revolt on Saint Domingue results in the Republic of Haiti.
1807	British Parliament bans the slave trade.
1808	The United States bans the importation of slaves but retains slavery.
1810–30	Independent movements in mainland Spanish America lead to abolition.
1822	Brazil's independence; slavery is retained.
1831	Nat Turner Rebellion in Virginia.
	Slave revolt in Jamaica.
1834	Slavery is ended in the British Empire; compensation is paid to slaveholders.
1835	*Male* revolt in Salvador da Bahia.
1836	Slavery banned in continental France.
1846–48	Slavery abolished in Swedish and Danish colonies.
1848	Slavery abolished in French Caribbean.
1850	British pressure curbs the slave trade to Cuba and Brazil.
1861–65	American Civil War; slavery ended in the United States in 1865 with the Thirteenth Amendment to the Constitution.
1863	Slavery abolished in Dutch colonies.
1870	Moret Law ("law of free birth") passed for the Spanish Caribbean; all children born from that date are born free.
1871	Rio Branco Law ("law of the free womb") passed in Brazil; it is similar to the Spanish Moret Law.
1886	Slavery banned in Cuba and the rest of the Spanish Caribbean.
1888	Slavery banned in Brazil without compensation for owners.

1 The Setting for New World Slavery: An Overview

"The traditions of both slavery and race are part and parcel of the evolution of Western culture. Nevertheless, the narrow correlation of slavery and race is a peculiarly American [New World] innovation."
        —Franklin W. Knight, *Slavery, Race, and Social Structure* (1974)[1]

Between the sixteenth and nineteenth centuries, the peoples of Africa, America, and Europe were linked to form new societies in what historian Robin Blackburn calls the "American crucible."[2] During that time, while native American populations were displaced, assimilated, or exterminated, millions of European and African peoples crossed the Atlantic, the majority of the latter without consent as African slaves.[3] Not until the middle of the nineteenth century did white European numbers dominate the Atlantic crossing. By then, Africans had made an indelible contribution to the epic reshaping of the Americas. The scale of the slave trade is striking: between 1500 and 1870, of 12.5 million Africans loaded on ships as slaves for the Americas, 10.7 million were landed there, some 85 per cent of them in Brazil and the Caribbean.[4] When slavery was at its most pervasive in the Americas, there were majorities of peoples of African descent on most Caribbean islands, in Brazil's northeast, and in parts of the southern United States. Slavery not only influenced the history of post-Columbus America but did so in different ways in the various settings where it took hold. What makes the history of African slavery in Brazil distinct from British, French, Dutch, and even Spanish slavery starts with timing, geography, and the outlook and purposes of the colonizers. African slavery's legacy includes mixed racial cultures in Latin America and the Afro-Caribbean and the

1

sharp black-white divisions in the United States, where any African ancestry defines one as African American, the so-called single drop principle.[5]

Slavery's uneven distribution led to "slave societies," such as those in Virginia, Cuba, Jamaica, and Bahia in Brazil. These differed from "slave-holding societies"—for example, in New England, the highlands of Mexico, Argentina, the Andes, the Amazon and Quebec, or for that matter above 40 degrees north latitude or below 40 degrees south latitude—where slavery had limited or little application because of climate, geography, and settlement objectives. To make the distinction clearer, what we understand as slave societies were those that were sustained and defined by African slavery. In slaveholding societies, the numbers of slaves were too small and their functions were incidental and not vital in the shaping of the society. Moreover, it must be emphasized that Europeans did not fix their own people as property. Slavery in the Americas was racially determined and settled exclusively on Africans or peoples of African descent, legally bound as property for life as chattels. The exception to this was the enslavement of natives, another matter of racial determinism, but a practice that was in decline early in the colonial period and was never as aggressively applied as was the case with Africans. In fact, the Spanish and Portuguese retreated from their early hopes of using extensive native labour for their plantations. Natives in the lowland tropical zones were either decimated by European diseases or were difficult to control or indoctrinate in the rigours of repetitive, disciplined agricultural work. Their numbers in some areas were simply too sparse.

African slaves underwrote the economic and political elites who emerged in Brazil, the southern British North American mainland colonies (the United States after the American Revolution), the Caribbean, and the mining zones of Spanish Peru, Brazil's Minas Gerais, and elsewhere. The first permanent settlements in Brazil depended on investments in sugar, and African slaves appeared as early as the 1550s, a dependency that grew to where an eighteenth-century Jesuit priest, appealing for a more humane treatment of slaves, could announce succinctly: "The slaves are the hands and feet of the sugar-mill owner [*senhor de engenho*] because without them it is not possible in Brazil to set up, maintain, and develop a plantation, nor to have a functioning mill."[6] A significant corollary to New World slave societies resulted in economic development in places physically distant from the farms, mines, and plantations of the Americas. Investment from non-slave-holding New England merchants in the sugar and rum trade made Boston a major North American financial, shipbuilding, and trade hub. Glasgow tobacco factors, Dutch bankers, and the congeries of shippers, processors, and intermediaries in Western Europe in the commodity markets and slave transportation business fed on the profits that flowed from the labour of African slaves. Slavery in the Americas coincided with the global revolution in finance, investment, and consumerism. It dovetailed with the Industrial Revolution, moving from the age of sail and water-driven mills to steam power, railroads, and the telegraph.[7] Slavery shaped the Americas' particular versions of "class," not only as it separated rich from poor whites, and all whites from slaves, but as it graded the latter increasingly in "castes" delineated in the gradations of colour from dark to light in the mixed racial populations of Latin America. Meanwhile, Western Europe became a cocoon for whites and whiteness, remaining largely aloof from racial diversification until the latter part of the twentieth century when it became a target for increased non-white immigration from its former colonies.

The Portuguese had access to slaves from the West African coast as early as the middle of the fifteenth century. They found existing slave trading patterns and met enthusiastic intermediaries. In the century before they went to America, they were using African slaves at home and in the Atlantic islands of the Azores, Madeira, and Cape Verde as were the Spanish in the Canaries. Moreover, in a balanced and delicate double standard, the Iberians (Spanish and Portuguese) with a long experience of slaveholding, acknowledged that Africans could be converted to Christianity, have Christian souls, and still become property and that while Christianity might lead to manumission (freedom) for some, this required the grace of the owner. On the other hand, the British and the Dutch who had no tradition of domestic slaveholding were for a long time hesitant to grant Christian status to slaves. Along with the French, they were unencumbered by the legal and customary restraints on Iberians and, as we shall see, were relatively free to devise their own codes in the colonies.

As for the slave trade, it did not matter if Africans were bound for North or South America or the Caribbean, they endured a frightening process as war captives or victims of calculated kidnap, a transit to ship, and then a long voyage to America. The shock, terror, and despair, along with the sickness and the ever-present dead and dying in transit that went with months of a squalid ordeal, were compounded by fears of what might await them in an unknown destination. For American-born slaves, the loss of a past beyond their birthright as chattels led to what sociologists have called "natal alienation." In a telling phrase, the sociologist Orlando Patterson refers to slavery as "social death," a teasing judgement that needs to be treated with caution, given the ways African and African American slaves dealt creatively with their demeaned status and roles.[8] Slaves were certainly victims, the ultimate "oppressed people," but recent studies of slave behaviour and gender and family issues by historians, ethnographers, and other social scientists have begun to depict them living in a vibrant world of survival and self-awareness, resisting and tempering the deeper effects of slavery. Still, even as historians write of slaves forging positive identities, slavery was maintained by physical force and laws enforced by the state. Slaves resisted and ran away in significant numbers in Brazil and the Caribbean or manipulated the system to suit their needs in North America where, it should be stressed, the opportunities for escaping or living in independent communities were much diminished. They plotted running away and/or murdering owners in a consistent pattern that stretched to the end of slavery. There are examples of hard resistance and well-organized uprisings from as early as 1531 in Spanish Panama, in Portuguese Sao Tome, off the African coast in 1536, and in the new slave plantations in the English and French Caribbean in the seventeenth century. But consistent resistance and defiance did not retard slavery's growth even if it inspired abolitionists who began to exert some influence after nearly three centuries of expansion.[9] When slavery faltered in the nineteenth century under political and abolitionist attack, its imprint on the Americas was already confirmed.

The sheer persistence of slavery in the Americas should not only give us pause but should alert us to a deep contradiction in "Western culture." The institution had taken root in an age of Christian zeal and matured and blossomed as a fully functioning institution in the "age of reason," the Enlightenment. Although by the late eighteenth century Europeans at home and many in the Americas began calling for universal and equal civic and human "rights," slavery not only survived in the United States, Cuba, and Brazil into the second half of the nineteenth century but actually boomed in those places. It would not go easily. A perceived champion of democracy, Thomas Jefferson (1743–1826), for example, died believing in the inherent inferiority of African Americans even as he deplored slavery but could see no practical way to end it.[10] Indeed, the revolutionary leadership of the United States acknowledged slavery as a property right in the Constitution. And even where and when slavery was abolished, it was only after often fierce resistance from slaveholders and assorted economic and political interests who adopted a strong proslavery ideology in all the major slave societies. Moral and economic arguments propelled an effective abolitionist movement in the British Empire after 1770, but moralistic voluntarism did not end slavery in the United States—that took the Civil War of 1861–65. Formal, legalized slavery survived to the eve of the twentieth century, in Cuba to 1886 and in Brazil to 1888. It has since cast a long racial shadow on the history of the American republics.

Slavery, Servitude, and Serfdom

As slavery in the Americas was racially defined, "race" should be understood as it was by contemporary Europeans who began with a classification of Caucasian at the head of a descending racial ladder to African, American Indian, Oriental, and Malay. These graduations were formalized in the taxonomies of eighteenth-century Enlightenment thinkers such as Carl Linneaus and J.F Blumenthal.[11] As for the sometimes amorphous categories of "servant" and "slave," these were long-established terms for positions ranging from voluntary, coerced, and obligatory to contract servitude and serfdom.

The word "slave" has an interesting etymology—it is *esclavo/a* in Spanish, *esclave* in French, *escravo/a* in Portuguese, and *slaaf* in Dutch. Drawn from references to Slavic peoples, the term came into general usage in Europe sometime in the ninth century CE. It tended to be used in a general sense to denote "servant," from the Latin *servus*, before it came to be narrowed into how we understand it today, that is, the servant as property. It denotes control as in the Czech word for slave, *robot*. Examples of slavery are deeply embedded in the historical record as conquerors enslaved the conquered and the powerful enslaved the weak and vulnerable. It was widely practiced in antiquity and stitched into Roman and Greek cultures. But the Romans and the Greeks before them did not confine slave status to any single racial group.[12]

In the most obvious sense, servitude is the right or assumption by one person to another person's "service" and involves some understanding of term limits, contract, or even reciprocal functions, something absent in the chattel slave's relationship to a master. The slave was a servant *without consent* and *without term*. That qualifier might also be applied to various forms of serfdom, where the status is hereditary and non-negotiable. Terms such as "serf," "villein," and "peasant" are generally found in agrarian feudalism. For centuries, Europe's serfs were allowed limited control over some land but were bound in legal ways to the land and were protected from abuse by a variety of specific civil and ecclesiastical laws that slaves did not always have.[13] In Russia, as historian Peter Kolchin has shown, hereditary serfdom certainly resembled some aspects of slavery in nineteenth-century United States, but there was little to compare Russian serfdom to servitude in Western Europe after the fifteenth century.[14]

The word "slave" was used colloquially and indiscriminately in the grim world of the nineteenth-century industrial factory. Writers as disparate as Karl Marx and the southern US proslavery advocate John Calhoun (1782–1850) used the concept of "wage slaves." Marx referred to the exploitation of wage labour by the capitalist system, and Calhoun defended slavery's benevolence (the slaveholder's protection of his property) against the cold anomie of wage workers in the northern states. For the Americas, we need to stress that the slave was not white and was subject to sanctioned alienation, humiliation, and physical abuse. In theory, the variations of Roman law found in Latin America do belie the frightful notion that the slave, property by definition, had no personal rights. In fact they did, and even under North America's harsher codes, the slave did have a "right" to "life," at least in theory. Whatever variations existed in law and language, the slave was defined as property. The economic historian Robert Fogel perhaps puts the meaning of slavery best as the "unlimited personal domination" of one person by another.[15]

Some kinds of service combine elements of poorly defined consent *and* coercion. In India, for example, into the twentieth century, poor, dependent, insecure masses of peoples and some culturally defined castes were routinely used for forced labour by landowners and aristocrats who needed no legal permission to do so. Were they slaves? Yes, by some measure of what coerced, involuntary labour means. In India and elsewhere, custom was a sufficient framework for the practice. For centuries, Korean peasants were bound to landlords in ways that resembled European feudal practices and that anthropologists have referred to as slavery, even though most of those peasants had disposal rights to the plots of lands they occupied.[16] In early modern Western societies, convicted criminals everywhere were stripped of rights and their keepers were given a level of control close to absolute. Were convicts slaves? Again, inmates in prisons, workhouses, almshouses, and other institutions for sequestering the socially deficient or malfeasant all retained some means of recovering their freedom. We need to recognize also that the slave who worked the oars of a Roman galley or tilled the fields of a Roman lord or served as a sexual companion, a secretary, an overseer, or an educated scribe had some way of appealing for manumission.

The majority of the world's peoples in the early modern period were agrarian, overseen by hereditary landed aristocracies or by military or political elites. There were no democracies as we understand it, and in most places deeply entrenched customs and conditions defined status. It began with whether one was without means (family connections, land, workshop, or craft) and was therefore dependent on others for subsistence or protection. Even with rising levels of mobility in some parts of Europe, status was often inheritable and drudgery was the lot of most. However, slavery as we have defined it was absent in most of Europe. To repeat, Europeans did not enslave their own people or even other Europeans who might, for example, be prisoners of war.

African slaves were present in Iberia before Columbus reached America. If not on the scale that would emerge in Brazil and the Caribbean, they were enough of a presence to set an important precedent. European agriculture and the labour needed for it was accommodated by settled clusters of peasants. In Iberia, even though African slaves were available, the organization and traditions of agrarian practices precluded their use as agricultural labour on any meaningful scale. The Americas provided the opportunity for a leap to cash crops on a grand scale that required extensive, available, and controlled labour.

Iberians went to the Americas with power and means. In Mexico and Peru, the Spanish superimposed themselves on the masses liberated from the conquered Aztecs and Incas. In the Caribbean, before they disappeared, natives were simply absorbed into the base of Spanish colonial hierarchy. The Portuguese encountered lowland tribal groups in Brazil and proceeded to either enslave them or press them into negotiated servitude, but malleable African slaves in abundance soon followed. Their arrival began as a stream, then a river, and then a flood, gathered in millions and transported thousands of kilometres.

The popular association of slavery with plantation fieldwork is misleading if taken to mean the fate of all or the vast majority of slaves. It does not apply to the mines of Peru and Brazil's Minas Gerais or to the workshops in Rio de Janeiro, Lima, and all the ports in the New World where slavery flourished. Slaves were also found on small mixed farm holdings and in ancillary work on large plantations. Slaves might be African by birth or, by the mid-nineteenth century, the product of several generations of African Americans in North America. There were large numbers of "free negroes" in many parts of Latin America and in the Spanish Caribbean islands but very few in the southern mainland colonies of the British Empire and its successor, the United States. Miscegenation was a major factor in shaping Brazil, as the mixed race permutations attest, and while it went on in North

America, it was legally prohibited there. However, in spite of the alleged openness in race relations in colonial Brazil, there was no free-floating undifferentiated mass of coloured people. Whites might marry mulattos (themselves the result of black-white liaison) but black-white marriage was uncommon, and while Brazil's reputation as condoning racial mixing has some validity, there were class boundaries marked by racial phenotypes. Historian Stuart Schwartz describes the behaviour of free coloured Brazilian women thus: "*Crioula* [a black born in Brazil] women married native-born blacks and sometimes *pardos* [free, usually mixed black and white], but light skinned women did not marry black men as a rule and preferred *pardo* men. In this pattern we see ... a hierarchy of color in which women seem to marry 'up,'" in a conscious adaptation to Brazil's racial gradations of status.[17] Shades of colour mattered.

Brazil's manumission laws did not mean that liberation was easy. As historian Katia Mattoso explains, the slave could be freed in any number of ways, "with or without formal proceedings, directly or indirectly, explicitly, tacitly, or presumptively, by contract between living persons or by will of the deceased, under private seal or sworn before a notary, [orally] or in writing." Most manumission required a written document for proof or a signed witnessed account, but this could be conditional. The freed slave's liberty could be revoked by the former master for any number of infractions including the ridiculous claim of "ingratitude."[18] Even if the former slave remained "free" as the vast majority technically did, that did not always mean prosperity or equal treatment. Manumitted slaves usually ended up as rural and landless labourers or as urban house servants or labourers in Salvador da Bahia, Rio de Janeiro, or Sao Paulo.

Slave populations everywhere in the Americas comprised mature and young slaves, healthy and weak slaves, defiant and passive slaves, African- and American-born slaves, and classes of slaves such as privileged house slaves, slaves who supervised other slaves, and in some cases former slaves who themselves owned slaves. In a theme inspired by Frank Tannenbaum's *Slave and Citizen* (1946), historians have run the gamut of comparative approaches, testing his suggestion that slavery was more physically oppressive in Brazil in particular and in Latin America generally than in the United States but also more open and fluid because of the legal manumission escape hatch. Tannenbaum invited debate on how the slave's experiences in various slave societies differed and how all of it revealed long-term influences on national development and race relations.[19] His approach rested to a great extent on the legal record, and while subsequent research and analyses have used a greater range of evidence and models to compare slavery in its various settings, and to test the relative severity of North American and Latin American slavery, his treatment of comparative race relations was original and provocative.

A Note on "Race"

"Race" is a sensitive and controversial term to distinguish genetic characteristics among various human groups. It notes genotypes (common genetic qualities) and phenotypes (the manifestation of those features in physiognomy and appearance). All humans, *homo sapiens,* constitute a single species, where all are capable of reproduction with all others. In fact, geneticists claim there can be more genetic variation *within* a "race" than *between* the "races."[20] Blanket racial stereotypes have been tied to culture, intelligence, and even morality. Sub-Saharan Africans are not all "black" (negro) and Europeans are certainly not "white," yet the terms are still used to determine dark to light skin with implicit categorical determinants. Social scientists now refer to race as a "social construct," suggesting that we now pull the term away from any biological reductionism. However, contemporary slavers and slaveholders and generations of peoples in the Americas and Europe understood race as a fixed biological characteristic and not a sociological one. Most early modern Europeans believed in versions of the medieval *scala naturae,* "the Chain of Being" that is God's design, whereby He and the angels were placed at the top of a ladder of ordered existence in which humans were ranked above plants, minerals, and animals. Christians were above Muslims and Jews, of course, or any belief system that was not Christian. Africans, Asians, and native Americans were lower or nonexistent on the Chain. Over time, abstract folk belief or theology gave way to quasi-science and, as historian Seymour Drescher argues, Europeans and North American whites adopted theories of "scientific racism" to cope with the end of slavery and to transfer the assumption of the racial inferiority of slaves to post-emancipation peoples of colour.[21]

At a low point in racialized politics in the early twentieth century, as millions of Slavs, Italians, and Russians, many of them Jews, flooded into North America, race took on some extravagant applications. For example, in the widely influential *The Passing of the Great Race, or the Racial Basis of European History* (1916), Madison Grant looked at ethnic, national, and cultural characteristics and alleged that history proved that the Nordic (northern European) branch of Caucasians was superior not only to "negroes" but to Mediterranean Caucasians. He used race to identify "ethnic" or cultural characteristics. His approving audiences, especially in the United States, were quick to accept his arguments, already reacting adversely to the new immigration and actively segregating freed African Americans under the law. Madison Grant was putting a twentieth-century twist on a much older and evolving notion of race. As millions of eastern and southern European immigrants poured into the post-slavery Americas, they were seen to be "polluting" the northern European stock in the United States, but the same ethnic groups were usually welcomed in Brazil as a much needed agricultural labour force in the wake of emancipation or as a useful European contribution to Brazil's modernization.[22] While eugenics debates and theories were circulating widely throughout the Western world, the American historian Ulrich B. Phillips published a formal study, *American Negro Slavery* (1918), which essentially saw the slave in the US South as having been properly suited, well-treated, and accommodated to what he claimed was a relatively benign system.[23] Phillips was hardly alone in his assessment of African American racial deficiency; the revered 1911 edition of the *Encyclopedia Britannica* claimed, unequivocally, that "mentally the negro is inferior to the white," an idea extrapolated and consolidated from practices of Renaissance Europeans who started the trade in African slaves.

People and Landscapes: Africa, circa 1500

The African continent lies between 35 degrees latitude north and 35 degrees latitude south, and most of it is tropical. It covers slightly more than 21 per cent of the land surface of the planet and at its widest point is about 6,500 kilometres from east to west. Africa's farthest western point is in present-day Senegal, and the closest African location to South America is in present-day Sierra Leone about 2,800 kilometres across the Atlantic from Recife in Brazil. The distance from north to south, from the shores of the Mediterranean to the Cape of Good Hope, is 7,700 kilometres. Morocco is only a few miles from Spain at the Strait of Gibraltar. To generalize the people as "African" and the whole as "Africa" obscures the continent's rich diversity. The Sahara Desert separates the fertile Mediterranean lands of the north from the rest of the continent and its savannahs, rainforests, and highlands. There are deserts in the southwest and prairie-like grass-lands in the far south. The great Nile and Zambezi River systems of East Africa nourish millions. The huge drainage basins of the Congo and Niger Rivers of West Africa water the core of the massive zone that provided the majority of slaves for the Americas. The fifteenth-century population of the continent was about 40 million people, comprising several hundred languages and thousands of dialects within five major linguistic families tied to hundreds of cultures and political and economic systems. Renaissance Europeans might from time to time have referred to specific peoples such as Hausa or Ibo, for example, but even when the slave trade was at its most commercial and when traders did understand specific African nationalities, one is likely to see in the record broadly inclusive terms such as "Guinea" or "Mina" or "Angolan."

There is also no common African physical "type": the tall Masai, the short Pygmy, and the dominant Bantu peoples of the continent's central and southern interior regions are clear examples of physiognomic variation. The bushmen of the southwest, the pastoralists of the plains and savannahs, the nomads of the Sahel, and the remote groups in the rainforests reveal a great social diversity. Some societies worked with iron, others were locked into hunting and gathering, and still others in sedentary agriculture. There were "warrior" societies; peaceful transient game herders; and river, lake, and seaside fishing cultures. Urban centres such as Mali and the great trading crossroads of Timbuktu and the Hausa city states added another layer of variety.

African politics were not static. The Mali Empire of West Africa was subject to shifting tides of power. It eventually fell to the impressive Songhay Empire that stretched inland from what the Europeans named Sierra Leone. In the late sixteenth century, it too collapsed. But the most common political units in West Africa were in small or even "mini-states." War was constant and just as likely to be inspired by slave acquisition as by political rivalries.[24] Although Islam had made inroads into sub-Saharan Africa and had converted some populations, local and traditional spiritual practices managed to survive. Europeans tended to find these practices mysterious or abhorrent or even amusing. They deplored the absence of anything resembling Christian monotheism. On the other hand, Africans found Christianity a vague and puzzling abstraction. An early eighteenth-century account of recently arrived slaves in Brazil who were being customarily baptized by the Portuguese notes:

> many do not even know who their Creator is, what they ought to believe in, what law they should keep, how they should surrender themselves to God, why Christians go to Church, why they adore the Church, what they should say to the priest when they kneel before him and he asks if they have a soul, or whether or not the soul dies, and where it goes when it leaves the body.

They would in time understand and practice those rites or versions of them. But, as the contemporary author notes, first they would learn their master's name and then "how many holes of manioc they must plant each day, how many bundles of sugar cane they must cut, how many loads of firewood they must collect."[25]

Africans who had been converted to Islam were viewed by Europeans as not only perverted but dangerous, given the doctrinal solidarity of Islam and Christianity's troubled history with it. The Moorish occupation of most of the Iberian Peninsula from the eighth century to the final foothold in Granada in 1492 had made the Portuguese and Spanish not only very much aware of Islam, of course, but also of Africa—without a clear understanding of what lay beyond the North African littoral. By comparison, since the end of the Roman Empire, Arab traders had gone south of the Sahara, west toward the Atlantic, and east to the Indian Ocean. During the first half of the fifteenth century, Portuguese maritime explorers and merchants made a crucial "discovery." They found Africans for sale along the coastline from Senegambia to Angola. Within decades, ports of departure dotted the coast and acquisition linkages stretched inland.[26] At the centre of the coastal arc defined by the Gulf of Guinea, the Bight of Benin, and the Bight of Biafra, the Portuguese were introduced to Fulani, Mandingo, Asante, Yoruba, Hausa, and Ibo peoples, among many others. That zone and contiguous West Central Africa eventually provided the great majority of the 12.5 million America-bound African slaves and the estimated 6 million more who were transported north by Arab traders during the same period.

European interest was specific. There was little meaningful penetration beyond the trading posts, and African political rulers and intermediaries controlled the trade in the interior. From early on, the Portuguese established permanent bases in a few West African coastal areas (Benguela, for example) and took part in some of the politics of the region. After 1500, they settled on the Indian Ocean in East Africa and later drew slaves from Madagascar and Mozambique. But for Europeans in 1500, Africa's appeal was along the West African coast. The Portuguese fixed their objectives on the human commodity. The great interior reaches of the continent remained uncharted by Europeans for generations until after the end of the slave trade in the nineteenth century when they were drawn to the continent's palm oil, rubber, minerals, cotton, and other commodities as the great imperial scramble for Africa began.

Sugar production had been moving west through the Mediterranean since the Crusades and had reached Spain and Portugal by the early fifteenth century. Then, after the occupation of the Atlantic islands with their promising climate and soils, and given the access to African slaves, sugar cultivation began in earnest. By the 1480s, Portuguese forays to the south as far as Cape Verde and west to the Azores were a harbinger of more exploration. Curiosity, ambition, and chance brought Iberians to Africa, out into the Atlantic, and then within decades to the American continent.

People and Landscapes: America, circa 1500

Strictly speaking, the continent named for the explorer Amerigo Vespucci is a single contiguous, elongated landform of nearly 14,000 kilometres running from the high Arctic to Patagonia, Cape Horn, and the Antarctic Ocean. It takes up about 29 per cent of the world's land surface. It measures 5,600 kilometres at its widest in North America and about 4,800 kilometres at its widest in South America at a point where the eastern extremity of South America is closer to Africa than it is to the Pacific on the other side of the continent. What makes this a single continent is the 50-kilometre wide membrane of the Isthmus of Panama, which links North America with the South America landmass. Central America or Mesoamerica refers to the southern part of North America and includes Mexico and the modern republics running south to Colombia and the other northern reaches of South America. There are other ways the continent is defined, including a convention that places Mexico in North America, or another, more common tripartite division based on Latin America, North America, and the Caribbean. The whole is often simply described as the Western Hemisphere although geography, culture, and history before and after Columbus make subdivisions inevitable. The Americas contain versions of the world's climates and landscapes and a biodiversity that includes both universal and unique species. One of the wettest zones in the world, the Amazonian rainforest is directly across the Andes from what is likely the driest place in the world, Chile's Atacama Desert. The Americas are both equatorial and polar. The Great Lakes are the world's largest body of fresh water. Great rivers such as the Amazon, Mississippi, and Mackenzie run through immense drainage basins. The drainage systems of these major rivers, the extent and size of the mountain ranges, and the great expanse of plains and forests compare to any in any other region of the world.

When Columbus arrived, he touched the edge of a vast array of cultures, societies, and languages and a continent of multitudes of people. The population of the Americas in 1492 has been the subject of great scholarly

debate and widely conflicting estimates drawn from arcane statistical specu-
lation. Recent generally accepted calculations put it at 54 million with large
concentrations in Mexico and the Andes.[27] Mere decades after Columbus's
arrival, disease, war, assimilation, miscegenation, and declining birth rates
had begun to eat away at those numbers. By the early seventeenth century,
natives had all but disappeared from the Caribbean; the northern European
impact made for such a serious erosion of the eastern North American native
population that by the nineteenth century it had been reduced to less than
25 per cent of its original size. The story was much the same in the Mexican
heartland and in parts of the Andes and in lowland Brazil. In 1500, there
were perhaps as many as 2,000 distinct languages in the Americas including
the Caribbean. Some language groups were extensive, such as the Quechua
of South America and the Algonquian of eastern North America, and some
were limited to a few thousand speakers in remote and isolated groups.
Social organization was as complex and sophisticated as the Inca Empire,
as large and hierarchical as the Aztec, or as rudimentary as the small clans
of hunter gatherers in the Amazon rainforests and the many thousands of
small nations everywhere.

That rich human complexity is still masked by generalized terms such
as "Indian" or "native American," "aboriginal" or "indigenous person" (in
Canada, the approved term is "First Nation"). When the Iberians arrived,
they made note of the stone-age cultures they found but generally over-
looked the continent's rich archaeology. Europeans noted the absence of
the wheel and what appeared to be crude technologies and hieroglyphics,
as well as incomprehensible spiritual, symbolic, and political rituals among
preliterate peoples operating at what seemed to them elementary stages of
development. Yet even without the wheel or draft animals, the Incas had
managed remarkable engineering feats in the high Andes with imagination,
experiment, and well-organized coerced labour. In awkward territory that
stretched for thousands of kilometres north and south, the Inca Empire had
created road networks, a sophisticated agriculture, and durable architecture. The political organization of aggregate millions in the Inca domain
and the range of the Aztec Empire in Mexico with its metal technologies
and infrastructure belie the notion of uniform "primitivism." Nevertheless,
for the Iberians the peculiarities and novelties of the Aztec, Mayan, and Inca
cultures actually fed their prejudices. They disdained ritual cannibalism and
stamped any number of creator myths and spiritual behaviours as pagan and
backward. Later, as northern Europeans settled North America, they too
encountered stone-age, wheel-less cultures but no immense consolidated

empires. Individual nations tended to be measured in hundreds or a few thousand rather than the millions found in the Andes or Mesoamerica.

The cultural anthropologist George Murdock spent a great deal of his long academic career compiling and analyzing global cultural data. One of his important extrapolations was that large settled agricultural societies were more likely to institutionalize slavery than were smaller communities whose approaches to slavery might be looser, more variable, or simply opportunistic. Slave status might be applied to permanent tributary groups in the Aztec Empire or war captives in societies as varied as the Tupinamba in coastal Brazil or the Haida, thousands of kilometres away on the north-west Pacific coast.[28] In Brazil, the cannibalistic Tupinamba kept slaves to promote status but also killed them for food in ritual ceremony. While the Portuguese were horrified by what they saw, they made the "degenerate" Tupinamba a target for coerced labour. Well into the eighteenth century, slave hunters flourished in Brazil and as far away as the trans-Appalachian region of North America.[29] Every colonizing power, in royal edicts or in charters, was obliged to treat natives as potential converts to Christianity as well as cohabitants. Priests such as Bartolomé de Las Casas in New Spain, the Jesuits, Quakers, and others throughout the Americas should be applauded for their sincere and passionate efforts to treat natives fairly, even when the efforts were tinged with arrogance. But even converted natives were never treated as equals.[30]

European explorers, settlers, adventurers, missionaries, soldiers, bureaucrats, and investors were awed by America's scale and grandeur. Although sometimes intimidated by the primeval "wilderness" and fascinated by or dismissive of its novel, exotic peoples, they were enticed by the promise of wealth or glory or both. They brought along European political and legal doctrines, social standards, declared territorial rights, religious orthodoxy, and military force. They came with a host of deadly microbial agents. Within decades of Columbus's landing, Spaniards had seen the Pacific at Panama and had occupied large swathes of South, Central and North America—they and the Portuguese in Brazil had begun to change the course of history. Shortly after 1600, northern Europeans began a similar process of transformation in the eastern woodlands of North America and the smaller islands of the Caribbean. They were also accompanied by deadly pathogens and an array of foreign animal and plant species and, eventually, Africans.

MAP 1.1 The Atlantic World of the Imperialists

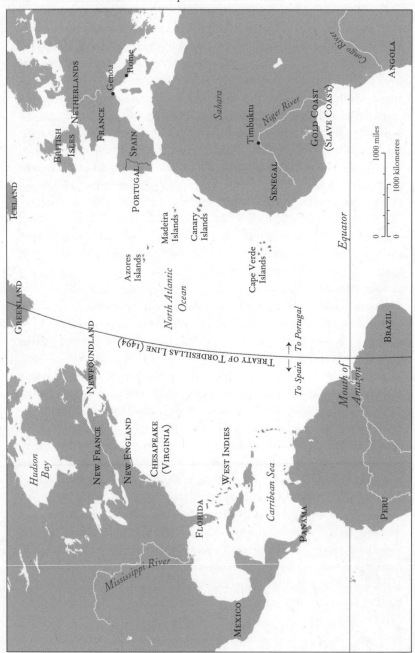

People and Landscapes: Europe, circa 1500

What is meant by Europe usually takes spatial outlines bound by the Atlantic Ocean to the west, the North Sea and the Arctic Ocean to the north, the Mediterranean Sea and its subsidiaries such as the Aegean to the south, and to the east by the Russian borderlands and the Baltic and Balkan nations. It is smaller than either the Americas or Africa with slightly more than 14 per cent of the world's land mass. In 1500, its population, having begun to recover from the Black Death of the mid–fourteenth century, was about 80 million.

Europe also had a coherence that was missing in Africa and America. Christianity, technology, art, and literature found their way across local or national boundaries. Communication in diplomatic, trade, intellectual, and religious affairs was made possible in Latin. In that language and with the new printing presses, volumes of new knowledge were disseminated. Despite being the continent's dominant spiritual medium, Christianity in the 1530s and later became as divisive as it was unifying following the bitter ecclesiastical split in the Church of Rome (Catholic) and the political and ideological impact of the Protestant Reformation, whose effects echoed into the 1600s and beyond. But the common God remained, and every European who went to Africa or America shared a spiritual superiority at least at the level of the deity. Europe was also a patchwork of cultural, linguistic, and political subdivisions; of nations, principalities, monarchies, city states, and localized communities; of dialects and customs. The general consolidation of smaller political units into nation-states turned out to be a decisive development.

A handful of those nations—Spain and Portugal initially; then France, England (Great Britain after 1707), and the Netherlands; and as minor colonizers, Sweden and Denmark—drew Africa and America together in a great interchange. Although these states were economic, religious, and imperial rivals distinguished by particular national traits, they shared two important qualities: first, they had emerged from the Middle Ages as something resembling the modern nation-state where assets, power, and policy were somewhat centralized and where trade and exploration could be financed, legitimized, and supported by a central governing power such as the Aragon-Castile dynasty and the Habsburgs in Spain, the House of Avis (Burgundy) in Portugal, the Bourbons in France, and the Tudor-Stuarts in England. There was no Germany or Italy but rather a large cluster of semi-autonomous principalities in the former, under the aegis of the Holy Roman

Empire, and city states such as Florence, Genoa, and Naples in the latter. The second shared quality of the Western European nations was that most were sited on the Atlantic or had close access to it, as in the Scandinavian case. Spain is both a Mediterranean and an Atlantic nation—Cadiz in the southeast and Coruna in the northwest are on the Atlantic. Portugal's coastline is entirely on the Atlantic. The maritime personality of Western Europe was well-established in the Baltic and North Sea trading routes and fishing zones and in sorties out into the North Atlantic. Genoese sailors, such as Columbus and John Cabot, might have cut their teeth in the shipping lanes of the Mediterranean, but vision and financing took them all the way to the Western Atlantic.

Traditionally, Europe's masses had been attached to a monarch, a lord, or a master; or with a location, the village or church, for example; or with a dialect. That was gradually changing as "nationality"—being English, Dutch or French, for example—became a cultural marker. In Africa and the Americas, group affiliation and identity took shape in the relative egalitarianism of smaller, co-operative communities, even those subsumed in empires; but Europeans increasingly saw themselves as part of larger, more complex polities that included important urban interchanges for intellectuals, academics, artists, merchants, craftsmen, entrepreneurs, and church leaders. Cities such as Florence, Bologna, Paris, Lisbon, and Seville were hubs of learning, and increasing rural manufacturing and social mobility indicated closer rural and urban integration.

This energy and complexity created contradictions. Historian Jonathan W. Zophy in *A Short History of Renaissance and Reformation Europe* (1999) quotes the Dutch humanist thinker Erasmus who praised the age's dynamic flowering of ideas "as if on a given signal, splendid talents are stirring" (1517) and who later bemoaned the era's wars and religious upheavals as revealing "the worst age in history" (1536).[31] Periodic famines and assorted often random epidemics of infectious and lethal diseases cut into life expectancy. Rates of infant mortality were high. Sustenance was intermittently threatened by shortages. A wet summer, blighted crops, or livestock diseases could wreak havoc on a village or a region. In some of the poorer neighbourhoods of Europe, hunger, malnutrition, and even famine were never far away. While there was increased social or economic mobility in the erosion of feudal social structures, the majority of Western Europe's peoples were still nominally bound to the land in legal and customary "ranks" from the "poorer sorts" to the "better sorts" to the peak of aristocracy to the Crown. What was egalitarian was a common spiritual canopy of the

Christian God, where the lowliest peasant was equal to the richest lord "in God's eyes." But social structure was important even to the often enforced sumptuary (dress) codes that lasted well into the eighteenth century. Along with other forms of deference, these were transported to the Americas and adapted to the racially set class structures there. We need to be clear, then, that Europe's masses did not inspire the conquest of the Atlantic. Rather, the men who led the way to Africa or the Americas were sponsored navigators, adventurers, explorers, traders, soldiers, priests, and political agents of monarchs or royal families. The commoners went as sailors or, in their wake, as servants. The European societies that formed in the Americas were hierarchical, and deference to superiors was expected of all common people. But in the New World, even the meanest Spanish or British servant expected deference from an African or a native American.

By the first half of the fifteenth century, Portugal and Spain had almost completed the *reconquista*, the centuries-long recovery of Iberia from Moorish domination. This signalled a victory of Christianity over Islam and the consolidation of the Christian kingdoms of Aragon-Castile and Portugal. The Portuguese settlements of the Madeira Islands and the Azores in the 1420s and the later acquisition of African slaves is a testament to a growing curiosity, ambition, and confidence. The sudden and dramatic appearance of America at century's end, however, was not foreseen. Christopher Columbus did not take Queen Isabella's contract to go west in order to find a place to make use of slaves. Indeed, it is no small irony that the European settlement of the New World began with the Spanish Crown's desire to contact and trade with China, a magnet for global commerce. Columbus chose to go west across the Atlantic to get to the east. An oceanic passage was certainly a daunting prospect because of the perceived void of the farther reaches of the Atlantic, but on balance it seemed the safest route to Asia. Travel accounts, the thirteenth-century experience of Marco Polo, and the wealth of Muslim long-distance traders confirmed the great riches to be won in Asia. But the prospects of traversing many thousands of kilometres through forbidding terrain across potentially hostile non-Christian empires made the Atlantic the preferred route for this Spanish venture.

A Note on Diets and Diseases

As noted, when Europeans intruded violently into the Americas, they brought along samples of the European environment, among them smallpox, influenza, whooping cough, measles, diphtheria, typhus, tuberculosis, and other infectious diseases. While sugar was perhaps the most important botanical species brought by the Europeans, they also introduced other edible plants including oats, barley, wheat, and some fruits as well as edible livestock such as pigs, sheep, and cattle along with draft animals, horses, and many smaller mammals.[32] Europeans took with them dietary preferences such as milk, cheese, and eggs and produced and drank their traditional distilled and fermented liquors, beer, and wine. They brought the weeds that went with their grasses and grains and the insects that depended on them. Native American dietary sources survived in the extended corn cultures and in the tomato, peppers, squash, potato, and cassava or manioc root edibles of the Andes. Native berries, fruits, fish, birds, and wild game were often merged with and sometimes superseded by European varieties. Some native groups, certainly in isolated regions, continued to avoid European foods and ate as they always had. They continued their use of strong plant-based intoxicants or medicines or chewed mood-changing herbs and plant leaf. American tobacco and chocolate revolutionized European consumption habits.

In a further example of the way diets were fused in the Atlantic interchange, African rice and root edibles accompanied the slave trade. Many Africans who arrived in America were used to goat and other meats and cereals such as millet. Their staple diets in many parts of the New World ended up with sorghum (a grain that was a staple in parts of Africa) along with local and European foods in Brazil and the Caribbean. In North America, the wheat, pigs, and chickens of the Europeans along with American manioc, corn, and potatoes made their way into slave diets, and as the flow of peoples and commodities circulated in the Atlantic, many of those same comestibles also made their way into African diets in Africa.[33]

While Europeans were taking their germs to America, they encountered some lethal infections in Africa. Those dangers and the power of local African merchants and princes was another deterrent to any serious European colonization of equatorial West Africa. Europeans were hit with malaria, yellow fever, a host of intestinal parasites (worms), and the inevitable dysentery, the "bloody flux." The tsetse fly and mosquito-borne infections such as dengue fever always threatened the health of European traders and agents. Northern Europeans also found the Caribbean uncomfortable, but Africa acquired a reputation as an especially dangerous place. The idea that the tropics could be the "white man's graveyard" was only a slight exaggeration. Mortality rates in the West African forts and ports were matched by those in the slave trade, where, as we shall see, white seamen were as much at risk as their miserable human cargoes. But Europeans persisted and put up with the threat of illness and death because, as it was clear from the start, slave trading promised to be a lucrative business for every white man involved in it.

Notes

1 Franklin W. Knight, "Slavery, Race, and Social Structure in Cuba during the Nineteenth Century," in Robert Trent Toplin, ed., *Slavery and Race Relations in Latin America* (Westport, CT: Greenwood, 1974), 2050.

2 The "New World became a crucible of new nations, values, institutions and identities." Robin Blackburn, *The American Crucible: Slavery, Emancipation and Human Rights* (London: Verso, 2011), 4.

3 See Alfred Crosby, *Ecological Imperialism: The Biological Expansion of Europe, 900–1900*, 2nd ed. (Cambridge: Cambridge University Press, 2004), Prologue, notes 1 and 5. See also Nicholas Canny, ed., *Europeans on the Move* (New York: Oxford University Press, 1994), summary in Chapter 10. See also Dudley Baines, *Emigration from Europe, 1815–1930* (Cambridge: Cambridge University Press), tables on page 3.

4 David Eltis and David Richardson, *Atlas of the Transatlantic Slave Trade* (New Haven: Yale University Press, 2010), *passim*. The thoroughness and sophistication of this work is impressive. The complete data base is available at http://www.slavevoyages.org/tast/index.faces and Tables 2.1, 2.2, and 2.3 in the present book.

5 The single drop thesis should not be confused with the various forms of Brazilian rules of descent. The single drop is specific to the United States and is described in Barbara Jeanne Fields, "Slavery, Race and Ideology in the United States of America," *New Left Review* 181 (May–June 1990) 95–118. See also the discussion in Nina G. Jablonski, *Living Color: The Biological and Social Meaning of Skin Color* (Berkeley: University of California Press, 2012), 134–68. Marvin Harris used the term the "rule of hypo-descent" in *Patterns of Race in the Americas* (New York: Walker and Co., 1964), 56–57 and Chapter 7. It flourished under the doctrine of "separate but equal" and post-Civil War segregation. C. Vann Woodward, *The Strange Career of Jim Crow*, 3rd ed. (New York: Oxford University Press, 1974 [1955]) is an important study of the ramifications of the simple black-white distinction after emancipation.

6 Robert Edgar Conrad, *Children of God's Fire: A Documentary History of Black Slavery in Brazil* (University Park: University of Pennsylvania Press, 1995), 55.

7 David Eltis, Frank D. Lewis, and Kenneth L. Sokoloff, eds., *Slavery in the Development of the Americas* (Cambridge: Cambridge University Press, 2004). This essay collection deals with markets, economic variables, and capital investment. See the "Introduction," 2–17.

8 Orlando Patterson, *Slavery and Social Death: A Comparative Study* (Cambridge, MA: Harvard University Press, 1982), 5–6; 38–39.

9 John W. Blassingame, *The Slave Community*, rev. ed. (Oxford: Oxford University Press, 1979), 101–05, and Herbert Klein and Fransisco Vidal Luna, *Slavery in Brazil* (New York: Cambridge University Press, 2010), 212–49, are useful in defining slave "agency." On slave resistance, see Herbert Aptheker, *American Negro Slave Revolts* (New York: International Publishers, 1974 [1943]); Laird Bergad, *Comparative Histories of Slavery in Brazil, Cuba and the United States* (Cambridge: Cambridge University Press, 2007), Chapter 7; Klein and Luna, *Slavery in Brazil*, Chapter 7. Blackburn, *American Crucible*, 354–64 clearly shows the link between slave resistance and its role in abolitionist propaganda. On North American slaves' "manipulation" of the system (the "accommodation" thesis), see Eugene Genovese,

Roll, Jordan, Roll: The World the Slaves Made (New York: Vintage, 1974), 285–309; 585–658. Gilberto Freyre, *The Masters and the Slaves: A Study in the Development of Brazilian Civilization* (New York: Knopf, 1946 [1933]) suggests some examples of a Brazilian version of the accommodation theory.

10 For white approaches, perceptions, and responses to Africans and African slaves, see Winthrop Jordan, *White Over Black: American Attitudes Toward the Negro, 1550–1812* (Chapel Hill: University of North Carolina Press, 1968), preface, 34–35, 216–63; and on the racial outlooks of Jefferson's generation, 429–81. Freyre offers a direct thesis on the degree to which African slaves shaped not only white attitudes but the larger society as well. He continues to influence the study of Brazilian slavery, national character, politics, and race relations. See the important appraisal of Freyre's work and reputation in David Cleary "Race, Nationalism and Social Theory in Brazil: Rethinking Gilberto Freyre" (Cambridge, MA: Harvard University Center For Latin America Studies, n.d.). For vivid descriptions of racial and caste attitudes in Brazil, see Conrad, *Children of God's Fire*, 217ff and 317ff. A useful selection of proslavery arguments with samples of racial biases in the antebellum US South is Paul Finkelman, *Defending Slavery: Proslavery Thought in the Old South* (Boston: Bedford/St. Martin's, 2003).

11 Stephen J. Gould, *The Mismeasure of Man*, rev. ed. (New York: Norton, 1996), 401–12.

12 M.L. Bush, *Servitude in Modern Times* (Malden: Blackwell, 2000), 6–68 is a useful comparative introduction. See also M.L. Bush, ed., *Serfdom and Slavery: Studies in Legal Bon*dage (London: Longman, 1996) for a selection of essays on the topic.

13 An accessible brief overview of the social context of European servitude and peasantry is in Jonathan W. Zophy, *A Short History of Renaissance and Reformation Europe: Dances over Fire and Water*, 2nd ed. (Upper Saddle River: Prentice Hall, 1999), Chapter 2 and "Notes on Further Reading."

14 Peter Kolchin, *Unfree Labor: American Slavery and Russian Serfdom* (Cambridge, MA: Belknap,1987). See also Richard Hellie, "Russian Slavery and Serfdom, 1450–1804," in David Eltis and Stanley L. Engerman, eds., *The Cambridge World History of Slavery*, Vol. 3 (New York: Cambridge University Press, 2011), 275–96.

15 Robert Fogel, *Without Consent or Contract: The Rise and Fall of American Slavery* (New York: Norton, 1989), 410.

16 Patterson, *Slavery and Social Death*, Part I, and index.

17 Stuart Schwartz, *Sugar Plantations in the Formation of Brazilian Society* (Cambridge: Cambridge University Press, 1985), 392; see also Conrad, *Children of God's Fire*, 211–13.

18 Katia M. Mattoso, *To Be a Slave in Brazil* (New Brunswick: Rutgers University Press, 1986), 157–58.

19 Frank Tannenbaum, *Slave and Citizen* (New York: Knopf, 1946); Stuart B. Schwartz, *Slaves, Peasants and Rebels: Reconsidering Brazilian Slavery* (Cambridge: Cambridge University Press, 1985), 3–4. Page 65, footnote 153 summarizes his thesis.

20 Two excellent surveys of the history of the uses of "race" are Ivan Hannaford, *Race: The History of an Idea in the West* (Baltimore: Johns Hopkins University Press for the Woodrow Wilson Center Press, 1996) and George M. Fredrickson, *The Comparative Imagination: On the History of Racism Nationalism and Social Movements* (Berkeley: University of California Press, 1997); see also Harris, *Patterns of Race*, 77–97 and especially Jablonski, *Living Color*, Part Two on the sociology of colour.

21 Seymour Drescher, "The Ending of the Slave Trade and the Evolution of European Scientific Racism," in Joseph E. Inkori and Stanley L. Engerman, eds., *The Atlantic Slave Trade: Effects on Economics, Societies and Peoples in Africa, the Americas and Europe* (Durham: Duke University Press, 1992), 361–93.

22   On Madison Grant's influence, see the brief note in Gould, *The Mismeasure of Man*, 227. On immigration, see Peter Bakewell, *A History of Latin America*, 2nd ed. (Oxford: Blackwell, 2004), Chapter 16. Immigration numbers for Brazil are available from Boris Fausto, *A Concise History of Brazil* (New York: Cambridge University Press, 1999), 142–46, 166–78. See also James Lockhart and Stuart Schwartz, *Early Latin America: A History of Colonial Spanish America and Brazil* (Cambridge: Cambridge University Press, 1984), 233–37, 372–77, 397–98.

23   Ulrich B. Phillips, *American Negro Slavery: A Survey of the Supply, Employment and Control of Negro Labor as Determined by the Plantation System* (Gloucester: P. Smith, 1959 [1918]). No historian approaches North American slavery without reference to Phillips's role in defining the subject as a scholarly enterprise. While Phillips is rightly seen as an apologist for a racially deterministic view of the slave, his research is impressive. He stands as an example of how the same material can stand for two opposing analyses of slavery. For an assessment of his influence and reputation, see Daniel C. Littlefield, "From Phillips to Genovese: The Historiography of American Slavery before *Time on the Cross*," in Wolfgang Binder, ed., *Slavery in the Americas* (Wurzburg, Germany: Konigshausen, 1993).

24   John Thornton, *Africa and Africans in the Making of the Atlantic World, 1400–1800* (Cambridge: Cambridge University Press, 1998), especially Chapters 3 and 4. Thornton's study is required reading on this subject. See also his naming and location of dozens of states, large and small and the maps that accompany his findings, x-xxxvi.

25   Conrad, *Children of God's Fire*, 57.

26   Patrick Manning, "The Slave Trade: The Formal Demography of a Global System," in Inkori and Engerman, *The Atlantic Slave Trade*, 117–41.

27   William M. Denevan, *The Native Population of the Americas in 1492*, 2nd ed. (Madison: University of Wisconsin Press, 1992), 291.

28   Patterson, *Slavery and Social Death*, Appendices A, B, C; George P. Murdock, "Ethnographic Atlas: A Summary," *Ethnology* 6 (1967): 109–236.

29   For a sixteenth-century description of the Tupinamba, see Stuart B. Schwartz, *Early Brazil: A Documentary Collection to 1700* (Cambridge: Cambridge University Press, 2010), 137–40. For North America, see Alan Gallay, ed., *Indian Slavery in Colonial America* (Lincoln: University of Nebraska Press, 2009).

30   Patterson, *Slavery and Social Death*, 72ff.

31   Zophy, *A Short History of Renaissance and Reformation Europe*, 1.

32   Crosby, *Biological Imperialism*, Chapters 7 and 8.

33   The best recent treatment of this topic is Judith Carney and Richard Nicholas Rosomoff, *In the Shadow of Slavery: Africa's Botanical Legacy in the Atlantic World* (Berkeley: University of California Press, 2009).

2 | The Atlantic Slave Trade

"That execrable sum of all villainies, commonly called the Slave Trade."
—John Wesley, *Journal*, February 12, 1772[1]

The Atlantic slave trade attracted commentary from the moment it began, but not until 1969 and the publication of Philip Curtin's *The Atlantic Slave Trade: A Census* did it receive the close scholarly attention and wider public awareness that it deserved. Curtin's careful examination of the scale and dynamics of the trade also showed the central role the African umbilical played in sustaining slavery in the Americas.[2] Curtin built on earlier but mostly forgotten studies, so his work's systematic statistical approach was akin to seeing the slave trade for the first time. The shock of his numbers sparked interest, of course, but so did his research and analysis of acquisition, logistics, market efficiencies, and capital accumulation, as well as the roles of Africans in the trade. He reiterated the trade's appalling dehumanizing conditions that earlier observers, especially abolitionists, had made and in summary revealed a market-oriented enterprise of surpassing magnitude whose tentacles reached into every corner of the Atlantic world.[3] Curtin inspired a generation of scholars such as David Anstey, Herbert Klein, David Eltis, James Walvin, and many others who have refined the data; rooted out additional African sources; and identified the ports of embarkation and debarkation, the numbers of ships involved and their home ports, their crews, and the mortality rates in the crossings. Now, Curtin's legacy can be seen in the work of David Eltis and his collaborators whose decades of analysis have been assembled in digital form and represent a landmark in scholarly research.[4]

There is no part of the record that does not evoke images of the abysmal enterprise, from the way Africans were caught in the slave gathering net to their ultimate fates. The chain as a grim appliance of capture becomes an extended metaphor for what awaited slaves. When tied to the statistics, the descriptions of shock, terror, humiliation, hunger, sickness, and death arouse our moral sensibilities as they did those of outraged abolitionists who began their attacks on slavery by focusing on the suffering endured in the "middle passage" from Africa to America.[5] Historians have since confirmed the mortality rates, the chains, the fetid atmosphere of the ships' holds, the "tight packing," and harsh discipline. But evidence also shows that mortality rates for slaves in transit were not always out of line with that of lower class transatlantic travellers in the age of sail, those many white servants and poor migrants who were squeezed into small spaces, "packed like herrings" as Gottlieb Mittelberger's vivid account notes and who suffered from dreadful spare diets, mortal infections, and the perils of Atlantic weather. Nevertheless, no white passengers, however awful their experiences, were chained or as tightly confined or physically abused as were slaves.[6] As we note below, slave ships eventually were custom designed to allow for space and some ventilation. Logic demands that we see in this the self-interest of the slavers and their need to protect their cargoes as effectively as possible. The "loss" of slaves because of malnutrition, disease, suicide, and injuries, even from excessive punishments, cut into profits.

Every European nation that colonized the Americas took part in the trade, and every agent has left a record, from the cold numbers on a bill of lading to identification of the slave's sex, age, disposition, and embarkation point. Log books and medical or managerial accounts of voyages go to the heart of the trade even if we are left with scant and often biased evidence of the captive slaves' experiences. The records of the buyers and sellers, shippers, merchants, insurance brokers, victualers, shipbuilders, outfitters, and sailors are detailed because this complex business needed accurate accounting all the way to the taxing powers of the state. The slave was caught or bought, processed, and fed into a system as a labour-producing commodity. Quite simply, the value of an individual slave in Bahia, for example, was measured by calculating cost and upkeep against the half ton of sugar that the slave produced annually.[7]

The Numbers

The most recent estimate of the numbers of African slaves sent to the Americas is 12.5 million, and the estimate of arrivals at ports in the Americas is 10.7 million, a difference of nearly 15 per cent because of the death rates in

MAP 2.1 West Africa during the Slave Trade

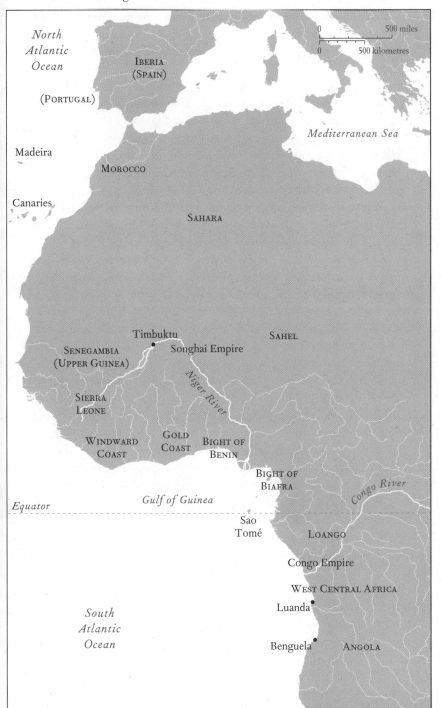

transit. In addition, some 6 million slaves were transported to North Africa and today's Middle East during the period of the Atlantic slave trade, and as many as 8 million people were enslaved in West Africa. The mortality rates in the Atlantic trade were matched or exceeded in the transit to North Africa and the Arab world. In addition, there are the unknown numbers of slaves who died prematurely in the seasoning process in the West Indies, Brazil, or elsewhere in the African slave diaspora. One estimate puts the death toll at 4 million overall for African slaves being shipped through and out of Africa, which, along with the overall numbers removed in the trade, caused a serious decline in population in some African ethnic groups. Those losses were compounded by the depletion of males in many catchment areas. The near consistent two or three to one ratio male to female slave cargoes meant that population stability or growth in Africa was further compromised by unbalanced sex ratios. Children were also removed in substantial numbers at an average of over 10 per cent over the course of the trade.[8]

Along a West African coastline of over 3,000 kilometres, from about 15 degrees north latitude to about 15 degrees south latitude, from Senegal to Angola, dozens of embarkation sites were established over the centuries, from simple pens to fortified enclosures and permanent bases with holding cells, living quarters, and wharves. Some 140 of those departure points have been identified, and while many were temporary or short-lived, others functioned for decades. For example, over time some 2.8 million slaves left from Luanda in Angola; over half of all America-bound slaves were shipped from sites south of the Bight of Benin; and nearly half were brought to the coast from the area that embraces Angola and the Congo River basin from the coast to the interior of West Central Africa (see Table 2.1, Table 2.2, and Map 2.1). They were carried in ships registered in New World ports such as Recife, Havana, Bridgetown, and Newport, Rhode Island. But several ports dominated the trade. Ships registered in Rio de Janeiro and Salvador da Bahia in Brazil and in Europe at Liverpool, London, Bristol, and Nantes carried approximately half of all African slaves to the Americas. British and Portuguese-Brazilian ships together carried 73 per cent of all slaves, with Portuguese-Brazilian ships accounting for nearly 47 per cent (5.85 million slaves) of the grand total, the majority after the last quarter of the eighteenth century. The British slave trade took off after the founding of the Royal African Company in 1672, and although its monopoly was dissolved in 1698 under pressure from free traders, British involvement in the trade was firmly established and grew at an extraordinary rate. After 1713, the Spanish *asiento* gave British ships exclusive rights to the Spanish

TABLE 2.1 Slaves Leaving Africa, 1501–1867

	Total[a]	Percentage of Whole	Average per Decade
1501–1550	63,400	0.51	12,780
1551–1600	213,370	1.70	42,500
1601–1650	668,500	5.33	133.654
1651–1700	1,207,000	9.64	241,600
1701–1750	2,560,900	20.45	511,840
1751–1800	3,934,600	31.42	786,860
1801–1850	3,649,000	29.13	729,640
1851–1867	225,800	1.80	132,353
Total	12,522,570	Rounded to 100	

a The totals in Tables 2.1 and 2.2 are slightly different because of the "rounding rules" used by Eltis and Richardson, *Atlas*, "About this Atlas," xxiii.
Adapted from Eltis and Richardson, *Atlas*, 23.
Complete data at http://www.slavevoyages.org/tast/index.faces.

TABLE 2.2 Slave Embarkation Zones, 1500–1867

	Upper Guinea[a]	Gold Coast	Bight of Benin	Bight of Biafra	West Central Africa[b]	South East Africa[c]	Totals
1500–1550	57,000	0	0	2,100	4,800	0	63,900
1551–1600	93,000	0	0	6,800	113,100	0	212,500
1601–1650	56,000	2,470	9,600	36,900	56,300	300	668,270
1651–1700	89,000	106,000	260,000	150,000	571,000	32,000	1,208,000
1701–1750	212,000	460,000	735,000	249,000	888,000	15,200	2,559,200
1751–1800	854,000	554,000	550,000	656,000	1,477,000	55,300	3,934,000
1801–1850	326,000	86,000	411,000	495,000	1,920,000	410,000	3,648,200
1851–1867	4,800	0	34,000	0	157,000	30,000	225,800
Totals	1,479,800	1,208,670	1,999,600	1,595,400	5,693,900	542,800	12,520,170

a Includes Senegambia.
b Includes Angola.
c Largely in the area of present-day Mozambique.
Adapted from Eltis and Richardson, *Atlas*, 89 (numbers rounded). Complete data at http://www.slavevoyages.org/tast/index.faces.

trade. For the most part, France served its own slave colonies and accounted for about 11 per cent of all slaves taken from Africa. Spanish registered ships accounted for 8.5 per cent of the whole and the Dutch 4.4 per cent. Ships registered in British North America and after 1787 the United States carried 2.5 per cent of the whole. The Swedes and Danes carried less than one-tenth of 1 per cent. British vessels registered in Liverpool, London, and Bristol took 2.7 million slaves (of the total British number of 3.25 million), mostly in the eighteenth century. Ships registered in Rio de Janeiro and Salvador da Bahia carried 2.8 million slaves to Brazil mostly in the first half of the nineteenth century (see Table 2.3 for points of arrival in the Americas).[9]

Liverpool and Rio de Janeiro became major ports largely because of the slave trade. By 1800, Liverpool was importing sugar, tobacco, and cotton from the Caribbean and the southern United States while its slave ships delivered the labour for those crops. There were few slaves in Liverpool itself, and those were held tenuously after a court in the 1772 Somerset case determined that slavery had no legal basis in Britain. After 1807, Parliament's banning of the slave trade ended Liverpool and the other British ports' participation in the trade but not before a vital Atlantic trade infrastructure had been derived from it. And slave-raised cotton, coffee, and tobacco continued to sustain British ports and industries.[10] On the other hand, Rio de Janeiro was home to thousands of slaves and free coloured people and was an entry and distribution point for the throngs of slaves headed into the interior, a role it maintained for decades after the British slave trade ban.

An older analysis of the Atlantic slave trade was modelled on the so-called triangular trade. This described a system where a ship left Liverpool, for example, with trade goods for Africa, picked up slaves, crossed the Atlantic, deposited the slaves in Jamaica, and took sugar back to Britain, completing the triangle. Several variants of this model existed, of course, and it fits a logistical assumption, but the triangular trade mechanism was simply one of a number of ways the commerce worked. By the eighteenth century, slave ships were being designed to carry slaves and little or no other cargo. Nearly two-thirds of those ships were engaged in a simple return sequence, from Africa to America then "deadheading" (sailing empty or near empty) back to Africa. As it grew in scale, the slave trade was less an adjunct to other commerce and increasingly a specialized system.[11]

TABLE 2.3 Slave Destinations, 1501–1866

	Total Number	Percentage of Total
Brazil	4,863,480	45.43
Mainland North America	391,060	3.63
Dutch Caribbean	443,700	4.14
Danish Caribbean	108,600	1.01
British Caribbean	2,318,200	21.65
French Caribbean	1,120,900	10.47
Spanish American Mainland	489,700	4.57
Spanish Caribbean	805,700	7.52
Europe	9,010	
Africa[a]	155,400	Combined with Europe 1.52
		99.95
Total	10,705,750[b]	

a   Includes 155,400 slaves taken from slave ships, liberated, and returned to Africa during the British ban on the trade after 1808.

b   The disparity between this figure and the numbers on Table 2.1 are explained by losses in transit from Africa to America.

Portuguese-Brazilian ships carried over 5.8 million slaves from Africa. British ships carried over 3.2 million slaves from Africa. Both the British and the Portuguese carried slaves for other colonial systems, including Spain's. See the numbers in Eltis and Richardson, *Atlas*, 23.

Of the slaves who arrived in the British Caribbean, 44 per cent disembarked in Jamaica and 21 per cent in Barbados. In the French Caribbean, 69 per cent of slaves landed in Saint Domingue. In the Spanish Caribbean, 68 per cent went to Cuba.

Adapted from Eltis and Richardson, *Atlas*, 200–03.

Complete data at http://www.slavevoyages.org/tast/index.faces.

Acquisition

Until the middle to late seventeenth century, slaves were not the principal commodity sought by Europeans in Africa. That is not to say that traders had not wanted slaves, but spices (pepper especially), animal hides, ivory, and gold were also major attractions. That changed with the growth of Brazil's sugar economy, the withering away of the native labour supply in the Americas, and the opening up of cash crop economies in the North American and Caribbean colonies. The demand and the prices for slaves were then pushed up, attracting trading specialists and exchange mechanisms in Africa along with European networks of capital investors, insurance brokers, ship designers, and builders. To be sure, slave trading was long established before the Portuguese arrived, and North African and Middle Eastern influence on sub-Saharan societies remained significant. But in the fifteenth century, the Portuguese intruded into a world of shifting political alliances, wars, kidnappings, and an active West African trade. It is likely that as much as 10 per cent of the sub-Saharan African population was enslaved at that time.[12] For the Portuguese, buying slaves came with a missionary responsibility to force Christian conversion on their acquisitions.

In a description of a Portuguese military expedition that took captives back to Portugal some time before 1460, the chronicler described the shock, despair, and fears of the defeated and enslaved Africans but consoled himself and his readers with the assurance that the slaves would now be converted to Christianity. When the royal share of the cargo was delivered in Portugal:

> The Prince was there mounted on a powerful horse, accompanied by his retinue, distributing his favors, like a man who wished to derive little material advantage from his share [he then gave away the slaves that were his due] since his main source of wealth lay in his own purpose ... the salvation of those souls that before were lost.[13]

The Prince was Henry the Navigator, who is discussed further in Chapter Three and who was instrumental in extending Portugal's maritime reach and the slave trade that followed. The apparently sincere blending of an aggressive Christian mission with the enslavement of "heathens" eventually faded, and religious piety became more and more a somewhat cynical accompaniment to the real objective of acquiring slaves. The Portuguese established political and economic relations with various African states, and Jesuit missionaries competed for African souls south of Islamic influence. For the most part, however, African peoples retained their regional or local spiritual and cultural practices until they were enslaved and then fed into the systems where their identities would be redefined.

The industry was never controlled completely by the Europeans but rather depended on African agents acquiring slaves in the interior and shipping them to the coast. In 1498, the Portuguese rounded the Cape of Good Hope for the first time, opening a sea route to Asia, with results discussed further in Chapter Three. On the east side of the continent, the Portuguese established a colony in Mozambique and took over half a million slaves from there in the nineteenth century. The northern Europeans who came after the Iberians to West and East Africa also dealt with African suppliers, merchants, and the local politicians who charged duties when European ships anchored off the coast. Regardless of the extensive African part in the trade, Europeans did shape it simply by expanding its scale and range and by keeping it profitable. Statistics show clearly the volume of slaves shipped from specific embarkation points. However, while their origins were not always identified, we can be sure that aggressive enslaving led to some regional depopulation.[14] Europeans traded for slaves with iron bars, alcohol, guns and gunpowder, tobacco, and great quantities of fabrics along with small manufactured items. Specie, in silver and gold coins and gold dust, was used along with small cowry shells from the Maldives atolls in the Indian Ocean. The shells were from sea snails dried and packed into reed baskets (as many as 12,000 to a unit) and introduced into economies from Asia and Polynesia to the northern reaches of North America. In parts of India and China, for example, they survived until they were replaced by copper coins or paper bills. As exchange, the shells floated in value, but because they came from a single and limited source, they had as much or more value as many other materials. They were used extensively in Africa both as jewellery and as money in the exchange nexus.

After a long period of price fluctuation, the cost of slaves rose steadily after the early eighteenth century, doubling by the end of the century, and then doubling again by the early to mid-nineteenth century.[15] The inflation was especially notable in the early nineteenth century in line with rising demand in Cuba and Brazil and higher transit costs because of Britain's attempted injunction of the trade. The expansion of the cotton economy in the United States after the end of the slave trade from Africa meant that the price of American-born slaves rose, too, in what was a closed domestic market. There the slave's value was tied to health, temperament, and productivity.[16] Contrived wars and kidnapping raids disfigured many local economies in Africa, where European goods upset local production in an area that was home to about half the continent's peoples as the slavers drew heavily on adults in their prime while taking a minority of children and older slaves.

Capture was the start of up to a year's pain, anxiety, humiliation, and alienation. In many communities, criminals were sentenced to slavery and became available to the market. Some slaves who ended up in America had actually volunteered their services to retire a debt but then had been swept up in a raid or in an opportunistic resale. There were random and private acquisitions, planned kidnapping forays, and genuine political or territorial conflicts with their inevitable prisoners, many of whom were spared death to be sold.[17] The delivery of slaves to the coast involved a chain of contacts and intermediaries who came and went as regional availability boomed and then ebbed. In the second half of the eighteenth century, an average of 80,000 slaves annually were loaded for the Atlantic crossing on some 200 to 250 ships representing every slave trading nation. Hundreds of small-scale acquisitions, first in the interior and then in individual or small groups put together by the coastal merchants and maritime traders, sent an average of 300 to 400 slaves per ship to America. The gross statistics given in thousands and then millions of human beings should be understood first in terms of small numbers who were captured, transported, and sold in thousands of individual transactions.

The term "coffle" is derived from the Arabic for "caravan" and was used to describe groups of slaves en route to coastal markets. The coffles gathered together several or even dozens of slaves, invariably shackled and linked one to the other with ropes. The transit to the coast, often from hundreds of kilometres away, was marked by bullying, hunger, disease, injury, and exhaustion. It is difficult to estimate the numbers of slaves who were lost, but it was certainly very high on some routes and worth noting given the attention paid to the mortality rates of the Atlantic crossings. In the most generalized way, we may cautiously estimate that in one or another stage of enslavement up to one-quarter of the unfortunate millions who were intended for slavery died before they could be delivered.[18] At the end of the trek to the coast, the survivors of the coffle were confronted with the ocean, the tall-mast ships offshore, and white men, all of them strange sights for interior peoples. The stress of the weeks-long journey took its toll on the will and strength of the slaves, but for most the full horror of their plight had just begun. Rumours that the white men intended to eat them, the mystery and fear of the branding by the Portuguese to identify the slave, the poking and prodding by African merchants and white buyers, and the ultimate transfer from the pen to the ship meant more humiliation. What awaited the slave were long days, weeks, or months as the ship sailed along the coast, picking up more slaves in groups, sometimes only a few individuals at a time, before setting off across the Atlantic. The slave was introduced to metal shackles, a tiny space, controlled access to fresh air and water, and food that often was alien to them.

The Middle Passage

The images of traders, agents, and intermediaries physically examining slaves at African ports of embarkation were matched at the other end in Santo Domingo, Recife, or Charleston. It is an image we should retain. White men went over slaves anatomically, in visual and tactile procedures that followed all slaves through all phases of their lives. Initially, traders looked for traits such as fear, arrogance, defiance, or docility. Certain facial features were preferred, and women were examined for their potential for fieldwork or for their matrimonial and child-bearing potential, especially in North America where slave populations were more permanently fixed and slave family units were encouraged. In Brazil at certain times, in some environments, female slaves were not welcome.[19] For the most part, the predatory white buyer or seller or intermediary self-consciously ignored his role in the debasement of the African captive. The same was true, of course, of the African merchants and princes who were crucial to the commerce. For whites, the testing of worthiness for slavery rested on notions of biological or cultural relativism that decided that the slave was morally or intellectually debased to begin with. The initial tests of worthiness of millions of Africans were repeated on millions of their offspring in the Americas who were bought and sold under similar conditions. The scrutiny in Africa meant that the slave, mostly young, who landed anywhere in the Americas left Africa as a physically healthy human being.

The ordeal of transit from African village to American wharf could take up to a year. For the reformers and abolitionists of the late eighteenth and early nineteenth centuries, the most notorious part of this process was the middle passage from Africa to America. Eyewitness descriptions from ships' captains, officers, physicians, and travellers were circulated in Britain and written in language that to this day evokes a shudder. The most common attack on the conditions of the human cargoes was on "tight packing." There was some overloading for enhanced profit, but even carefully measured capacities in custom-designed ships led to horrific conditions below decks where slaves were laid out in fetal poses like spoons in a drawer or in alternating rows placed head to toes. Illustrations added graphic force to abolitionist literature. Slaves, usually segregated by sex and sometimes linguistic background, spent up to two months in a swill of feces and vomit, where an outbreak of dysentery could turn a hold into a deadly compound. Stories, no doubt true, were circulated describing infected slaves being thrown overboard. Samples of deaths during the Atlantic crossing varied from 8 per cent to 18 per cent, which was roughly what white crews experienced. Moreover, the loss of, say, 10 per cent of very healthy young adults in a one- to two-month Atlantic crossing is a stunning reminder of the potency of contagious diseases in crowded quarters. As the Brazilian-bound Mahommah Baquaqua put it in a rare example of the slave's perspective: "We were thrust into the hold in a state of nudity [and] we were obliged to crouch upon the floor or sit down; day or night being the same to us." And in another much cited slave recollection, Olaudah Equiano noted that the heat below decks and the lack of space:

> almost suffocated us [and] the air soon became unfit for respiration, from ... loathsome smells, and brought on a sickness among the slaves, of which many died.... This wretched situation was again aggravated by the ... chains, now become insupportable; and the filth of the necessary tubs [buckets as latrines], into which children often fell and were almost suffocated. The shrieks of the [segregated] women, and the groans of the dying, rendered the whole a scene of horror....[20]

By the eighteenth and nineteenth centuries, ships entering ports often had to be quarantined because of smallpox. A British doctor in the 1840s assigned to a Royal Navy ship intercepting Brazilian-bound slaves during the British ban was shocked by what he saw. He noted naked "mothers with infants [trying] to suck a few drops ... from the lank, withered and skinny breasts of their mothers" and "presenting as woeful a spectacle of misery as it is possible to conceive." He found many men "afflicted with confluent small-pox" and others "with purulent ophthalmia, and the majority of what remained, with dysentery, ulcers, emaciation and exhaustion." His descriptions of the hunger and thirst and the pus from advanced stages of infectious eye disease, which led to permanent blindness for many, and the cowering, terrified "wretches" whose fear was palpable are vivid and painful. The stench of weeks of built-up "disgusting effluvium," rotting meat, and bilge water was overwhelming. His account describes an extreme but not rare example.[21]

Ships were designed to allow a minimal level of fresh air and sustenance and as much security as possible, but it was profit and not humanitarian concerns that pushed ship owners, officers, and crews to minimize the loss of slaves. But 300 slaves crammed into a 150-ton vessel, even one designed for human cargo, left little more than a few square feet per slave. Exercise was limited, sustenance uncertain, and crews were always on guard against slave uprisings. Historians have estimated that some 300,000 to 350,000 seamen of all nationalities took part in the slave trade during its history, and at any time during the eighteenth century several thousand sailors were engaged in the transportation of slaves, usually in crews of about 20 to 30 sailors per ship. The composition of some crews included freed blacks and mixed coloured, especially on Portuguese and Brazilian ships, who, in the latter case to be sure, added a peculiar relationship to the cargo. This vast floating "proletariat" often spent years at sea, cruising in coastal waters or simply anchored off the African coast.

Dealing with human cargoes meant that slave ships likely attracted sailors who accepted and perhaps relished roles that required them to apply physical punishments and humiliations to their charges. Otherwise, the appeal of the trade, as with most seaborne occupations, might have been the opportunity for obscurity for escaped criminals, runaway husbands, and servant deserters, or the promise of higher pay than in other maritime trade. The perils of ocean travel in the age of sail were great for everyone, and the slave ship was not a place for the faint of heart or the compassionate. Not only did white sailors die en route in comparable numbers to the slaves they tended, but the "white man's graveyard" took its toll on Europeans in equatorial Africa or tropical America. Desertions were inevitable. The numbers of sailors who went ashore in Africa or the Caribbean in search of sex or rest and who stayed ashore permanently was another variable in the complex world of the slave trade. Slave ship sailors deserted in larger numbers than elsewhere in maritime trade. On another level, any seaman with serious moral objections to transporting captive human cargoes could not last long in the trade. The case of John Newton (1725–1807) is instructive. His reaction to his experiences on a slave voyage brought about a deep religious conversion and commitment. His evangelical disposition stayed with him throughout the rest of his life. He became a Church of England clergyman and a renowned hymnist. With the poet William Cowper, he composed the *Olney Hymns* that included the memorable "Amazing Grace" ("I once was blind but now I see"). His abolitionist tract *Thoughts Upon the African Slave Trade* (1788) contributed to the growing British antislavery movement of the late eighteenth century. He lived long enough to see some fruit from his labours, dying in 1807 just as Parliament passed the act banning the British slave trade.[22]

Every European maritime and slave trading nation built and designed ships for trade, for passenger travel, and for war. Portugal and Brazil, the largest carriers, were also the most active in slave ship design. By the eighteenth century, most ships ranged in size from 150 to 300 imperial tons. Even by contemporary standards, these vessels were small in comparison to other cargo-carrying ships, being rarely more than 120 feet long with narrow beam widths and tight deck surfaces that determined the few square feet of space allotted to slaves, with only slightly more space for crew. As calculated from cargoes and tonnage data, the ships usually carried 1.6 slaves per ton so that a customized slave carrier of 150 imperial tons was designed to carry about 250 slaves. The correlations were not exact, and slave traders experimented with deck design and estimates of how much water and food to carry aboard for each slave and crew member for a voyage of several weeks. What is notable about the slave ship and its conditions and the slave trade in general is how it was much the same for the British, the Portuguese, the French, and all others. The physical treatment of a slave on a Portuguese ship bound for Brazil was much the same as it would be for a slave on a French or British ship bound for Martinique or Jamaica, respectively. What was different was what awaited the slave at the end of the voyage. Slave ship crews were on average twice as large as crews on other merchant ships. Feeding, guarding, and exercising large numbers of captives demanded a higher than usual crew to tonnage ratio.

The slave ship functioned as a prison. A minimal diet of 2,000 calories a day per person required ships to carry several tons of grains and dried and salted meat. Slaves were fed twice or three times a day. The most common meal in the eighteenth century was boiled rice or other grain with some yams and perhaps some dried meat, fish, or vegetables. Scurvy afflicted slaves and crews alike. One estimate shows that a 65-kilogram barrel of water needed to be stowed for every person aboard. Delays for storms or calm seas could add enough time to a voyage to deplete a ship's stores. Shipwrecks and successful slave revolts occurred often enough to raise insurance costs. There were occasional crew mutinies, a not unexpected outcome considering the conditions. But slave mortality was the main concern for profit-seeking shippers. There are accounts of slave suicides or of slaves so depressed they refused food and water and wasted away. Slaves did perish from wounds incurred from punishments, but in the end the chief killers were the fearsome smallpox or the "bloody flux." The end of the voyage brought another adjustment, from being captive in cruel circumstances to property in transit, to bartered commodity in a strange role in a strange place in America. Yet in spite of the alienation and confusion, Africans of various ethnic backgrounds found common ground in their common plight in ways that survived in the Americas through a bonding in colour, culture, and class.[23]

Slaves were sold in mostly small lots in the debarkation markets. A shipload of 300 slaves might find up to 100 separate buyers, once again evidence of an industry predicated on the sum of many small transactions from the villages of the Congo or Angola to the dozens of loading sites on the West African coast to the wharves and markets of Salvador, Kingston, Havana, Charleston, and a dozen other New World ports. Slaves usually lost their African names and were renamed by merchants, buyers in Africa or America, or their eventual owners. Usually they were given simple tags like Tom, Juan, Pierre, or Nancy or classical names like Cleo, Caesar, or Cato. In the English system "Sambo" appeared with some frequency. From the earliest period to the end of slavery, everywhere in the Americas, slaves awarded themselves surnames that might reflect their owners or modified African recovered names. But inventories, deeds, censuses, sale advertisements, or runaway notices seldom acknowledged a surname for a slave.[24]

Simultaneously, as the volumes of slaves crossing the Atlantic rose at a spectacular rate in the late eighteenth century, and as the public was made increasingly sensitive to the frightful details of the trade, the abolitionist movement in Britain took off. As we shall see, a strenuous series of campaigns against the trade pressured Parliament to outlaw it in 1807 as a prelude to abolishing slavery in the British Empire in 1834. Thereafter, the British put pressure on the Spanish and Brazilian trade. The United States, in its 1787 Constitution, allowed slavery and the slave trade to continue but included a provision to end the trade as of 1808. Otherwise, the Constitution confirmed slavery as a property right and allowed for the domestic trade in slaves.

Chapter Seven below follows the convoluted trail of abolitionism and the commercial opportunism and cynicism that kept the slave trade alive for decades after the initial flash of abolitionist hope. From the late 1700s through the early decades of the 1800s, neither the French Revolution's idealism, nor the United States' trumpeting of rights, nor the independence movements and slave-ending revolutions in Spanish America did anything to deter the trade in slaves. It continued, illegally in some ways and legally in others, until the second half of the nineteenth century. The argument that the attacks on slavery in the "age of revolutions" began to sound the death knell of the institution needs to be tempered by the fact that even after Britain and the United States outlawed the Atlantic trade, over half a million slaves were landed in Cuba and a million and a half in Brazil. Slaves were landed in Puerto Rico as late as 1864.

Notes

1 W. Reginald Ward and Richard P. Heitzenrater, eds., *The Works of John Wesley: Journals and Diaries V 1765–1775* Volume 22 (Nashville: Abingdon Press, 1997), 307.

2 Curtin, *The Atlantic Slave Trade*. See the sections in J.C. Miller, *Slavery and Slaving in World History: A Bibliography*, Vol. I (Millwood: Kraus, 1993), in the entries numbered from 9001 to 10, 344 and in Volume II (Armonk: ME Sharpe, 1999), entries numbered 3473 to 3894 for a sense of the impact of Curtin's work. Klein, *The Atlantic Slave Trade*, Introduction, has a useful comment on the literature.

3 Klein, *The Atlantic Slave Trade*, Introduction.

4 See the superb Eltis and Richardson, *Atlas of the Transatlantic Slave Trade*. Their immense database can be accessed at http://www.slavevoyages.org/tast/index.faces. See also James Walvin, *Atlas of Slavery* (Harlow: Pearson Education, 2006).

5 Tannenbaum, *Slave and Citizen*, 16–36 has a brief overview of the trade and should be compared to Klein's 1999 *The Atlantic Slave Trade* as an example of changing historiographical approaches. See also Klein's older *The Middle Passage: Comparative Studies in the Atlantic Slave Trade* (Princeton: Princeton University Press, 1978).

6 On the "tight packing" question, see Klein, *The Atlantic Slave Trade*, 130–60; Klein, *The Middle Passage*, 73–94; Lisa A. Lindsay, *Captives as Commodities: The Transatlantic Slave Trade* (Upper Saddle River: Prentice Hall, 2008), 89–96. For a notorious example of the conditions of white servant passengers in the eighteenth century, see Gottlieb Mittelberger, *Journey to Pennsylvania* (Cambridge, MA: Belknap, 1960), 12–15. Mittelberger noted that adults were given a space of two feet by six feet, "packed like herrings," and he recorded "smells, fumes, horrors, vomiting" as well as "fever, dysentery, heat, constipation, boils, scurvy ... mouth rot ... filthy water ... thick with dirt, and full of worms," and the "ship's biscuit ... full of red worms and spiders' nests." He noted that 32 children had died (perhaps a third of those on board) and that those under seven years of age "rarely survive."

7 Elizabeth Abbott, *Sugar, A Bittersweet History* (Toronto: Penguin, 2008), Chapter 5 offers a brief overview of production values. There is a huge literature on the economics of slave productivity. The recent wide-ranging anthology of Eltis *et al.*, *Slavery in the Development of the Americas* shows how sophisticated economic models and analyses are being applied to the slave trade and slave-based commodity production. See also Gad Heuman and James Walvin, eds., *The Slavery Reader* (London: Routledge, 2003), Part 6.

8 Manning, "The Slave Trade."

9 Eltis and Richardson, *Atlas*, 21, 37, 39.

10 David Brion Davis, *The Problem of Slavery in the Age of Revolutions: 1770–1823* (Ithaca: Cornell University Press, 1975), Chapter 10.

11 Klein, *The Atlantic Slave Trade*, Chapter 6.

12 Thornton, *Africa and Africans*, Chapter 4.

13 Conrad, *Children of God's Fire*, 10.

14 Klein, *The Atlantic Slave Trade*, Appendix (tables); Eltis and Richardson, *Atlas*, Tables 1–6; Walvin, *Atlas of Slavery*, Chapter 8. On population decline in Africa because of the slave trade, see Thornton, *Africa and Africans*, 72–73.

15 David Eltis and David Richardson, "Prices of African Slaves Newly Arrived in the Americas, 1673–1865: New Evidence on Long Term Trends and Regional Differentials," in Eltis, *et al.*, *Slavery in the Development of the Americas*, 181–218.

16 Laird Bergad, "American Slave Markets During the 1850s: Slave Price Rises in the United States, Cuba and Brazil in Comparative Perspective," in Eltis, *et al.*, *Slavery in the Development of the Americas*, Chapter 7.

17   Thornton, *Africa and Africans*, Chapter 4. See also the brisk and readable "The Slave Trade" in Richard Hofstadter, *America at 1750: A Social Portrait* (New York: Vintage, 1973); Elizabeth Donnan, ed., *Documents Illustrative of the History of the Slave Trade to America*, Vol. II (Washington, DC: Carnegie Institution, 1931) in which "The Travels of Mungo Park," 632–42, is a standard contemporary account.

18   Klein, *The Atlantic Slave Trade*, 103–60.

19   Klein, *The Atlantic Slave Trade*, Chapters 4 and 5.

20   Lindsay, *Captives as Commodities*, 90; Robin Law and Paul Lovejoy, *The Biography of Mahommah Gardo Baquaqua* (Princeton: Markus Wiener, 2007), Introduction. On Equiano, see Angelo Costanza, ed., *The Interesting Narrative of the Life of Olaudah Equiano* (Peterborough: Broadview, 2004), 73. See also Bergad, "Slaves in their Own Words," in his *Comparative Histories*. A worthy compilation of graphic images with an emphasis on French sources can be found in Isabelle Aguet, *La Traite Des Nègres* (Genève: Editions Minerva, 1971).

21   Thomas Nelson, *Remarks on the Slavery and Slave Trade in the Brazils* (1846), quoted in Conrad, *Children of God's Fire*, 43–48.

22   Emma Christopher, *Slave Ship Sailors and Their Captive Cargoes, 1730–1807* (New York: Cambridge University Press, 2006) is the best current study of the topic. See also Marcus Rediker, *The Slave Ship: A Human History* (New York: Viking, 2007). For the use of slaves on Portuguese and Brazilian ships including slave sailors on slave ships, see Klein and Luna, *Slavery in Brazil*, 66–67. On John Newton, see David Dabydeen, John Gilmore, and Cecily Jones, eds., *The Oxford Companion to Black British History* (Oxford: Oxford University Press, 2007), 343–44; and Bruce D. Hindmarsh, "John Newton," in *Oxford Dictionary of National Biography* (Oxford: Oxford University Press, 2004). Marcus Rediker, *The Slave Ship: A Human History* (New York: Viking, 2007) offers a sensitive portrayal of Newton in Chapter 6.

23   Klein, *The Atlantic Slave Trade*, 93–95. See the example in Eltis and Richardson, *Atlas*, 211.

24   For North America, see Genovese, *Roll, Jordan, Roll*, 443–50; for Brazil, see Schwartz, *Sugar Plantations*; for the English Caribbean, see Richard Dunn, *Sugar and Slaves: The Rise of the Planter Class in the English West Indies, 1624–1713* (Chapel Hill: University of North Carolina Press, 1972), 252.

3 | Slavery and the Shaping of Colonial Latin America: 1500–1800

"When there are such lands there should be profitable things without number."
—Christopher Columbus, *Journal of the First Voyage*, November 1492

The Legacies of Prince Henry the Navigator and Christopher Columbus

Fifteenth-century Iberia was perhaps the most culturally complex region of Europe with its Moorish architecture and place names, newly arrived sub-Saharan African slaves, free coloured people, converted Jews, converted Moors, and a revitalized Christian majority of bishops and priests, princes, lords and peasants, merchants and artists. It was also among the most dynamic. The century ended with a great flourish: in 1492, practising Jews were expelled, the last of the Moorish rulers were dispatched from Granada, Columbus reached the Caribbean, and the Pope agreed to divide the world between Spanish and Portuguese expansionists.

Portugal's Prince Henry (1396–1460), the fourth son of King John I of the House of Avis, was a major figure in the earliest phase of New World slavery. His policies, outlook, and actions led the way to Africa and out into the Atlantic. He was an energetic Christian, a patriotic Portuguese, and an enquiring, experimental, and ambitious intellectual. His reputation as a Christian expansionist took hold when he established a foothold in North Africa at Ceuta in Morocco in 1415. Henry was and remains celebrated as a nautical pioneer, acquiring the title of "Navigator" in the nineteenth century, although not because of any personal exploits on the high seas, because there were none. He founded a maritime school at Sagres that produced Vasco da Gama, who sailed around the Cape of Good Hope in 1498 and across the Indian Ocean to the Indian port of Calicut, and also Ferdinand

Magellan, whose crews made the first global circumnavigation in 1521 on behalf of Spain. Henry encouraged innovative design for the caravel and later the *nao* or carrack as ocean-going vessels. His part in the early stages of European exploration and expansion cannot be overstated. By having coasts and islands mapped and advancing "dead reckoning" navigation, rudimentary astronomy, and innovative, sturdier ship construction, Henry contributed to the seagoing revolution that set the stage for one of Europe's smallest nations to establish settlements and trading posts in Africa, India, China, Southeast Asia, and the Americas all before 1600.

As early as the 1450s, Henry's sailors (*marinheiros*) had gone south along the West African coast searching for souls to save, exchanging slaves for gold, dealing with Muslim traders, and establishing a beachhead on what would become the "slave coast." By the time Henry died in 1460, repentant for what he saw developing in the slave trade, African captives were making their way by the thousands into Iberia, often as slaves for noble families and affluent urban merchants, and more importantly to the Atlantic islands to harvest and refine sugar. In the space of a few decades, the Portuguese ventured into the Atlantic, colonized Sao Tome on the African coast, Madeira, the Cape Verde Islands, and far to the west, the Azores. By the time Columbus sailed into the Caribbean, the Spanish had acquired from Portugal and occupied the Canary Islands, just off the coast of Morocco. Those islands were known in antiquity and familiar to North Africans and Mediterranean Europeans alike. Indeed, Catalan sailors had likely sailed beyond Northwest Africa into the Atlantic in the thirteenth century. Chinese sailors had certainly visited East Africa, and the Vikings had been to what is now Newfoundland, long before the Iberians ventured into the great spaces, but neither had stayed. The Portuguese were leaders in probing the Atlantic, but the Spanish completed the crossing with the commission given to the Genoese sailor Cristoforo Colombo (1451–1507), Cristobal Colon to the Spanish and Christopher Columbus to the English.

When his three-vessel fleet made landfall in the Bahamas in October 1492, it was greeted by natives whose appearance, behaviour, and temperament were recorded by Columbus as exotic and peaceful. The natives had no inclusive term for their islands or for the mainland that lay beyond. The humanist and historian Peter Martyr (1457–1528) coined the term "New World," and by the early sixteenth century, it and "America" (named for the explorer Amerigo Vespucci) began appearing on maps to identify the land the Spanish referred to for some time as *las Indias* and the people as *los indios*. The explorers, cartographers, and traders who followed Columbus tended to describe the local Ciboney, Arawak (Taino), and Carib peoples as primitive and mostly friendly, notwithstanding some of their warlike traits and ritual cannibalism. Columbus kept journals of his four voyages throughout the Caribbean, and his descriptions were the first to reach Europeans. His accounts contain a mix of curiosity and condescension. He noted that the natives he encountered believed that he had descended "from the sky, and in this belief they received me, after they had overcome their fear." Amerigo Vespucci noted their absence of religion, calling the natives "Epicurean" and in a telling phrase, "very desirous of copulating with us Christians."[1] In any case, any favourable impressions of natives did not deter the Spanish and the Portuguese from enslaving them.

By the early decades of the sixteenth century, African slaves were arriving in the Caribbean. The Spanish also brought with them Christian zeal, Iberian steel, and horses. The initial Spanish assumption of exclusive domain in the Western Atlantic was challenged by the Portuguese, and in 1492 the Treaty of Tordesillas was signed by Spain and Portugal under the auspices of Pope Alexander VI. It was adjusted in 1494 when a line was drawn at longitude 39 degrees and 53 minutes west. Spain was given "rights" to all that was west of that line, taking in *all* the Americas, and the Portuguese assumed all that went east from the line, that is, Africa, India, and by 1529 much of Asia up to the Philippines archipelago. Such were the presumptions of the Iberians and the bilateral authority of the "infallible" Pope that the world at least on paper could be divided into exclusive imperial hemispheres. The fateful revision of the treaty in 1494 pushed the line of demarcation to the eastern section of South America in what would be Brazil, the only Portuguese perch in the Americas (see Map 1.1).

In the space of a lifetime, Spanish colonization began to reshape the Greater Antilles and Central and South America in campaigns marked by death and social reconstruction. Hernando Cortes (1485–1547) landed in Mexico in 1518, not with sugar cuttings but with guns and men in armour. African slaves accompanied Cortes as military support, along with emissaries of the Church of Rome and a clutch of lethal diseases. Preceded by an advance army of deadly microbes, another *conquistador,* Francisco Pizarro (ca. 1478–1541), overran the Inca Empire in the Andes in the 1530s by force, diplomacy, and deceit. He destroyed much of Inca civilization without ever understanding it. In what proved to be a pattern for the future, Spanish conquerors grafted their settlement designs to Aztec and Inca systems of tribute and peonage, invoking the *repartimiento*, or in the Andes the *mita*, official procedures for attaching native labour for Spanish purposes. There was limited demand for African slaves in the *hacienda*s of South and Central America. No great cash crop economy was developed, and a New World neo-feudal system was stamped on the footprint of the Aztec and Inca regimes. In other ways, over time, African slaves along with native labour were used specifically in the gold and silver mines of New Spain (Mexico), New Granada (including Colombia and Venezuela), and Peru.

The Spanish Caribbean was another matter. Early on, Africans were brought to Cuba, Puerto Rico, and Santo Domingo (the island of Hispaniola, present-day Haiti and Dominican Republic). Columbus likely took some sugar cane cuttings from the Canaries on his first voyage, but most status- and profit-seeking Spaniards headed for the mainland, lured by land, gold, silver, and native labour. Indeed, gold and silver underwrote the Spanish Empire in America up to the early nineteenth century. In the Caribbean, settlement languished until the northern Europeans and their slaves took over the Lesser Antilles in the seventeenth century. Until the late eighteenth century, Spanish sugar production was limited to supplying its own American market. By contrast, when sugar came to Brazil, the Portuguese already had an eye on the European market.

In 1500, Pedro Alvares Cabral, sailing south from Portugal to round the Cape of Good Hope on his way to India, veered so far off course to the west that he made landfall at the easternmost point of South America. He understood it to be a Portuguese claim but saw little of value and went on his way. Eventually, assorted runaways and wanderers but more importantly some Portuguese entrepreneurs did settle along the northern shores. The area was initially known as *Terra da Santa Cruz* (Land of the Holy Cross), but "Brazil" took hold informally at first and then officially. When British and French interlopers went after the region's timber (brazilwood was one of the varieties available and was prized for its dye properties), Portugal decided to make a more formal stake in the land. Sugar was planted after 1510. The colony was established formally when an official fleet landed in 1532 and set up an administrative centre at Salvador da Bahia. A bishopric was established there in 1554. African slaves accompanied the administrators, priests, and merchants. A long stretch of the littoral (the coastal zone) was organized into 12 captaincies, units with administrative and economic authority. But the commissioned *donatarios* (grantees) were mostly incompetent and only two survived, one in the south and one in the north at Pernambuco where, with financial backing and native and African labour, sugar fields and mills appeared within a few years.[2] From a poor colonial outpost, Brazil then grew in importance to rival Portugal's interests in India and Asia.

The late medieval European market for Mediterranean sugar was limited by modest supply that kept prices high and prohibitive for all but the wealthy. The rising production in Madeira, the Azores, and the Spanish Canaries changed that, and it was changed again by the end of the sixteenth century when rising volumes of slave-produced South American sugar arrived in Europe. By then *engenhos* (mills, usually combined with sugar fields; *ingenios* in Spanish) dotted the landscape of coastal Brazil.

Sugar is a sweet carbohydrate, a confection, and a dietary supplement. Either as a sweetener or a base for rum, Brazilian brandy, and molasses, regular access to abundant supplies of sugar changed European culinary and consumption habits, and demand for it changed the course of Brazilian history. By the eighteenth century, sugar had been joined by the other American slave-based cash crops—tobacco, cacao (the chocolate bean), cotton, and coffee. Brazil's growth was helped by rich soils, a hot and humid climate, abundant land, and scarce or declining native resistance. Planters, refiners, merchants and shippers, improved shipbuilding technology, and eager European consumers combined to create an empire of sugar, where the cost of every pound of sugar was measured against the value of the African slaves who maintained it.[3]

Spain's population was approaching 6 million in 1500, but the peasantry that formed the nation's majority was not recruited for the colonies. Official policies discouraged wholesale peasant resettlement to its American colonies, because Spain's military exploits in Europe during the sixteenth and seventeenth centuries required an accessible pool of military aged men enlisted from the lower classes. But a steady flow of Spanish entrepreneurs and opportunists did cross the Atlantic. Portugal, with a small population of between 1 and 2 million, had little or no peasant or servant surplus, but several thousand Portuguese—church officials, government bureaucrats, planters, farmers, and merchants—emigrated each year to Africa, Asia, and America during the colonial period. The flow of white Portuguese to Brazil remained steady through the colonial period so that by the early nineteenth century whites comprised about one-third of the recorded population even as Africans were arriving in staggering numbers. Between 1500 and the early nineteenth century, perhaps half a million Spaniards, half a million Britons, several hundred thousand Portuguese, and smaller numbers of German, Dutch, and French migrants landed in the Americas. Their motivations varied, but the lure of improved economic or social status was all the incentive they needed. By contrast, African slaves came to the Americas at roughly a six to one ratio over white Europeans, a ratio that rose steadily from the first importations.[4]

Before 1600, much of the labour for Brazil's sugar production came from Brazilian natives as servants under Portuguese control; as contract, barter, or wage labour; and as slaves sold to the Portuguese by other natives. But there were impediments to the long-term use of native labour. One was the absence in the South American lowlands of a tradition of disciplined sedentary agriculture, and another was the constant assault of European diseases on pristine native gene pools. On the other hand, large numbers of Africans were familiar with the seasonal rhythms of crop cultivation and were also able to survive the worst of the epidemics that ravaged native populations. In the early colonial period, *engenhos* used both native and African labour.[5]

Africans in Spanish America were streamed into the Caribbean or Vera Cruz plantations or the alluvial deposits and underground mines of Peru, Mexico, and Colombia where, well into the eighteenth century, they mingled with native labour.[6] Urban Spanish American slaves made shoes and clothes or worked as sailors, porters, construction workers, and personal aides. While significant numbers of African women were brought to the Americas in the sixteenth and seventeenth centuries, the ratios of women to men in the African slave cargoes diminished over time to one or two females to three males.[7] Following African precedent, female slaves were usually assigned to fieldwork in Brazil. But women were also taken into affluent Latin American households and used as wet nurses, domestics, seamstresses, cooks, and concubines.

Status and the Early Latin American Slavery Codes

We can be sure that the early Portuguese traders and Prince Henry himself knew that Roman law acknowledged slavery as legally and morally acceptable and that no African was enslaved without the enslaver assuming a right to do so. The slave had only tenuous rights in these circumstances. For the Portuguese and Spanish and to some extent the French, the legacies of Roman law formed the basis of codifying slavery, and those laws were taken to their colonies. In Spanish America, the legal framework, not simply for slavery but for colonial governance in general, was taken from *Las Siete Partidas* (the "seven part" codes or laws), a medieval set of legal, moral, and social statutes and principles. The Portuguese relied on a mixture of what was considered "natural law," God's divine order, and appropriate borrowings from Roman law. In 1603, the *Codigo Filipino* with specific references to slavery and the slave trade was issued and was retained in Brazil beyond its independence in 1823. The language used to explain legalized slavery for the Portuguese could be very decisive. The Brazilian legal historian, Agostinho Malheiro put it this way:

> From the moment a man is reduced to the condition of a *thing*, from the moment he becomes the property of another person subject to his *power* and *authority*, he is regarded as legally *dead*, deprived of every right ... as Roman Law previously established.... This is expressly laid down in various old Portuguese laws....

Malheiro goes on to say that while the 1824 Constitution, which was to be an enlightened correction to the ills of the past, absolutely prohibited the whip, torture, branding, and other acts "suitable only to barbarians.... [T]his was understood to mean *except in the case of the slave*" [emphasis added].[8] And long before the Romans codified slavery, Aristotle's *Politics* had determined, pithily, that "he is by nature a slave who is capable of belonging to another." New World slaveholders did not need to read Aristotle to apply the principle. In the case of the French, the Dutch, and the British, there was a process of innovation, of creating laws in America for slavery, where none existed at home. In other words, the northern Europeans in North America and the Caribbean designed and applied on site a unique set of codes that were original American laws. The British case was especially telling in that Africans were in the colonial population *before* codes were written, and those codes were carried over into the new United States in direct or modified form. All slave codes and ordinances spelled out permissible punishments and the disposal rights of masters. But while law can tell us much, it can never explain the day-to-day and unrecorded relations, thoughts, and actions that sustained slavery.

The question of how slaves were treated in various settings is a vexing one compounded by time, place, and occupation. Treatment mostly depended on the moral or psychological temperament of owners; the restraining influence of the Church or the legal system; and the indifference, aggression, or even tolerance of overseers. Slaves on large plantations were subject to more discipline than other slaves. Urban slaves such as household servants, merchant's helpers, or qualified tradespeople often had marketable skills and could be hired for wages that went either to master or slave or both. The numbers of free persons of colour in the Spanish and Portuguese settlements was a significant demographic and cultural feature of colonial Latin America. Freed Africans engaged in sexual and formal marital relations with natives and free mixed race peoples (see Chapter Six). However, the apparent fluidity and openness in Latin American slavery is no longer accepted unequivocally by historians as a sign of inclusion, fairness, or colour blindness. Historians note that Brazilian slavery was not only physically harsh but less flexible than the laws suggest. And we might ask the question: did the prospects of a moral identity, manumission, and a path to self-purchase (a legally formalized process called *coartacion* in Spanish and *coartacao* in Portuguese) make the Iberian slave less oppressed than those subject to the more restrictive Dutch, French, or Anglo-American codes? What difference did it make if the slave was at the mercy of a system that even in relatively liberal circumstances humiliated and routinely beat him or her and which in the final tally decided how and when manumission might be granted? In Brazil, slaves were maimed for offences against the prerogatives of masters, subject to emotional and psychological anxiety, and sometimes worked to an early death. All this despite the protests and objections of sympathetic observers and commentators. Not for all slaves and not all the time, of course, but as a rule of thumb slavery everywhere was marked by threatened, actual, or implied violence, and the prospect of sale and separation in the case of slave families.[9]

Portuguese and Spanish practices were shaped by Iberian precedent; well-established slave codes stemming from a longer, direct experience with slavery, however modest in scale; and the oversight of the Crown and Church.[10] But we now see that Iberians did not regard slaves with any more care than did other Europeans, the laws and the power of the Church notwithstanding. The long span of the slave era should temper easy conclusions. Still, when we do look at the approaches of the northern Europeans after 1600 there can be no doubt that their legal codes, economic theories, and racial attitudes were responsible for slave regimes that differed substantively from those of the Spanish and Portuguese. As Chapters Four and Five note, local northern European colonial elites set their own rules prohibiting manumission.[11] Those differences meant that on the eve of the US Civil War in 1860, 90 per cent of the "coloured" peoples in the southern United States were slaves, but a slight majority of "coloured" people in the Spanish Caribbean were free, as were a majority of Brazil's "coloured" population.

Slavery and the Shaping of Colonial Brazil

After the 1530s, the settlement of the Brazilian coast from Pernambuco in the north to Spanish claims in the south was well underway despite native attacks on *engenhos*. In a pattern that was repeated all over the Americas, retaliation pushed natives farther and farther inland, enslaved them, or subsumed them into mixed race communities. Sadly, natives themselves became disease carriers, infecting inland populations even before the Portuguese contacted them. By the end of the sixteenth century, natives had been displaced along Brazil's coastline.

As sugar cultivation was pushed inland, settlement was encouraged by the merging of the Spanish and Portuguese Crowns in 1580. Greater military assets were now available, law and order tightened, and French and British encroachment effectively curbed. The massacre of the remaining members of a French Protestant (Huguenot) settlement near Rio de Janeiro in 1555 was a sharp example of combined imperial interest and sectarian protectionism. Brazil was emphatically Portuguese and Catholic.

The landscape was, however, raw, generally poorly organized, and almost uniformly rural. Although Portuguese Jesuits did establish schools and missions, Brazil lacked Spanish America's urban cultures and well-organized Church infrastructure, administrative hierarchy, and universities. But after 1550 and into the early seventeenth century, investment, slaves, and sugar spurred development, pushing the frontier farther into the interior and confirming permanent settlement. Nearly 30,000 African slaves were landed at Brazilian ports between 1570 and 1600, the first of the millions who would follow.[12]

By the early seventeenth century, Brazil's coastal population was made up of scattered native remnants, African arrivals, some white immigrants and white *crioullos* (Brazilian-born Portuguese), and growing numbers of mixed coloured. To the Portuguese, natives of original stock were *negros da terra* (local blacks) and Africans were *negros de Guine* and also, simply, *negro* as a convenient or dismissive way of defining all non-whites. It was also commonly used as a synonym for slave. Colour and heredity began to form an interesting racial taxonomy to identify the emerging mixed white-native people, known as *mamelucos, mesticos,* or *caboclos* in Portuguese; or *mulattos* (mixed white-black, sometimes spelled with one "t"); or *cafuzos* or *zambos* (mixed black-native). In time, those groupings gave way to a dazzling number of pigmentation variations and encouraged a practice of using subtle identifications based on shades of colour. For example, a twentieth-century experiment asked a group of 100 Bahians to identify the racial characteristics of pictures of nine people. They came up with 40 different definitions, all expressed in colour variation, many of which are untranslatable. The descriptions for a *mulatto* were qualified as "*branco mulato, mulato bem claro, mulato sarara, mulato escuro* or *mulato claro*" and show the difficulty in identifying mixtures that continued to be more complex over time.[13]

The sugar economy and the African slaves who sustained it meant that by the last part of the sixteenth century a European-run Africa-to-America axis was in place. In 1576, Portuguese traders, militia, and African allies helped to retard a threat to the Kingdom of the Congo. A trading station was set up at Luanda, far to the south of the original slave trading zone, and the catchment area for slaves was enlarged. By then, the transition from native to African slave labour in Brazil was nearly complete, and the Spanish *asiento*, a licence to foreigners to ship slaves to the Spanish colonies, sparked a rise in Portuguese slave trading. In the settled areas of Portuguese Brazil in 1600, there were about 30,000 whites and over 50,000 natives and mixed races. Of 30,000 African slaves who had arrived in Brazil in the previous 30 years, only 15,000 were counted in 1600. An early pattern appeared where mortality, runaways, and manumissions meant that slaves had to be constantly imported to maintain levels or to ensure expansion. In 1800, there were nearly 1 million African or Afro-Brazilian slaves in a total coloured population of about 1.75 million, although a startling 2.5 million African slaves had been imported into Brazil up to that point.[14]

By the middle of the seventeenth century, 90 per cent of Brazil's wealth came from sugar exports. Even when Caribbean sugar undercut Brazil's monopoly in the late seventeenth century and its share of the market dipped, sugar remained at the core of Brazil's economy and continued to be the key sector through the gold mining boom in the eighteenth century. In 1585, some 120 *engenhos* (the plantation-sugar mill complexes), over half of them in Pernambuco, were producing a few thousand metric tons of sugar. In 1630, an estimated 350 mills produced some 20,000 metric tons of sugar annually. That growth stretched the geographical range of the crop, raising production as it did. By the middle of the nineteenth century, Brazil's sugar production reached 200,000 metric tons a year and Cuba's twice that much. This occurred after the collapse of Haiti's sugar economy in the 1790s when sugar producers in Spanish Cuba and in Brazil went on a binge of slave importation. Between 1800 and the 1860s, some 700,000 Africans were landed in Cuba and an astonishing 2.2 million in Brazil, where coffee and cotton plantations joined sugar as high volume export commodities. Much of this occurred after the United States and Britain had withdrawn from the slave trade and when abolitionist talk circulated widely throughout the Atlantic world. The Portuguese defied British pressure, though in 1827 newly independent Brazil promised to end importation by 1831. But it casually reneged on the promise.[15] Brazil's role as the hemisphere's greatest importer of Africans began early and ended late.

Planters invested heavily in land, draft animals, buildings, machinery, and technicians (metal workers and millers). Mills were driven by water or oxen, but from the cane cutters to the boilers, human energy made it all go. The *engenhos* were miniature fiefdoms, employing some free labour as well as 80 to 120 slaves on the larger average estates of 1,000 hectares. The *enghenieros* (planters) were the tiny tip of the pyramid of mostly petty slaveholders on much smaller plots of land in the shadow of the grandees' prestige and political power.[16] Life for slaves on small holdings was unlikely to be any more congenial than life in the *engenho*, and the intimacy was often more than painful for the handful of slaves found on those holdings. The Muslim Mahommah Gardo Baquaqua, introduced in Chapter Two, left one of the great slave autobiographies. He was bought by a Brazilian smallholder who had a "wife, two children and a woman who was related to him. He had four other slaves." The master held daily worship sessions, forcing his slaves to kneel and repeat his scriptural phrases in what was to the slaves a foreign tongue. In an effort to get the slaves to respond the owner held a whip:

> and those who showed signs of inattention or drowsiness were immediately
> brought to consciousness by a smart application of the whip. This mostly
> fell to the lot of the female slave, who would often fall asleep in spite of the
> images, crossings, and other like pieces of amusement.

His touch of sarcasm is perhaps an afterthought, but his keen mind saw the pain and absurdity in slavery, and he notes, "I was ... placed at hard labor, such as none but slaves and horses are put to." He was also sold and resold in the swirling smallholding labour market of Brazil, all the while keeping silent while suffering near constant verbal and physical abuse. His itinerary (or odyssey) is unique in its scope. He was taken from Djougou in what is now Benin and shipped from Ouidah (Widah) to Pernambuco, thence to Rio de Janeiro and Rio Grande do Sul, and then as a sailor to New York, several thousand kilometres away, where he escaped to become part of the black abolitionist community. He spent time in Boston, in Chatham, Canada West, and two years in the Haitian Republic before returning to New York and then to England in 1855.[17]

What Baquaqua described for the early nineteenth century might be applied all the way back to 1500. Slavery was work, physically demanding, repetitive, tiring, and, unlike free labour, often brutally enforced and always edging to humiliation. Fieldwork was the bane of the slave. According to testimony, the hours spent stooped over weeds or crops in tropical heat was a commonly remembered agony. The use of draft animals supplemented but never replaced human hands, backs, and implements such as hoes, axes, shovels, machetes, and hammers. In coastal Brazil after land was cleared, small pieces of seed cane were planted and tended for a year or more until the cane was mature and ready to cut. The harvested cane was hauled to the mill and crushed by wooden rollers driven by a cog mechanism turned by water, oxen, or in some cases human power. Larger *engenhos* used the task system, assigning a specific job to a particular slave or group of slaves that when completed allowed the slaves to rest. This division of labour was used in fieldwork and among the skilled maintenance workers and boiler workers where boilers often ran all night. The regimentation of life for the *engenho* slave began for most with an assembly at dawn, and even when assigned tasks were completed, some gardening or laundry or other personal chores needed attention.[18] Injuries and illness were tolerated or anticipated, as were defections and death, and Brazilian slaveholders adapted early to a steady replenishing of their labour force from what seemed an endless supply of Africans.

Whites dominated the skilled and supervisory jobs, and there was a clear division of status whereby on large *engenho* mixed coloured slaves or paid free coloured labour were found away from the fields where the work fell mostly to the black slave, especially newly arrived Africans, including women. There the whip or painless incentives, such as time off for religious holidays, helped to maintain the flow of sugar.[19] Before the advent of steam power, Brazil's production model was efficient for its time and influenced the Caribbean sugar economy as an important example of knowledge transfer. As for the apt "factory in the field" image for the *engenho*, it bears noting that apart from shipbuilding, mining, and arms manufacturing, few early modern production systems were as sophisticated as the cane to granulated sugar process. It not only depended on favourable weather but on labour efficiency and tight coordination. After the crushing of the cane, a refined sugar was produced by boiling, skimming, filtering, and settling. White and brown sugars along with residual molasses were produced. The sugars were granulated by hammering and then packed in bulk in casks or as cakes or loaves. Every bit of the recovered crop was marketable. The process would be as punishing for the slave in the nineteenth century as it was in the sixteenth century.[20]

In any analysis of this centuries-long industry, the effects on the slave, and after abolition on indentured servants or peasant labour, must be seen as a continuous assault on the body and mind. Nothing in tropical Africa could prepare the slave for the enervating demoralization of the tropical Brazilian or Caribbean sugar culture. Even during breaks in the cycle, slaves were busy raising pigs and cattle; growing some edible crops; and maintaining or repairing the tools, sheds, and other paraphernalia that went with production. The reach of the *engenheiros* was wide, and local independent farmers were often contracted for additional sugar cane, making some of them dependent on the larger producers.

The Dutch in Brazil

Earlier teasing intrusions by northern Europeans into Iberian-held territory resumed in the early seventeenth century when Brazil's economic potential and flimsy political infrastructure became a target of the Dutch. The failure of the Portuguese Crown in 1580 had led to a joint monarchy and the protective weight of the Spanish Habsburgs. At the same time, the English, French, and Dutch had begun to ignore Spanish and Portuguese claims to hegemony in the Americas, Africa, India, East Asia, and Europe itself. The French in particular tested Portuguese resolve in Brazil and intruded into the slave trade in Africa. English privateers, most notably Sir Francis Drake (ca. 1540–96), raided Spanish bullion ships with regularity in the 1570s, and Sir John Hawkins (1532–95) had broken into the Spanish slave trade as early as 1562 with limited success. By the early seventeenth century, the newly independent Dutch Republic assumed a serious role in Atlantic slavery.

The Dutch Netherlands rose from a geographically awkward extension of Spain's Habsburg Empire to become a global power in the seventeenth century. The Dutch wars of independence from the 1560s to the 1640s alone tell a remarkable story, but the way the small nation of about 1 million people influenced international relations is even more compelling. By the second half of the seventeenth century, it was the world's most powerful maritime trading nation, and its people were the richest per capita in the world. It is estimated that in the middle of the seventeenth century, there were 10,000 Dutch vessels plying the world's oceans, including the world's largest cargo ship, the *fluyt*. A few hundred smaller Dutch ships were carrying slaves from Africa to the Americas. The Dutch briefly displaced the Portuguese as the leading slave trader. They shipped an average of 2,500 Africans a year to the Americas, and in one especially busy year, 1644, they carried 7,000 slaves across the Atlantic. The Dutch talent for commerce stemmed from their open, inventive financial institutions; civic harmony; a need to be self-sufficient in industry, education, and technology; a military system that backed their enterprises; and, most important, a penchant for maritime trade. This practical and innovative Protestant republic tolerated Jews and Catholics and at the same time became one of the Atlantic's most aggressive buyers and sellers of Africans.

In many ways, the Dutch approach to economic success in the world rested on a tradition of order and efficiency and on joint stock companies that were similar to the English models. The Dutch East India Company was chartered in 1602 and the West India Company in 1621. The former, with its own armed forces, attacked the Portuguese in Asia and Africa and eventually took control of what came to be the Dutch East Indies, present-day Indonesia. The West India Company claimed a place in North America (New Netherland, later New York). Then, in an audacious display of force, it entered Brazil in 1624, took control of Pernambuco, and remained there until driven out in the 1650s by combined Spanish and Portuguese forces. The enterprising Dutch then made their way north and entered the Caribbean with sugar production in mind and an orderly and ruthless approach to the slave trade. Their mission was enhanced by unique banking expertise and accessible financial credit, logistical skill, and the support of a coherent state apparatus.[21] If they had any moral qualms about slavery, they put them aside. Curacao in the Dutch Antilles soon became a fully developed slave society, and with strategic insight the small neighbouring island of Aruba was used to raise cattle to feed plantation slaves. Moreover, the failure of the Dutch in Brazil's northeast did not deter them from taking over a Spanish claim in the far north of eastern South America, north of Brazil, in Guyana, now Surinam, adjacent to French and British Guyana. But the Dutch reach had limits, and three wars with England sparked by trade issues in the middle of the seventeenth century sapped its military resources, economy, and territorial reach. The tiny nation had overextended itself, but it had made an enormous impression on the slave trade.

Growth and Diversification in Colonial Brazil

To contemporary observers, colonial Brazil was for generations a rough, often inhospitable place with a distended settlement pattern featuring clusters of plantations and small farms with a polychromatic population. The line between settlement and the frontier was a thin one, and from the earliest days, natives and African slaves had run away into an unpoliced hinterland. However, there were few opportunities for slaves freed by self-purchase or formal manumission, and most stayed close to home, often in poor circumstances. But for runaways, there were self-sufficient havens known as *mocambos*. After 1700, the word *quilombo*, taken from an Angolan word for "encampment," was used to mean the same thing. Hundreds of these settlements rose and fell during the colonial period, and some endured for long periods as substantial communities. Surviving through farming and raiding, they operated in a semblance of political order with councils, militias, and cultural solidarity. The largest and most famous (or notorious) was Palmares in Pernambuco, a fortress and symbol of African resistance as well as a threat to colonial authority. It was a complex, fully functioning micro-state and at its zenith was home to over 10,000 people and allowed a politics where some former slaves, with no hesitation, became slaveholders themselves.[22] After a full-blown military campaign, Palmares was reduced in 1694 by a force of local militia and the hard-nosed *paulista bandeirantes* ("followers of the flag" from Sao Paulo), a loose assemblage of explorers, scouts, and native slavers.

Somewhat similar communities of escaped slaves, at times mixed with freedmen, existed elsewhere in the Americas, especially in the Caribbean. They remind us of slaves' restless seeking for freedom and of many ex-slaves' abilities to maintain independent communities. But they were also seen as serious threats to the system by encouraging defiance, running away, and revolt; and the official response to them was tighter controls, heavier punishments, the employment of "bush captains" to hunt down runaways, and military force as a last resort. The reprisals for revolts or plots were harsh. During a six-month uprising in Minas Gerais, Brazil, in 1757–58, 3,900 pairs of rebel ears were returned for bounty. However, revolts recurred. Religion sparked a series of riots in Bahia in the early nineteenth century, and a Muslim-inspired uprising in 1835 threatened something like a "holy war" against masters, government officials, and white Christians (see Chapter Seven).

While the *paulista bandeirantes* played a decisive role in the destruction of the Palmares *quilombo*, they have a more storied, heroic reputation in Brazil as frontiersmen. They should be better known, perhaps, for their principal role, which was raiding and capturing natives for the slave trade, a lucrative business that drove these hunters deep into the interior. By the end of the seventeenth century, the *bandeirantes* had led the way to large alluvial gold deposits in what would become Minas Gerais ("General Mines"), some 250 kilometres inland from Rio de Janeiro. Encouraged by official policies and gold and later diamond mining licences, Minas Gerais boomed and drew in

Africans to the point that by the end of the eighteenth century it had one of the largest concentrations of slaves in all of Brazil.[23]

The history of Minas Gerais reveals the difficulty and expense of maintaining a permanent slave population in the mining economy. The plantation model simply did not work. Manumissions were common, as mine deposits petered out. The cost of keeping unproductive slaves made it easier for investors to let them go, sell them off if possible, and then buy new slaves when needed. Adding to the region's racial and social mix, Portuguese whites were drawn to the mining zones as managers, engineers and mechanics, merchants, and government officials. Rio de Janeiro became an important commercial entrepôt and an entry point for the adventurers, speculators, and African slaves headed to the mines. By the early nineteenth century, it was Brazil's busiest debarkation point for African slaves and an urban mélange of nationalities and classes; a hive of commercial and political bustle; and a busy intersection of slaves, free coloured labourers, traders, bureaucrats, and merchants.[24]

Minas Gerais was wedged between Sao Paulo in the south and Bahia to the north. Its rapid growth pushed Brazilian settlement and slavery to what would become the administrative units of Goias and Mato Grosso, both of which lay far beyond the 1494 Spanish-Portuguese boundary and ran to the edge of the Amazon rainforest. Most important, the growth in Minas Gerais continued to pull Brazil's centre of gravity away from Bahia and Pernambuco. The first mining boom was over by 1750, but by then several permanent inland towns had been established, seeded by the hardscrabble mining camps, and calmed by the ubiquitous Church. Permanence brought a measure of law and order to the Minas Gerais frontier along with tax collectors and Crown bureaucrats. Within decades of being sparsely populated backcountry, it had become an important economic and political Vice Captaincy. Its settlement completed the distribution of slavery and mixed coloured majorities to all regions of colonial Brazil, while in the far north slavery helped move the investment and settlement zone north of Pernambuco in the Vice Captaincies of Maranhao and Para.[25] (See Map 3.1.)

By the middle of the eighteenth century, Brazil had become an important source of Portuguese wealth. The steady rise of European imperialism forced every rival nation to militarize, improve colonial governance, and adopt protective economic systems. Portuguese colonial policy was rationalized in the middle decades of the eighteenth century under the direction of the Crown favourite, the Marquis de Pombal (1699–1782). Pombal was Portugal's de facto secretary of state with enormous civil authority.

MAP 3.1 Brazil, ca. 1800

His approach to national interest and international relations drew on his Enlightenment values, market savvy, and the need for a more rigorous administration of Portugal's colonies. The theory that imperial peripheries should feed the metropolitan economy led to policies that in Brazil meant more sugar, gold, and slaves. Pombal's administrative reforms in the sometimes free-for-all of the Minas Gerais goldfields inspired more orderly planning, economic development, and rising slave populations everywhere in Brazil. His impact on colonial Brazil was a lasting one and should remind us that the "Age of Reason" did not immediately equate with a revolution in moral responsibility, at least so far as African slavery was concerned. While he was instrumental in ending legalized slavery in Portugal in the 1760s, Pombal's policies had the reverse effect in Brazil. Moreover, in order to bolster metropolitan control, he attacked Jesuit schools and missions and certainly retarded educational progress, effectively ending the Jesuits' attempts to curb the abuses of natives and slaves. He and his peers everywhere in Europe and America, and their law-making authority in the organization of slavery and the slave trade, confirm the paradoxes embedded in bureaucracies composed of rational men. In Pombal's version of "enlightenment," by striking down the Inquisition in Portugal, he curbed the terror and arbitrary power of the Church's watchdog while also blunting the Church's often benevolent influence on slave management in Brazil.[26]

As the Brazilian economy diversified, growth in the agrarian *fazendas* (landed estates or farms) and in the *engenhos* of Bahia and Pernambuco continued, and, as food and tobacco production made headway, African slavery found its way into every economic sector. The livestock economy in the south not only used slaves in cattle ranching and the grain and feed industries but also in small factories that produced tons of dried beef as a staple food for slaves in other parts of Brazil. Slaves were used in manufacturing and as deck hands on merchant ships, as whalers and as port workers, and after 1760 in the production of raw cotton. Brazil was on its way to becoming self-sufficient in food while it expanded sugar, cotton, cacao, tobacco, gold, whale products, and beef production. Urban culture emerged in several places: Salvador da Bahia, for example, was larger than any North American city of the time, and by the end of the eighteenth century Rio de Janeiro was the second largest city in the Americas after Mexico City. Other characteristics of late colonial Brazil emerged in the so-called free coloured "peasantry" that formed in the small mixed farm agriculture that grew food for plantations and towns. But slavery remained pervasive, and small landowners and even former slaves availed themselves of slave labour. White

TABLE 3.1 Selected Population Figures, Brazil, 1800 and 1872

	Total	White	%[a]	Slaves	%	Free Coloured	%
Ca. 1800[b]	2,552,071	714,579	28.0	969,786	38.0	714,579	28.0
1872[c]							
North (includes Bahia and Pernambuco)	4,971,407	1,778,435	35.7	508,846	10.2	2,684,126	54.0
Centre (includes Minas Gerais and Rio de Janeiro)	3,400,380	1,431,209	42.1	752,013	22.1	1,217,158	35.8
South (includes Sao Paulo)	1,558,691	964,600	61.9	249,947	16.0	344,144	22.1
Total	9,930,478	4,174,244	42.0	1,510,806	15.2	4,245,428	42.8

a   Percentage of whole population.
Adapted from:
   b   *Cambridge History of Latin America*, Vol. II, 607. The total includes an additional 153,124 "Indians" (6 per cent of total);
   c   Bergad, *Comparative Histories*, 120–21.

and mixed race farmers producing simple subsistence or surpluses, often using a few slaves, added complexity to the bigger world of *engenhos* and the mining and cattle ranching industries. (See Table 3.1 for selected population figures for Brazil.)

The diversification had some ironic consequences. For example, by 1800 slave-produced Brazilian tobacco was being used in Africa to buy slaves, and Brazilian slaves were providing 30 per cent of Britain's imports of raw cotton even as an antislavery movement was gaining momentum there. As the ideological shocks of the American and French revolutions reverberated through Europe and the Atlantic world, colonial Brazil continued to import record numbers of slaves to Rio de Janeiro and Sao Paulo in the late eighteenth century and early nineteenth century. There was no place in the Portuguese Empire like it, and certainly none of the northern European colonies in the Caribbean and North America resembled its demographic, economic, political, and social characteristics. A new society had taken root in the southern tropics dominated by a plantation culture where nearly 75 per cent of its peoples were settled in the littoral. Brazilian slaveholder mentality was such that planters were loath to buy too many African women, in part for fear of the costs of raising slave children.[27] The system needed a steady importation of large numbers of Africans to sustain it. Without those imports, the slave population of Brazil would have declined; by the early nineteenth century, more than two-thirds of Brazil's plantation slaves were African-born. This stands in stark contrast to the steady natural increase in the slave population of North America after 1750 and the resulting African American majority in the slave population.

Two centuries had seen African and European cultural, religious, and linguistic habits merging into unique Afro-Brazilian social and religious customs, music, and storytelling. Slaves and free coloured peoples forged new cultural identities. European and African musical instruments were blended to form new rhythms, sounds, and meanings. African and local customs were joined and passed across communities and handed down to generation after generation, always taking on what the constant flow of new Africans brought with them, adding fresh spiritual energy. This blending of the older oral forms in the coloured community with whatever specific African songs, icons, gods, and folk myths arrived daily or weekly shaped Brazil in ways that continued to the end of the slave trade. White planters, bureaucrats, priests, and merchants viewed these trends with scorn, for the most part, and denigrated African and Afro-Brazilian practices. Laws were written to curb non-Christian icons, worship, and the public dancing and celebration that stimulated coloured people inside and outside slavery. The practices continued despite the restraints. White Brazil on the other hand did its best to replicate the music, art, theatre, and literature of Europe, and some progress was made in developing local art and literature. Arts and scientific societies did emerge, fashioning themselves on European models.[28]

In 1933, the Brazilian sociologist Gilberto Freyre (1900–87) published an eccentric, stimulating, and controversial study of Brazil's development in *Casa Grande e Senzala* (published in English translation in 1946 as *The Masters and the Slaves: A Study in the Development of Brazilian Civilization*). His version of Brazil's history and culture sought to counter the notion that a backward Brazil had been hobbled by its slow path to modernization because of class, castes, and racism. Freyre argued that in fact Brazil's peoples had overcome a difficult tropical environment meliorated, as he put it, by the interplay of races. Brazil's settlement had created a racially and culturally interrelated population that made the nation if not quite a racial "democracy" then at least an example of the positive impact of Africans on the making of a new society. Freyre maintained that "in place of a hard and dry, grinding effort at adaptation to conditions wholly strange, the contact of European culture with that of the aborigines was smoothed by the oil of African mediation."[29] He did not deny the harshness of slavery and the rough rural world in which it operated, but he argued that wide-spread miscegenation had a positive effect on Brazil. What might be closer to reality, at least by the first part of the twentieth century when he made his claim, was that race in the shaping of modern Brazil was a more complicated matter than the simple black-white division in North America. Whether or not Freyre's thesis speaks to a genuinely balanced interracial society and to long-term benefits to Brazil, his often flamboyant discussion of sexuality and the African benefits to white personality ("the oil of African mediation") still arouses debate among historians. As much as any other intellectual, Freyre influenced politicians, educators, and the national consciousness of twentieth-century Brazilians. While his thesis is no longer accepted, his tantalizing suggestion that Portuguese adaptability to African influences was beneficial stands in serious contrast to the older Anglo-centric North American perspective that prevailed until recent shifts that acknowledged the strong African American influence on US culture.[30]

Slavery in Spanish America, 1500–1800

From the moment Columbus laid claim to parts of the Caribbean and the coastline of northwestern South America, Spanish *conquistadores,* explorers, missionaries, mining entrepreneurs, land-hungry petty aristocrats, government officials, and slave traders went about instituting some of the most enduring features of the Americas, including the Spanish language, Catholicism, and populations of *mestizos* (white-native mix). For a start, of all the European intruders, only the Spanish encountered two very large empires in America, the Inca in Andean South America and the Aztecs in Mesoamerica. Approximately half of all the natives in all the Americas were within the orbit of those empires.[31] Most of the survivors of the millions "liberated" by the *conquistadores* from either Aztec or Inca rule became Spanish peons. In Mexico (New Spain), for example, while gold and silver attracted investment and buoyed the Empire, the most permanent outcome of the conquest was a trend to *hacienda* culture and the appropriation of the labour of millions of natives and, later, *mestizo* peasants. Otherwise, imperial Spain did not fix on a dominant agricultural export commodity.

With the exception of the sugar plantations of Vera Cruz and its mining operations, Mexican society developed with modest African importation. However, the Spanish-speaking Caribbean today has significant numbers of African descendants; over 80 per cent of the present Dominican Republic (Santo Domingo) population is of African descent; the figure for Cuba is 35 per cent. Mexico's records indicate less than one-tenth of 1 per cent African descendants in its population while Peru has 2 per cent. Colombia has the highest proportion in Spanish South America of 4 per cent black and 14 per cent mulatto. Before the sugar boom in Cuba at the end of the eighteenth century, Spain imported only one-sixth the number of slaves brought into Brazil. After 1800, however, over half the slaves ever brought to Spanish America arrived, and almost all went to Cuba.

White European immigration in the late nineteenth and early twentieth centuries made a deep impression on the demographics of Spanish America, especially in places such as Argentina and Chile, neither of which had a significant African population during the colonial period.[32] Mexico became the New World's greatest *mestizo* culture, as first *peninsulares* (Spanish-born immigrants) and then *criollos* (Spaniards born in the New World) mixed freely with native populations. Over time in Colombia, parts of Mexico, and most importantly at Potosi in Peru (the area is in present-day Bolivia), as many or more natives than Africans were used for mining. Well into the eighteenth century, Christian missionaries fanned out to the farthest edges of the Empire, often ahead of settlers. A problem with the sprawl of the Empire and its tenuous outposts can be seen in the Pueblo Revolt of 1680 when one of the few post-Conquest native uprisings against Spanish rule occurred near Santa Fe, in what is now New Mexico. Natives rose up against decades of Franciscan efforts to smother native spirituality with Christian rites. The mission was destroyed. The Pueblo experiment was conducted nearly 2,000 kilometres north of Mexico City, the hub of New Spain. No other imperial power spread itself so far or so thin with such grand objectives.

Portuguese Brazil developed in a zone bordered by the Atlantic Ocean, the edges of the Amazon rainforest, the southern Andes cordilleras, and the Spanish Vice Royalty of La Plata. It moved gradually east to west and north to south in a continuous extension of settlement frontiers. The British colonies were confined by the Appalachian Mountains, the French to the north, and the Spanish to the south. The French claimed large parts of North America but only settled a small strip along the St. Lawrence River in Quebec and in Acadia on the Atlantic; and the Dutch settled briefly on the east coast of North America and then in Dutch Guyana (Surinam). After 1787, the new United States grew episodically to the west. The northern Europeans settled the confining islands of the Lesser Antilles. But Spain was everywhere: on the Atlantic and the Pacific as far north as California and in the mountains of Peru, the deserts of northern Mexico, the pampas of La Plata, the jungles of Central America, and the Caribbean's Greater Antilles.[33]

Cities, even if most were hardly more than large towns, were very important to official Spanish settlement policy. The trend began in 1521 on the ruins of Aztec Tenochtitlan with the superimposition of Mexico City, which by 1580 was home to as many as 100,000 people, and then to Lima in 1535, Buenos Aires in 1536 (abandoned in 1541 and then restored), Acuncion in 1537, Bogota in 1538, and Caracas in 1567. Across the world, in the Philippines, Manila was founded in 1571. The great silver lodes of Potosi were discovered in 1545. By 1580, the city housed as many as 120,000 people and had become by 1650 the largest city in the Spanish-speaking world, even though the chief commercial and administrative capital of Peru was at Lima. Cathedrals were built in strategic regional locations, and in contrast to Portugal's failure to establish universities, Spanish America's first universities were established early on in 1551 in both Lima and Mexico City.

As a major distribution centre in the Andean silver economy, Lima imported African slaves who carted silver, unloaded supplies, and worked in construction or in trades connected to food preparation, clothing, shoe-making, and metalwork. In the seventeenth century, slaughterhouses and hat factories employed hundreds of African slaves. In this early colonial urban setting, slaves were held singly or in small groups by merchants, royal officials, and craftsmen. By the middle of the seventeenth century, perhaps as much as half of Lima's population was African or mixed coloured, bound or free. The Spanish preferred slaves from the Western Sudan, where it was presumed the males were more disciplined and intelligent, and Sudanese women in particular were seen to be attractive and strong. The direct Spanish participation in the slave trade in its infancy allowed their agents some role in the selection of slaves, a practice that became difficult in the later mass culling of Africans after the early eighteenth century. The preferences reveal a persistent commercial approach, an appraisal of the slave as commodity.

What greeted the first few generations of slaves in the Spanish colonies set the scene for the next few centuries. Spanish law ostensibly allowed for basic human rights for the slave (the slave was a person). Although the *Siete Partidos* were profoundly important in that light, we must keep in mind that slave laws or codes were usually abridged, edited, ignored, or enforced according to local practices or needs. This was true of every European slave society in the Americas, from Bahia to Barbados to Virginia. Still, the *Siete Partidos* meant that there was a mechanism for manumission, self-purchase, racial intermarriage, and Christian identity. That in no way softened the power relationship between master and slave, and the Spanish system could be as oppressive in some cases as it was benign in others. As in Brazil, an African slave with a set of legal protections and some latitude was still a slave under strict Christian control. As early as 1501, Moors, Jews, heretics, and even recent converts to Catholicism were effectively banned from Spanish America. Christians were to have a monopoly on slaveholding.[34]

Spanish American Regionalism

Over two and a half centuries, Spanish policies shaped four distinct settlement environments in America. Mexico, the least slave dependent, had and still has the largest population of any jurisdiction in Spanish America. The classic Mexican *hacienda* functioned as a self-contained community with a civil authority and a church in the environs. A second sector encompassed the sugar complexes in Santo Domingo, Cuba, and Puerto Rico, which up to the late eighteenth century produced sugar and other crops mostly for the Spanish American market. A third and lucrative sector involved the mining settlements in Peru, Colombia, and Mexico. Before the Cuban sugar boom, the largest concentration of African slaves in Spanish America was in mining camps and towns. In some of the most exhausting work environments in the New World, mining was the fate of the lowest of the *bozales* (new arrivals from Africa; *bossales* in Portuguese) and the source of the wealth that raised Spain into its "Golden Age" in the sixteenth and seventeenth centuries. Slavery was also a factor in a fourth sector, which was, as noted, the urban world of commerce and manufacturing. There, the most skilled and expensive slaves worked in household occupations; in shop work with metals, textiles, and leather; and as bakers, handymen, liverymen, carpenters, and household servants.

The variety of settings for slavery reminds us that fieldwork was not the lot of all slaves in all places. Plantation slaves in Cuba worked in ordered groups on individual holdings that eventually numbered in the hundreds and were sometimes employed in family units. Miners worked in gangs in camps with perhaps 50 slaves, usually all male, in brutal conditions in isolated places. In the cities, slaves were in small groups or in single occupations. The *obrajes* (textile and clothing workshops) that sprang up in the Spanish American cities allowed for flexible arrangements between masters and slaves. As noted, a regular practice everywhere in Latin America was for masters to hire out their slaves for profit. Manumission rates were constant, and after the start of the eighteenth century, the number of free coloured was greater than the numbers in slavery in most places, including the gold mining areas of Spanish America.

The most widespread form of gold extraction was placer mining, consisting of sluicing, panning, or surface dredging and digging for alluvial deposits in river beds and banks. This was heavy and typically monotonous work and only intermittently exciting when new deposits were found. Slaves had permission to recover gold for themselves on their standard "days of rest," and shrewd masters offered incentives to them in a system of shared profit. Silver mining was a more sophisticated industry, requiring underground work and refining technology. The Spanish had learned a great deal from the Inca and Aztec operations but also brought along advanced equipment and more efficient production techniques. Refining experts, metalworkers, and gangs of either native or African labour helped make silver the major source of Spain's vast wealth. As with gold mining and refining, the work was punishing; silver in particular was dangerous to lungs, limbs, and eyes. It was refined by smelting but also by a process called "amalgamation" where mercury was used to produce the purest silver. Water- or ox-driven mills along with furnaces and liquid metals maimed, burned, and poisoned workers who, it must be remembered, were driven to produce by force or enticements or both. The opportunity for slaves and contract native labour to earn money or freedom was always subject to decisions made by masters. At times, some flexibility favoured the slave, as for example in the cacao plantations of Venezuela where slaves had access to cacao trees for their own means.

Still, there was little or no status integration, and the persistence of terms such as negro, mulatto, quadroon, and other descriptors in the records speak clearly to a persistent racialism. Those terms were nothing, of course, when compared to the offensive, derisory slang used to identify coloured people everywhere in the Americas.[35] It was as true in Spanish America as it was in Brazil that even the newest lower class white Iberian immigrant was immediately superior in legal status, opportunity, and social standing to anyone of colour. The role of the Catholic Church in any supposed amelioration of the slaves' treatment must be viewed with caution. The Church certainly restrained cruelty when it chose to intervene, but it tolerated the rights of masters to their routine punishments. Outside the formal authority of the Church of Rome, the Jesuits in particular were known for their strict codes of discipline and, like other Catholic orders, kept slaves themselves. Moreover, the principle of manumission was not always a case of slaveholder enlightenment or fairness. In truth, there might have been no further use for the slave, or the owner could profit from a slave paying for his own freedom (*coartacion*). Whether they were stern or amiable, steady or erratic, slave owners were inevitably practical men with selfish objectives. If there were callous patriarchs, there were also temperate, even kind masters. In the case of American-born slaves, in most settings older, feeble, orphaned, or infirm slaves were cared for. That practice was more common in the North American British colonies and United States than it appears to have been in Latin America, where manumission rates and the charity of the Church or the free coloured community offered some means of welfare or old age security for the infirm.[36]

If the Church was ubiquitous in Spanish America, so too was a bureaucratic structure that had no equal in the Americas. In Spain, the Council of the Indies designed imperial policy and the Board of Trade administered trade, exploration, and other organizational features of the Empire. In Spanish America, regional government was centred in *audiencias* (the divisions that contained major courts and in many cases conform to today's Spanish-speaking nations), *capitanias* (captaincy generals), *gobiernos* and *cabildos* (towns, community governments), and the *haciendas* (estates) of the *latifundia* (agrarian society). *Capitanias* were established for administrative and military purposes, and several of them composed the largest subdivisions—the Vice Royalties of New Spain, and Peru, and in the eighteenth century, New Granada and La Plata. By comparison, Portuguese Brazil was a single Vice Royalty, and its captaincy generals resemble today's states such as Sao Paulo or Pernambuco. The administration and legal authority of Spanish America was intended to be run from Europe. Judges, colonial governors, and military commanders were appointed by the Crown; royal tax collectors roamed everywhere, collecting the Royal Fifth, the standard share for the Crown of all economic activity. Jesuits and other Catholic orders were equally busy.

Some of the methods for distribution of land or commercial licences in Spanish America had precedents in Spain or in the Atlantic Islands. An older method, the *encomienda*, was a "commission" to manage a large estate and the people on it, and it was taken to America to streamline settlement. It was a reward system for preferred recipients, such as *conquistadores* or court favourites, who were granted something approximating the status and reach of a colonial landed aristocracy. However, after a few generations, abuses by the *encomienderos*—mostly their treatment of the natives under their control—led to the easing and abandonment of the policy.

Over time, Spanish American politics were increasingly defined by a rising self-conscious white *criollo* class of local politicians, artists, and entrepreneurs whose identities were increasingly American and who, by the late eighteenth century, began to resent the cumbersome and intrusive bureaucracies of the homeland. In Mesoamerica and South America, rising majorities of *mestizos* changed the human face of the Empire and, along with European, black, and native peoples and their mixed progenies, shaped Spanish America's regional characteristics. By the end of the eighteenth century, Latin America had gone through a remarkable process of depopulation to repopulation, the scale of which remains one of the most striking demographic revolutions in recorded history. The population of all of the Spanish settlements in America in the 1790s was approximately 12.5 million, with about half in Mexico with specific pockets of African and mixed African, native and white peoples, and large concentrations of *mestizos*. We should recall William Denevan's estimates for 1492 which claimed some 40 million natives in what was to be Spanish America and Brazil.[37] In the settled parts of Brazil in the 1790s, a tripartite division of newcomers dominated the population. Only 6 per cent or so of the recorded population of about 2.5 million was native, about 38 per cent slave, 28 per cent white, and 28 per cent free coloured.[38] While healthy independent groups of natives survived in some highland regions and in the Brazilian interior, the impact of colonization on natives is shocking. The places now known as Brazil, Mexico, Peru, Colombia, and Guatemala, for example, had been remade not simply by European political and economic systems but in fundamental demographic ways. These were truly new worlds and the process was repeated with important distinctions in the Caribbean and North America.

Notes

1 Quotes from Columbus and Vespucci can be found in Eric Nellis, *An Empire of Regions: A Brief History of Colonial British America* (Toronto: University of Toronto Press, 2010), 16.

2 Stuart B. Schwartz, "First Slavery: From Indian to African," in Heuman and Walvin, *The Slavery Reader*, 83–102.

3 On the history of sugar with extensive material on slavery and production techniques, see the encyclopedic, still useful Deerr, *The History of Sugar*; see also Abbott, *Sugar, A Bittersweet History*. On the economics of slavery and the slave trade, the selections in Inkori and Engerman, *The Atlantic Slave Trade*, and in Eltis *et al.*, *Slavery in the Development of the Americas* are accessible to the non-specialist.

4 Canny, *Europeans on the Move*, 263–83.

5 Schwartz, "First Slavery."

6 Herbert S. Klein and Ben Vinson III, *African Slavery in Latin America and the Caribbean*, 2nd ed. (New York: Oxford University Press, 2007), 30‑32, 78‑81.

7 David Eltis and David Richardson, "West Africa and the Trans-Atlantic Slave Trade: New Evidence of Long Term Trends" in Heuman and Walvin, *The Slavery Reader*, 42–57.

8 Conrad, *Children of God's Fire*, 237–38.

9 For Brazil, see Conrad, *Children of God's Fire*, Introduction.

10 Lockhart and Schwartz, *Early Latin America*, Chapter 7.

11 For example, see Fogel, *Without Consent or Contract*, 393ff.

12 Bakewell, *A History of Latin America*, Chapter 13; on the numbers, see Eltis and Richardson, *Atlas*, 203.

13 Harris, *Patterns of Race*, 57–58. The full list is branco, preto, sarara, moreno claro, moreno escuro, mulato, moreno, mulato claro, mulato escuro, negro, caboclo, escuro, cabo verde, claro, aracuaba, roxo, amarelo, sarara escuro, cor de canela, preto claro, roxo clara, cor de cinza, vermelho, caboclo escuro, pardo, branco sarara, mambebe, branco caboclado, moreno escuro, mulato sarara, gazula, cor de cinza clara, creolo, lourro, moreno claro caboclado, mulato bem claro, branco mulato, roxo de cabelo bom, preto escuro, pele. See also the similar note on Brazil in Jablonski, *Living Color*, 164.

14 Eltis and Richardson, *Atlas*, 203.

15 For Brazil, see Klein and Luna, *Slavery in Brazil*, Chapter 5; for Cuba, see Franklin W. Knight, *Slave Society in Cuba in the Nineteenth Century* (Madison: University of Wisconsin Press, 1970), 3–46 and Table 1.

16 Klein and Luna, *Slavery in Brazil*, 115–48. See also the contemporary (sixteenth century) descriptions of the *engenho* system in Schwartz, *Early Brazil*, 198–233.

17 Law and Lovejoy, *The Biography of Mahommah Gardo Baquaqua*, Introduction. The quotes are from 158–59.

18 Schwartz, *Slaves, Peasants, and Rebels*, 39–63.

19 Schwartz, *Slaves, Peasants, and Rebels*, 45–48.

20 Fausto, *Concise History of Brazil*, 144; Schwartz, *Early Brazil*, 199ff.

21 Henk Den Heijer, "Dutch Caribbean," in Robert L. Paquette and Mark M. Smith, *The Oxford Handbook of Slavery in the Americas* (Oxford: Oxford University Press, 2010). See also the useful comments in Deerr, *History of Sugar*, 163, 181, 208–28, 231, 259; Peter C. Emmer, "The Dutch and the Slave Americas," in Eltis *et al.*, *Slavery in the Development of the Americas*, 70–88; Johannes Postma, "The Dispersal of African Slaves in the West by Dutch Slave Traders," in Inkori and Engerman, *The Atlantic Slave Trade*, 283–300.

22 Schwartz, *Slaves, Peasants and Rebels*, 103–36.

23 For Minas Gerais, see Laird Bergad, *Slavery and the Demographic and Economic History of Minas Gerais, Brazil, 1720–1888* (Cambridge: Cambridge University Press, 1999). See also Klein and Luna, *Slavery in Brazil*, 35–73.

24 See Conrad, *Children of God's Fire*, 117–24 for a vivid description of slaves at work in the city of Rio de Janeiro.

25 On the development of new resources in the Brazilian north with a focus on African-Brazilian linkages, see Walter Hawthorne, *From Africa to Brazil: Culture, Identity and an Atlantic Slave Trade, 1600–1830* (New York: Cambridge University Press, 2010).

26 David Brion Davis, *The Problem of Slavery in Western Culture* (Ithaca: Cornell University Press, 1966), 239, 399. Bakewell, *A History of Latin America*, 368–74.

27 Richard Follett, "The Demography of Slavery," in Gad Heuman and Trevor Burnard, eds., *Routledge History of Slavery* (New York: Routledge, 2011), 119–37. Follett notes that fertility rates in Minas Gerais were higher than those in Bahia, for example.

28 A.J.R. Russell-Wood, *Slavery and Freedom in Colonial Brazil* (Oxford: One World, 2002), 95–103.

29   Freyre, *The Masters and the Slaves*, 78.

30   Freyre, *The Masters and the Slaves*, 256; Cleary, "Race, Nationalism and Social Theory in Brazil," 9. Cleary provides an important review of Freyre's thesis and his influence on the politics, historiography, and popular culture of Brazil. See also Tannenbaum, *Slave and Citizen*, 119.

31   Denevan, *The Native Population*, 291.

32   Geoffrey Barraclough, ed., *The Times Atlas of World History*, rev. ed. (London: Times Books, 1984), 208–09; Bakewell, *A History of Latin America*, 449–50. For Brazil, see Fausto, *History of Brazil*, 160–70.

33   Barraclough, *The Times Atlas of World History*, 158, 160–62, 164–65.

34   Klein and Luna, *Slavery in Brazil*, 22–23.

35   See, for North America, George Rawick, *The American Slave: A Composite Autobiography. Volume I: From Sundown to Sunup: The Making of the Black Community* (Westport: Greenwood, 1972). This contains samples from the Federal Writers Project of 1936–38 which interviewed 2,300 ex-slaves. The entire collection is also available online from the Library of Congress as *Born in Slavery: Slave Narratives from the Federal Writers Project, 1936–1938* found at http://memory.loc.gov/ammem/snhtml/snhome.html. The advice for interviewers regarding dialect and slang are instructive. It is worth noting that when the ex-slaves use the term "nigger," it has a different denotation than when used by whites as an insult. The word was taken up by African Americans as an assertive counter, a matter of pride, even, in the 1960s. Much of the twentieth-century derisory English slang is parodied in an accessible orthography in the song "Colored Spade" in the musical *Hair* (1967).

36   For North America, see Genovese, *Roll, Jordan Roll*, Book Two, Part 2. For Brazil, see Russell-Wood, *Slavery and Freedom*, Chapters 8 and 9.

37   See Chapter 1, note 26.

38   Bakewell, *A History of Latin America*, 294ff and 334; for Brazil, see Patterson, *Slavery and Social Death*, Appendix C, Table N15.

4 | The Making of the Black Caribbean, 1650–1800

"The Island is divided into three sorts of men, viz: Masters, Servants and Slaves. The slaves and their posterity, being subject to their masters forever, are kept and presev'd with greater care than the servants who are theirs but for five years, according to the law of the Island. So that for the time, the servants have the worser lives, for they are put to very hard labour, and their dyet very sleight."

—Richard Ligon, *True and Exact History of the Island of Barbadoes* (1673 edition)[1]

The Islands

The Caribbean Sea (See Map 4.1) is set between the Atlantic Ocean to the east and several mainland nations to the west, and the islands in it extend in a great arc east and south from Cuba to Trinidad, Curacao, and Aruba between 10 and 25 degrees north latitudes.[2] There are three distinct archipelagos: the Bahamas, strictly speaking an Atlantic cluster; the Greater Antilles, that is, Cuba, Hispaniola (present-day Haiti and Dominican Republic), Jamaica, and Puerto Rico; and the Lesser Antilles, comprising the many small Leeward and Windward Islands and Barbados. Most of the islands look out to the Atlantic from their eastern shores. There are over 115 islands by definition; over 3,000 islets and smaller sand or coral islet "cays"; and hundreds of labyrinthine channels, inlets, and natural harbours.

By the start of the seventeenth century, the Spanish had investigated most of the islands and had settled the Greater Antilles. Then the Dutch, English, and French occupied many of the smaller and heavily forested islands. By the time sugar came to the Lesser Antilles, the native societies that greeted Columbus were mostly gone.

The English and Race

In the early phase of European settlement, the smaller islands were home to as untidy a collection of inhabitants as the New World ever saw: a ragged population of misfits, outcasts, opportunists, deserters, political and religious exiles, escaped criminals, anarchists, and runaway slaves and servants who regularly made up the crews for the privateers and pirates who cruised the Spanish Main. But what emerged was something close to the tripartite structure described by Ligon, above, as "Masters, Servants and Slaves." Another observer, Henry Whistler, described Barbados in 1655 as "a dunghill whereon England doth cast forth its rubbish. Rogues and whores and such like people are those that are generally brought here." That sour description could be repeated in any other European language throughout the Lesser Antilles. Whistler's loose proletarian cast included a great many Africans in bondage. He noted "French, Dutch, Scots, Irish, Spaniards they being Jews, with Indians and miserable Negors born to perpetual slavery, they and their seed." Some of the gentry, as he defined the slaveholding planters, already owned 100 or more "slave apes" and encouraged the males to take "as many wives as they will have" for the children they produced, who could then be sold "from one to the other [planters] as we do sell sheep."[3]

Whistler's use of "apes" in reference to Africans harkens back to the English traders who followed the Portuguese into Africa a century earlier, in the age of John Hawkins, and reported seeing Africans with "ape like" features copulating with apes. The Iberian exposure to Africans was more tactile than the English experience. As early as 1550, there were over 9,000 African slaves among Lisbon's 100,000 people, held in small groups or individually; they were a conspicuous, tolerated part of everyday life in a cosmopolitan city. Historian Herbert Klein notes that because of that familiarity and the history of direct contact with Moors, Iberian prejudices were more tempered than the views of sixteenth-century English observers who seemed both fascinated and appalled in turn by what they saw as African "oddities." As historian Winthrop Jordan notes in an important discussion of "first impressions," the English in particular were fixated on "blackness" as a visual and metaphorical descriptor and were preoccupied with Africans' "lasciviousness" as "keen and lustful." Elizabethan English

MAP 4.1 The Caribbean, ca. 1800

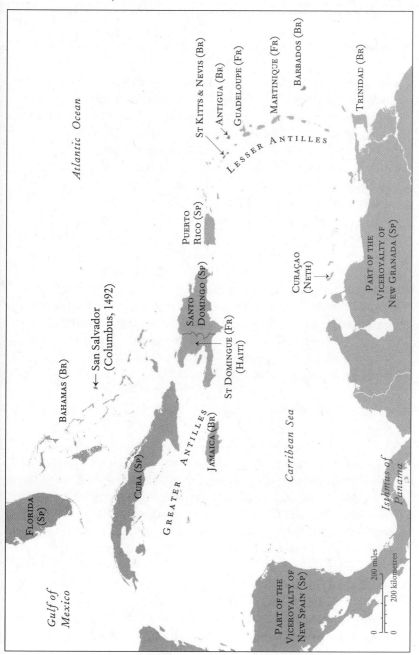

reporters were wont to offer descriptions of the African males as being "furnisht with such members as are after a sort burthensome to them." The female pudenda and male penises, the latter "large propagators," intrigued English observers. The Iberians were certainly not free of such "impressions" but for the most part did not record the same levels of cross-cultural revulsion. And although American natives were considered to be heathen and "epicurean," they were usually less offensively stereotyped, even by the Iberians. Africans were not only heathen but patently more distant from many European ideals of human appearance and behaviour.[4]

The English descriptions of Africans as disgusting and unsightly were not unusual in the confused and crude xenophobia of the age. Images of Africans as hardly removed from primates marks a disturbing commentary on some early perceptions that did not, however, deter the English from embarking on a long history of enslaving Africans for their colonies in the Caribbean and North America. In fact, it seems to have prepared a rationale for their systematic degradation of Africans. Even if we allow that Ligon's categories were simplified or Whistler's exaggerated, Barbados, settled in 1627, had clearly become a slave society when they recorded their impressions a generation later. Within a few decades, the smaller Caribbean islands were transformed by northern Europeans from libertarian havens for pirates, adventurers, and outcasts into a sugar producing zone. It was then that the northern Europeans made a belated but serious and comprehensive investment in the New World.

Northern European Initiatives and African Slavery

There are many reasons why permanent settlement of the New World by northern Europeans was 100 years behind the Iberians, but the most plausible is a general lack of interest or political will. English and French explorers were in the Western Atlantic on the heels of Columbus. John Cabot, the Genoese Giovanni Cabotto (ca. 1450–99), sailed to Newfoundland and the northern coasts by 1497 on behalf of the English. Nothing came of his reports except descriptions of great stocks of cod, geography, climate, and the ocean currents of the northwestern Atlantic. The brilliant Jacques Cartier (1491–1557) founded a short-lived settlement at present-day Quebec in 1535. As noted earlier, French Huguenots had a brief experience in Brazil, where French and English interlopers had interrupted or co-opted Brazilian merchants; John Hawkins transported Africans to the Spanish in the 1560s; and Francis Drake attacked Spanish resources in the Caribbean and Venezuela in the 1570s without any scheme to settle. Between 1585 and 1587, the Elizabethan adventurer Walter Raleigh next attempted a settlement on Roanoke Island, just off the coast of what is now North Carolina. Its failure delayed but did not end the developing English trend to settle in the Americas.

At the start of the seventeenth century, the earlier feelers became a rush of settlement. The English essayist, propagandist, and imperialist Richard Haklyut (1552–1616) published a series of proposals for economic growth in the Atlantic and urged a diplomatic and military curb on Spanish power. His writings reflected a growing sense of English pride and nationalism that was bolstered by the destruction of the invading Spanish Armada in 1588 off the coast of England, an event that remains a milestone in the rise of English national identity and patriotism. The appeal of American colonial assets, the quieting of domestic tensions, and increased dynastic and ecclesiastical stability in both France and England, plus the independence of the Netherlands, all inspired formal approaches to overseas colonization.[5]

In 1606, the London Company (a commercial joint stock company) was granted a charter that gave it governing rights and trading monopoly for most of the North American Atlantic seaboard between Quebec and Florida. The result was the permanent settling of Virginia in 1607 and the charter model for other English colonies. By the 1630s, colonies had been established in Massachusetts and Maryland; by the early eighteenth century, 13 mainland colonies had been settled. This American branch of the "first British Empire" eventually consisted of 26 colonies stretching from Newfoundland to Guyana. The French established Acadia in 1606 and Quebec in 1608 and then arbitrarily claimed most of the interior of North America west of the English and north and east of the Spanish colonies. The Dutch established New Netherland (present-day New York) after 1614. Then, rapidly, the Europeans occupied, chartered, and settled the islands of the Lesser Antilles.

The English claimed the Atlantic island of Bermuda in 1620 and St. Kitts (named Ste. Christophe by the French) and Nevis in 1623. Barbados was formally occupied in 1627, and Jamaica was taken from Spain in 1655. The French colonized Guadalupe and Martinique in 1635 and then moved resources into the western part of Hispaniola (Santo Domingo) in the 1660s, renaming it Saint Domingue (now Haiti), and made it the most productive sugar colony in the Caribbean. By 1636, the Dutch were permanently established at Curacao and Aruba; earlier, in an event that remains a staple datum in the history of the North American colonies and US history, an enterprising Dutch captain deposited 20 "negars" as John Rolfe noted, at Jamestown in 1619. There were no slave codes in Virginia, and it is not clear who purchased those Africans as "servants," but, as we note in Chapter Five, the story has become part of the debate over the origins of African slavery in the United States.[6]

On some islands, small-scale landowners eventually raised coffee, tobacco, indigo, nuts, and fruits—but sugar was the agricultural *raison d'être*. Over time, it created great wealth for a very small class of planters and investors and soaked up nearly 5 million Africans, with the vast majority arriving after 1700.[7] Capitalists brought with them law and order, military and court authority. Naval bases were built and sea lanes cleared of pirates. Deforestation was rampant, as it was in all the Americas, providing timber for export as well as fuel for the sugar boilers. Roads, wharves, and settlements followed, the latter reflecting European architecture modified for the tropics. State authority made the Caribbean safer for commerce and investments, and security was no longer threatened by criminals and buccaneers but instead by state rivalries. The Caribbean became a crucial naval theatre, from the Dutch wars of the seventeenth century to the various Anglo-French wars, down to the Seven Years' War and beyond into the American Revolution and the Napoleonic Wars. But the various slave societies survived all these conflicts, maturing as they went along, even as control of some islands changed hands.[8] Slaves came in and sugar went out, and as it did white Caribbean settlers imported beer, wine, and clothing—especially finery for the elites—furniture, specialty construction materials (including bricks), medicines, and foodstuffs from Europe and North America.[9]

As native populations withered away, the repopulation of the Lesser Antilles swelled within 200 years from a few thousand Africans and whites in the early seventeenth century to over 2.5 million blacks and mixed coloured, with only a small minority of whites. A new world shaped by sugar was being stamped on the islands. As historian Ralph Davis puts it:

After 1660 England's sugar imports always exceeded its combined imports of all colonial produce; in 1774 sugar made up ... half of all French imports from her West Indian colonies; over the colonial period as a whole more than half Brazil's exports ... were sugar. Sugar made up almost a fifth of the whole English import bill of 1774 far surpassing the share of any other commodity.

Caribbean society was dominated by greedy and opportunistic men where only "a quite rich man could establish or buy a sugar plantation," and tobacco and cotton were "small men's crops."[10] The economy of the British Caribbean grew steadily as tobacco gave way to sugar production. Between 1680 and 1800, when slaves comprised nearly 90 per cent of the population, sugar production in Barbados rose from 8,000 to 19,000 imperial tons annually. By then, Jamaica had become the major sugar producer in the British Caribbean. In the early nineteenth century, it exported 78,000 imperial tons annually from the labour of 324,000 slaves. In French Saint Domingue, average sugar production reached 80,000 imperial tons a year in the 30 years before the great slave uprising of 1791.[11]

While a great racial divide was at work, Ligon's tripartite categories were not as neat as his language implied. Class distinctions in white society were laddered in the status and wealth rankings of planters, managers, merchants, government officials, lawyers, soldiers, sailors, and white mechanics. While these overlapped socially at certain levels and economically or politically in matters of interdependency, there were ultimately lifestyle differences between a petite aristocracy, a petite bourgeoisie, and an assortment of white specialists in and around the plantations, refineries, warehouses, docks, and merchants' offices. The Europeans in the French islands divided along lines denoted by *grandes blancs* and *petites blancs*. In the Spanish Antilles, freshly minted titles were handed out to a class of presumptive New World aristocrats. In Trinidad and the Dutch "freeport" of St. Eustatius, races, classes, and nationalities intersected in a more fluid atmosphere, but political influence went with wealth as it did in all slave societies.

Within his generalized subdivisions, Ligon identified an important English form of servitude, the indenture. This was a popular legal device where a master negotiated a contract with a servant, each agreeing to a limited term of service, usually of four to seven years. This bound the servant to the master and his authority, while the master was obliged to ensure the servant's welfare and supervise his or her Christianity. At the completion of the contract, the servant was allowed some means of support and released. The punishments for any breach of the agreement by the servant could be severe: runaways could have their terms doubled; whipping, branding, the lopping off of an ear, or other mutilation was allowed. A disproportionate number of white servants "signed" their agreements with a cross, which was affirmed by a literate witness as the servant's "mark." White servants occupied stations ranging from fieldwork and other manual labour to house servants, carters, supervisors, blacksmiths, or carpenters. But Ligon's prescient remarks do anticipate the eventual switch from white indentured servants to African slaves: the latter could be kept for life and were seen to be more malleable. In any case, mortality rates for indentured servants were unacceptably high, in part due to overwork and diseases in tropical conditions too oppressive for most northern Europeans. Therefore, what had seemed a prohibitive cost of buying Africans became easy to justify. Here it must be stressed that any dependence on white indentured labour would have failed to drive the sugar economy. White servant numbers were too limited and the flow uneven in part because of white reluctance to do fieldwork. And even with incentives for voluntary servitude, or the more desperate kidnapping of unwary young men—in the contemporary term "Barbadoed" to the Caribbean—the white pool of potential workers was a fraction of what Africa could provide. The French also tried free white labour until it could not be sustained and like the English turned to African slaves. Males who survived their service contracts entered local society and joined independent merchants, tradesmen, colonial officials, garrisoned soldiers, and the white mechanics who ran the sugar refineries. White females who completed their servitude usually were stuck in service or found suitable marriages.[12] All the while, whites were fast becoming a minority on the French as well as the English islands.

Ligon did not bother to identify the "slaves" as African; that would have been obvious to his readers. They sat at the bottom of his ladder even as they began impressively to support it. By the middle of the eighteenth century, the populations of the Lesser Antilles tended to be predominantly male, adult, enslaved, and coloured and ran through the inevitable African-white, mulatto-white, mulatto-mulatto, or African-mulatto permutations in shades and status. Unlike the Spanish Caribbean, manumission rates were very low, but frequent miscegenation was constant and meant that the slave populations in the French, English, and Dutch systems combined Africans, Afro-Caribbeans, and mixed white-coloured slaves. In British Jamaica in 1800, the free coloured population amounted to a mere 10 per cent of the entire coloured population that included some residual native mixture. Following wars in North America and some frontier native slave hunting, natives from the mainland were also sold into the Caribbean.

The agro-industrial sugar plantation was organized around clear gradations of unskilled, semiskilled, and skilled labour whether it needed 20 or 200 slaves. For slaves, the ranking was clear: from cutting sugar cane to mending copper kettles. Household slaves were somewhere in the mix, above the field hand but perhaps below skilled carpenters, blacksmiths, and other tradesmen or the ultimate in coloured status, the slave "driver." On larger estates, white resident managers and overseers supervised operations, and any advanced occupations for coloured people were held by males. Females were valued for their endurance and generally assigned to field-work. Until the nineteenth century, male slaves were in the majority in the British and French Caribbean, and most were unmarried. As for the development of a "slave community" on any island, it is difficult to see in extended or aggregate form, from island to island, plantation to plantation, or plantation to small holding. Nevertheless, shared racial or bonded status or background often led to tacit solidarity or social communion, and indi-vidual plantations often encouraged a setting for shared social conscious-ness and cultural and spiritual cohesiveness in the slave quarters. Over time, escaped slaves, especially on the larger islands such as Jamaica and Saint Domingue, became settled in communities not unlike the *quilombos* of Brazil or the *palenques* in the Spanish colonies. These "Maroons," as the English and French described them, while not numerically dominant, added another dimension to the evolving cultural and social characteristics of the Caribbean. The term *maroon* is derived from the Spanish *cimarron* and took hold to describe the mountain refuges used by runaways (*cima* is Spanish for "top"). The term also shows up in North America to describe escaped slave communities.

As in Latin America, urban slaves, particularly the skilled, lived more comfortably than fieldworkers. Some free coloured people found their way into the ancillary economies of the sugar islands, reaching to the edges of the white controlled commercial, legal, and military infrastructures. Island militias leaned heavily on free mixed coloured populations in all the impe-rial systems, and during crises even slaves were enlisted for defence.[13] A rather interesting gender demographic developed in Jamaica's slave and free coloured population where females were in the majority by the early nineteenth century, reversing the earlier male to female ratios. There is some evidence that lighter skinned mixed coloured people pulled away in social and economic matters from Africans and darker skinned people, as in Brazil, to the point in some cases of attempting to "pass" for white. In the end, however, there was no legal, economic, social, or cultural racial integration and no white enthusiasm for it.[14]

In a significant way, not only did white to black population ratios decrease over time, but on many islands the actual numbers of whites fell. The remaining white population included a ruling elite of resident plant-ers, managers, political and bureaucratic placemen, and professionals. The demographic and social trend was toward a coloured majority of slaves with a small percentage of free coloured. In a typical example, in Antigua

TABLE 4.1 Selected Population Figures, British Caribbean

	Year	Total	White	Slave	Free Coloured	% Free Coloured to Slave[a]
Barbados	1680	44,143	5,361	38,782	0	0
	1748	62,324	15,192	47,025	107	0.2
	1801	82,292	15,887	64,196	2,209	3.3
	1833	100,242	12,797	80,861	6,584	7.5
Jamaica	1658	5,900	4,500	1,400	0	0
	1722	87,100	7,100	80,000	800	1.0
	1775	216,000	18,700	192,800	4,500	2.3
	1800	340,000	30,000	300,000	10,000	3.2
Antigua	1678	4,480	2,308	2,172	0	0
	1745	31,430	3,538	27,892	0	0
	1817	35,800	2,100	31,500	2,200	7.0
	1834	35,100	2,000	29,100	4,000	13.7
Trinidad[b]	1777	1,410	340	200	870	81.3
	1810	31,263[c]	2,495	20,821	15,003	42.0
	1834	44,715	3,632	22,359	18,724	45.5

a   Percentage of free coloured in total coloured population, free and slave.
b   Under Spanish rule to 1797.
c   Includes 1,683 "Indians."

Adapted from Dunn, *Sugar and Slaves*, 88 for 1680 Barbados; David W. Cohen and Jack P. Greene, eds., *Neither Slave Nor Free* (Baltimore, MD: Johns Hopkins, 1972), 338; Patterson, *Slavery and Social Death*, 477–79 for Barbados, Jamaica, Antigua, and Trinidad.

in 1678 there were 2,308 whites and 2,172 African slaves and in 1817, there were 2,000 and 31,500 respectively. That pattern was repeated everywhere in the British and French islands (see Table 4.1 and Table 4.2). Apart from the Loyalists who fled to the West Indies during and after the American Revolution, there was no meaningful white migration to the Caribbean after the early to mid-eighteenth century, except to the Spanish colonies. The nature of the islands' economies, a combination of their small limited land base and the valid opportunities elsewhere from Canada to Argentina, meant that the Lesser Antilles would not attract a fraction of the millions of European migrants who flocked to North and South America in the nineteenth and into the twentieth centuries. Only in the Spanish Caribbean did white populations grow over time. In 1830, even after massive African

TABLE 4.2 Selected Population Figures, French Caribbean

	Date	Total	White	Slave	Free Coloured	Free Coloured Percentage[a]
Martinique	1700	21,379	6,597	14,225	507	3.4
	1751	79,386	12,068	65,905	1,413	2.0
	1802	91,988	9,826	75,584	6,578	8.0
	1835	116,031	9,000	78,076	29,955	27.7
Saint Domingue	1681	6,648	4,336	2,312	0	0
	1739	132,539	11,540	117,411	3,588	3.0
	1789	490,108	30,831	434,429	24,848	5.4
Guadalupe	1700	10,875	3,825	6,725	325	4.6
	1788	101,971	13,466	85,461	3,044	3.4
	1834	c. 126,684	c. 15,000	96,684	c. 15,000	13.4

a   Percentage of total coloured population.
Adapted from Patterson, *Slavery and Social Death*, 480–81.

importation, there were 532,935 whites in the Spanish Antilles (nearly half the total population) compared to 88,043 in the combined British, French, Dutch, and Scandinavian islands, some 10 per cent of the whole in those islands. Here was the "black Caribbean" in the full sense, concentrated in the Northern Europeans' Lesser Antilles colonies.[15]

The Importance of the Codes

As noted, the Spanish and Portuguese came to America with codes for and experience with African slavery. That was not the case with the northern Europeans' colonies. There was nothing like the Spanish *Las Siete Partidos* or the Portuguese "natural law" or the *Codigo Filipino*. There was no codified slavery in the British Isles, France, or the Netherlands, even though some coloured servants were held without contracts, and colonists constructed their own codes after they settled in America. What Ligon and Whistler described for Barbados was formalized in 1636 by the Barbados governor and council. Their charter authority allowed them to make regulations such as "Negroes and Indians that came here to be sold, should serve for life, unless a contract ... to the contrary." In 1661, the Barbados Assembly passed "The Master and Servant Act," which clarified the status of white indentured servitude and "negro" slavery and then followed it with an act "for the better ordering and governing of negroes." The codes had the force of law in the chartered British colonies. While Barbados was spelling out its slave codes, the same was being done by the assemblies in Maryland, Virginia, and the Carolinas after 1660. English colonial strategy created "monopolies" such as the East India Company, the Virginia Company, the Massachusetts Bay Company (1629), the Hudson Bay Company (1670), and the Royal African Company (1672). The latter held a monopoly on the slave trade in the Empire until it was ended in 1698 under pressure from free trade merchant interests. Whether strictly for commerce or to combine trade with territorial occupation or to get rid of Quakers or Puritans, the English created an empire in America that ostensibly was under the ultimate authority of Crown and Parliament but which allowed settlement to proceed within the needs and objectives of the charter holders.

The resumption of Stuart rule in England in the 1660s signalled the beginning of a global imperial policy and the organization of new colonies in America. But by then the foundations of local authority had been laid down. The English charter model tended to encourage white immigration so that on the eve of the American Revolution the 13 North American colonies had the largest concentrations of white people in the New World, with a substantial minority of slaves, some 40 per cent of the whole in the southern colonies but less than 10 per cent in the northern colonies. No one in Parliament or at Court and no slave trader or plantation owner sat down to design the system; it emerged along with England's pragmatic imperial models and settlement patterns. There was tighter regulation of trade in the Navigation Acts of 1650 and 1660; along with the Dutch wars and the growing tensions with the French and Spanish empires, huge investments were made in the Royal Navy. A Board of Trade was established in 1696 and was a major step in the rationalizing of England's trade policies in a way that was similar to Colbert's French model, the Council of Commerce, and the older Spanish system, the *Casa de Contratacion*. The union of the Scottish and English Parliaments in 1707 created what would come to be Great Britain, and the Empire flourished as an economic entity. As it did, about 1.5 million Africans were imported into the British Caribbean along with the majority of the 400,000 who were sent to the North American colonies and the United States before 1808.

Models of economic protectionism were developed everywhere in the seventeenth century. The English and Dutch had each combined the functions of chartered colonies with national objectives, as had the French. The latter allowed companies and entrepreneurs along with Jesuits and

Franciscans to settle New France and the Caribbean islands. But the apparent fragility of colonial society made the colonies vulnerable to foreign seizure and encouraged Louis XIV, the Sun King, and his chief minister Jean-Baptiste Colbert (1619–83) to design a plan for colonial development. The Crown attached New France (Quebec) and the Caribbean islands in the 1660s as extensions of the realm with direct administrative control coming from France. In 1685, Louis signed into law the *Code Noir,* a far-ranging decree with provisions for controlling slaves and the free coloured populations in the French colonies. The new emphasis on royal organization and control sought to blunt the influence of the British Royal African Company and the French *Compagnie de Senegal,* but the French West India Company of 1664, designed in part by Colbert to dominate the trade, was dissolved in 1674 under pressure from competing free trade interests. The slave trade then operated on *laissez-faire* principles while enjoying the approval and protection of the state.

The *Code Noir* is an extraordinary document. No other European nation issued anything as comprehensive as national policy. It represented the French state's desire for a single body of laws to define and manage slavery after it had begun in practice. Like the English Barbados edict of 1636 that declared slaves as permanent chattels, the *Code* defined the slave as "movable property." Otherwise, the *Code* is a French original. It went so far as to declare the Protestant religion illegal, and it banished Jews from any French overseas territory, in part because of their association with the Dutch. The racial thesis attached the womb as property, with an interesting proviso: if the "husband," that is, the father, was a slave and the mother free, the progeny were to be free, but if the mother was a slave and the father free, any child was born a slave. The *Code* sought to control the free coloured population with a string of restrictions, but it first and foremost applied an absolutist approach to slavery in the French overseas territories. It skipped around some of the provisions of Roman law such as ease of manumission, independent income (as in the Iberian colonies), self-purchase, and matrimonial volition and was at pains to state the absence of legal or social rights for slaves as chattels.

On paper and in practice, a major slave nation was created overnight. In 1724, the edict was amended slightly (for New Orleans), but the basic content remained down to the French Revolution of 1789. There had been no slavery in continental France, but the Colbert-Louis XIV initiative looked directly at France's formal extensions in the New World. Over the next 100 years, over a million slaves were landed in French America, and before it collapsed in the Haitian Revolution, the sugar colony of Saint Domingue became the largest slave-based sugar economy in the Caribbean.

Running through the 60 articles in the *Code Noir* as a national policy are some of the most savage control mechanisms applied by any slave society. The death penalty was mandated for assaulting a master or "teacher," for stealing cattle or horses, or for running away a "third time." Methods of punishments such as chaining and whipping for misdemeanors were actually prescribed in the document. Branding with the *fleur de lis* or the amputation of an ear were permitted for runaways. The death penalty for a third offence might seem counterproductive given the cost of replacing the slave. But then what was the resale value of habitual runaways? The British colonial authorities were also harsh in their prescribed sentences but took a more measured approach to capital punishment. As noted, many of the British colonial codes were held over by many of the colonies that, as states, formed the United States. Interestingly, the French, for all the severity of the *Code Noir,* considered freed slaves to be French subjects, that is, with access to the same legal rights as all French colonial subjects, something that did not apply to freed slaves in the Anglo-American systems.[16]

As for the Dutch, their practices lacked the formal details of the British colonial codes or the *Code Noir,* but their regulations were firmly administered. Dutch slavery evolved into a set of practices that by the late seventeenth century were as brutal as any. For example, in a curious use of "black," the Dutch and the English had accepted the "black legend," a particular kind of ethnic profiling that had nothing to do with Africans. Rather, it was used to condemn the Spanish for their cruelty, and the "black" in the black legend alluded to Spanish wickedness. The legend had emerged in the sixteenth century as a slur on Spanish character and as a hypocritical comment on the desolation Spain visited on the Americas. It went with Protestant charges of the Spanish Church's anti-heresy practices with the Inquisition. The legend survived, even as the northern Europeans decimated native populations in North America, enslaved millions of Africans, and employed disciplinary methods that rank with any for cruelty. How ironic it is that the anti-Spanish Dutch adopted a punishment known as the "Spanish Buck" where a recalcitrant slave had his arms locked to his knees, held by a cross stick, then tipped forward and whipped until the skin disappeared.[17]

At the end of the eighteenth century, the Caribbean was the most intensively African region in the Americas. There were comparable pockets of black majorities in South Carolina, Bahia, and elsewhere, but no single colonial jurisdiction in North America or Latin America could match the

90 per cent black majorities of Jamaica or Saint Domingue and much of the Lesser Antilles. But the region was on the cusp of great upheaval as we shall see in Chapter Seven. The French Revolution sparked a series of uprisings by free coloured peoples in the French Caribbean. In unrelated ways, the British abolitionists gained parliamentary support during the last decades of the eighteenth century at the same time as the Constitution of the United States was guaranteeing the right of individuals to keep slaves as property. While the British began to fix an end to the trade, slavery itself in the British Caribbean did not end until 1834. On the eve of the Saint Domingue (Haitian) uprising, there were nearly half a million slaves in the colony, double what it had been a generation earlier. There were fewer than 50,000 slaves in Spanish Cuba when Saint Domingue imploded, but what followed were the most dramatic rises in both sugar production and slave arrivals in Caribbean history. Nearly three-quarters of a million slaves were brought into Cuba before the slave trade was ended in the 1850s, and sugar production reached nearly half a million imperial tons annually during that time. This figure represented about one-third of the global production of cane sugar.[18]

Slavery boomed in North America after 1804, driven by cotton. Brazil became independent in 1822 and began the greatest volume of slave importation in its history. The Spanish colonies in the Caribbean kept slavery going to the end of the nineteenth century. When slavery ended in Jamaica in 1834, Cuban planters during the same period were importing an average of 13,000 slaves annually. The Haitian Revolution and the ending of slavery in the British Caribbean might have promised a future without slavery in the Caribbean. But Cuba's boom ensured that it would be otherwise. Elsewhere, slavery expanded its reach in the United States and Brazil.

Notes

1 Richard Ligon, *A True and Excellent History of the Island of Barbadoes*, Abridged (Caribbean Affairs: University College of the West Indies, n.d.), 10.

2 Those countries are Belize, Colombia, Costa Rica, Guatemala, Honduras, Mexico, Nicaragua, Panama, and Venezuela.

3 Jordan, *White Over Black*, 65 (spelling modernized). On Barbados, see Matthew Parker, *The Sugar Barons: Family, Corruption, Empire and War in the West Indies* (New York: Walker and Company, 2011), 38–66; 88–102.

4 Jordan, *White Over Black*, 34–35, 216–63. Jordan's four-decades old comments about white attitudes (meaning English attitudes) are still among the best on the subject. See also Klein and Luna, *Slavery in Brazil*, 251ff, for notes on racism.

5 See Peter Mancall, *Hakluyt's Promise: An Elizabethan's Obsession for an English America* (New Haven: Yale University Press, 2007); for a sample of Hakluyt's thesis, see "A Discourse concerning Western Planting," in Jack P. Greene, *Settlement to Society, 1607–1763: A Documentary History of Colonial America* (New York: Norton, 1975), 2–4.

6 Edward Countryman, ed., *How Did American Slavery Begin?* (Boston: Bedford/ St. Martin's, 1999); Alden T. Vaughan, "The Origins Debate: Slavery and Racism in Seventeenth Century Virginia," *Virginia Magazine of History and Biography* 97 (1989): 311–54.

7 Eltis and Richardson, *Atlas*, 200–02.

8 Franklin W. Knight, *The Caribbean, The Genesis of a Fragmented Nationalism*, 2nd ed. (New York: Oxford University Press, 1990). Much of the material in this chapter is drawn from this source. See also Richard S. Dunn, *Sugar and Slaves*; Hilary Beckles, *White Servitude and Black Slavery in Barbados, 1627–1715* (Knoxville: University of Tennessee, 1989); Klein and Vinson, *Slavery in Latin America and the Caribbean*, especially Chapters 3 and 5.

9 Knight, *The Caribbean*, 117.

10 Ralph Davis, *The Rise of the Atlantic Economies* (Ithaca: Cornell University Press, 1973), 251, 259–61.

11 For population and sugar exports, see Knight, *The Caribbean*, 364–69. For sugar production, see Deerr, *History of Sugar*, Chapters 11–14 on production numbers and labour issues.

12 Bush, *Servitude*, 58–68; Beckles, *White Servitude*, Chapter 6. See also David Galenson, *White Servitude in Colonial America* (Cambridge: Cambridge University Press, 1981) for a detailed study of servitude in North America. The models apply in general to the British Caribbean. The literature on British indentured labour models emphasize its importance in British law.

13 Knight, *The Caribbean*, Chapter 4.

14 Knight, *The Caribbean*, Chapter 5. See also Jablonski, *Living Color*, Chapters 10–13.

15 Stanley L. Engerman and B.W. Higman, "The Demographic Structure of the Caribbean Slave Societies in the Eighteenth and Nineteenth Centuries," in Franklin Knight, ed., *The Slave Societies of the Caribbean*, Vol. III of *General History of the Caribbean* (London: UNESCO, 1997).

16 Klein and Luna, *Slavery in Brazil*, 195–96. On the *Code Noir*, see Sue Peabody and Keila Grinsberg, *Slavery, Freedom, and the Law in the Atlantic World: A Brief History with Documents* (Boston: Bedford/St. Martin's, 2007), 31–36.

17 Den Heijer, "Dutch Caribbean."

18 Eltis, "The Slave Economies of the Caribbean: Structure, Performance, Evolution, and Significance," in Knight, ed., *The Slave Societies of the Caribbean*, 105–37.

5 | Slavery in Prerevolutionary North America: The Making of the "South"

"Negro slavery was to become a vitally important institution [in the Chesapeake] and, later, to the southwards. In the tobacco colonies it is possible to watch Negro slavery develop, not pop up full-grown overnight.... Negro slavery ... was neither borrowed from foreigners, nor extracted from books, nor invented out of whole cloth, nor extrapolated from servitude, nor generated by English reaction to Negroes as such, nor necessitated by the exigencies of the New World. Not any one of these made the Negro a slave [in English mainland North America], but all."[1]

—Winthrop Jordan, *White over Black*.

From Servant to Slave

Anthony Johnson, an African, might have been one of the 20 "negars" landed at Jamestown, Virginia in 1619, or he might have come in 1621 from Angola as Antonio. He serves as an example of Winthrop Jordan's complex and tragic causality. He began his life in Virginia as a servant and later amassed over 200 acres of headright land grants for bringing into the colony five black servants of his own. The headright system of 1618 was a means to encourage settlement, by which any person who brought in a settler, usually a servant, was granted free title to 50 acres. By the 1650s, Johnson had established a successful operation in Virginia and was a slaveholder himself. One of his slaves petitioned the court for his freedom on the grounds that he was an indentured servant whose term had expired. Johnson countered with the claim that the petitioner was his slave "for life" and that no indenture existed. Johnson had no qualms about keeping another "negro" in formal bondage yet assumed that he, personally, was somehow exempt from the growing trend in Virginia that suggested all Africans could be kept for life. He later moved to Maryland where he leased land, and he died there in 1669. He even managed to set up his sons with deeds to land before his Virginia estate was expropriated and he was retroactively deemed to be "alien." Johnson had run into the new slave codes of the 1650s and 1660s. He had gone from servant to landowner to slaveholder himself and then to "alien." Johnson, an Angolan, had taken on an English name, married freely, and raised several children. His story is important because it illustrates a trend. The "ancestry of inferiority" principle was early on applied to Africans and their progeny first in practice and then in law.[2]

When Johnson died, Virginia and Maryland were on their way to defining racial slavery in law in the way it had already taken shape in the Barbados Council's declaration of 1636 that "Negroes and Indians ... should serve for life" if they did not have an indenture contract, a policy that was continued in the "Master and Servant Act" of 1661. The test of legitimacy rested on the principle of "contract" in Barbados and in the Johnson case in Virginia. The nebulous, indeterminate definitions and roles for servants and slaves were clarified with codes that delineated legal status by race. In the 1660s, elected assemblies in Virginia and Maryland passed laws that in one form or another would survive for 200 years. The Chesapeake planters did not refer directly to Barbados for their codes but like the Barbadians simply legalized what was already happening. In 1664, the Maryland Assembly passed "An Act Concerning Negroes & other Slaves":

> That all Negroes or other slaves ... within the Province, and [those] hereafter imported ... shall serve Durante Vita. And all Children born of any Negro or other slave shall be Slaves as their fathers were for the terme of their lives. And forasmuch as diverse freeborn English women ... to the disgrace of our Nation doe intermarry [that is cohabited or otherwise have coital relations] with Negro Slaves ... the Issue [child] of such women ... shall serve [become the property of] the Masters of their parents.[3]

There is a great deal going on in that statute and in the unequivocal phrase *durante vita* (for the duration of life). The reference to "other slaves" is to native slaves.

The tone and specifics of the act are self-serving and advance the proscription against miscegenation. All English jurisdictions in the seventeenth century prohibited illicit sex, including extramarital or premarital sex, and applied penalties for "fornication" and the fathering or mothering of "bastards." But the Maryland code also punished interracial sex with heritable bondage. Moreover, another section of the 1664 act condemned white women who "married," that is, had coital relations with a slave, to be the property of the slave's master. The odds against those liaisons were high because there was a two or three to one ratio of white males to white females in late seventeenth-century Chesapeake so that white female servants or widows were in great demand and under intense scrutiny. White males were under less scrutiny and female slaves were not always protected. In any case, the Chesapeake laws opened the way to the "single drop" doctrine, first in a patrilineal status for mixed race children and later when laws added matrilineal descent. But sexual relations continued between white males, usually masters, and black slave women, an exercise in power relations that lasted to the Civil War era. Generations of "mulattos" were absorbed into slavery, and their status was certainly not affected because of lighter colour or white paternity.

More codes followed in the Chesapeake and later in the Carolinas. They eventually included clauses explaining the rights of disposal (the selling of slaves as taxable property), specific bans on interracial marriage, anti-literacy rules, slave to slave marital rights or restrictions, tax rates, and special categories of slave crimes (resistance, mostly) and the punishments to go with them. A 1705 summary of Virginia's codes appeared in Robert Beverley's *The History and Present State of Virginia*. Beverley, a Virginia born planter and slaveholder, likely had some part in the drawing up of the statutes he describes. His comprehensive overview is clear and instructive:

> [In Virginia] Servants they distinguish by the Names of Slaves for Life, and Servants for a time. Slaves are the Negroes, and their Posterity following the Condition of the Mother, according to the Maxim, *partus sequitur ventrem*. They are call'd Slaves in Respect of the Time of their Servitude, because it is for Life. Servants are those which serve only for a few Years, according to ... their Indenture, or the Custom of the Country ... the Male Servants and Slaves of both Sexes are imployed together ... in sowing and planting Tobacco, Corn, &c ... Female-Servants [are] ... rarely or never put to work in the Ground, if she be good for any thing else ... Whereas on the other hand, it is a common thing to work a Woman slave out of Doors.[4]

The Latin *partus sequitur ventrem* was used, as a matter of legalese, to say that the child inherits the status of the mother—the matrilineal determinant to go with the patrilineal. Beverley's memorable statement, "Slaves are the Negroes, and their Posterity," clarified any earlier confusion over the differences between black and white servitude. Here, race came to define the slave. And, as a 1705 Virginia code put it, "All Negro, mulatto and Indian slaves ... shall be held as real estate." Virginia had become a slave society, not from original purpose but after a sequence of failures, rebirth, and redefinition.

Slavery and the Roots of Sectionalism

In 1607, Virginia became the first of the original 13 North American colonies to be settled permanently. It was the southern part of the London Company Charter of 1606. The English charter system encouraged a degree of flexible local political and legal authority forbidding only laws that were inimical to the laws of England. Thus, when the councils and assemblies of Virginia and other colonies adopted codes defining chattel bondage, they did not violate English law, which contained nothing concrete that either condoned or banned chattel bondage. The issue was not properly addressed in England (Great Britain after 1707) until the late eighteenth century on the eve of the American Revolution. By then, Virginia had long since become a full-blown slave society as had Maryland and North and South Carolina. In 1733, Georgia, the last of the original 13 colonies to be chartered, was established in part as a refuge for London's poor, with strict codes of sobriety and conduct and a ban on slavery. When the experiment failed, Georgia was opened to planter settlement and slavery in 1752.

From the beginning of the eighteenth century, a steady flow of slaves into the southern colonies was offset by a steady flow of white immigrants into the northern colonies and a remarkable rate of natural increase in both. In 1650, a simple comparative statistic shows that after 150 years of settlement and change, the white population in all of Spanish America was estimated at about 6 per cent of the whole.[5] After 150 years of settlement and change, in 1750, the population of the 13 British colonies, from Canada south to Florida and west to the Appalachians, comprised 70 per cent whites and 20 per cent blacks, with a 10 per cent native population in the margin. However, the distribution was uneven. The non-native population in the northern colonies was 95 per cent white and in the settled areas of the southern colonies 60 per cent white and 40 per cent black. An even more remarkable statistic shows that the population of British North America was as much as five times greater than it had been when only natives had occupied the territories. As much as the advent and scale of slavery shaped North America's distinctiveness, its whiteness shaped it too. By the 1750s, the Caribbean was 90 per cent black, Brazil was a mixture of black and mixed coloured with a white minority, and Mexico was distinctly *mestizo* with pockets of blacks and natives and, as noted, a white minority.

Between 1607 and 1625, the Virginia Company sent managers and servants (white Englishmen and other Europeans) into the area with no real prospects of profit. The colony became a death trap for thousands of white servants who perished from disease, starvation, and native resistance. Incompetence, the absence of gold or any other resource, false expectations, and bad initial planning combined to doom the company. But if the Roanoke Colony of 1585 had been a disaster and abandoned, Virginia was a disaster that was *not* abandoned because just before it collapsed completely a few entrepreneurs saw their future in tobacco.[6] A legislative assembly, the aptly named "House of Burgesses," was formed in 1619 by the survivors. The representatives distributed land to themselves and to immigrant investors who in turn contracted English indentured servants for labour. The original charter was abandoned and replaced in 1625 with a Royal Charter that left the old company rules and activities in place but which stabilized the community's future. The profits from tobacco came to be what sugar was to Barbados, and as the transition from white indentured labour to slaves sped up after 1660, a decisive shift was made in the shaping of colonial North America. A cultural and economic division opened up between a slave-based South and a white North.

The 1629 charter of the Massachusetts Bay Company was held by a group seeking to purify (hence "Puritan") the Church of England in America. In the ringing phrase of the Company's religious and civil leader John Winthrop, it was to make a "city upon the hill." The model for settlement in Massachusetts was the Church congregation with a communitarian town government. Families were granted enough land to be self-sufficient but hardly enough to produce surpluses. Servants were largely confined to domestic and some commercial occupations. Grants usually contained enough land to be willed to children with the objective of perpetuating a congregational, corporate, family farm society. The legacies of Winthrop and his successors stand in sharp contrast to those of the mercurial adventurer John Smith (1580–1631) or the entrepreneurial John Rolfe (1585–1622) and the planter elites (the "plantocracy") and slave society that took root in Virginia.

The congregational pattern was gradually extended, sometimes in modified form, to the emerging settlements in New England. The important commercial ports of Boston, Newport, and Salem were vital to New England's ultimate importance in the imperial world of politics and trade. Cash crops were out of the question, and livestock or grain yields were not large enough to support much servant labour and certainly not slave labour. Nevertheless, slave codes were written in all the northern colonies, regardless of slave numbers. There were several hundred Africans in Massachusetts by 1660, a tiny percentage of the whole, and they were found in the colony's ports. A 1641 Massachusetts law had banned slavery but had included a clause that excepted "captives taken in just wars [that is, natives]" or "strangers [Africans] ... sold to us." Native prisoners of war were candidates for slavery, and after the Powhatan Wars in Virginia and the Pequot and King Philip's Wars in New England, native captives were sent as slaves to Caribbean planters.[7] White servants could also be bought and sold but only for the terms of their contracts. Rhode Island banned slavery altogether in 1670, but the law was ignored. In any case, African slaves were not a factor in the shaping of any of New England's colonies including Connecticut and New Hampshire and never made up more than 2 or 3 per cent of the region's aggregate population.

Lodged between New England and the slave South, the "middle colonies" (the later "mid-Atlantic states") of New York, Pennsylvania, New Jersey, and Delaware were more socially, ethnically, and religiously pluralistic and economically diverse than New England. Land holdings were generally larger and agricultural surpluses were possible in some of the more fertile valleys. In fact, Pennsylvania grains and meats fed slaves on some Caribbean islands. During the eighteenth century, the numbers of slaves in Pennsylvania fluctuated between 6 per cent and 8 per cent of the whole population in an area that attracted a higher proportion of white immigrants than any comparable space in all the Americas. The northern slave population was concentrated in coastal towns doing dock work, shop work, carting, household service, and general labouring. By the middle of the eighteenth century, few slaveholders held more than one or two slaves and those were found in places such as New York City where a substantial minority of 14 per cent of the overall population was black. But the main thing to note here is that the rural North, as a whole, was emphatically white. The rural South was a different matter, although it had taken its original shape on a white servant base.

A 1625 census listed 40 per cent of Virginia's population as "servants" without reference to race. A century later, 40 per cent of the whole population was slave, that is, black and in bondage. In 1676, as the transition to slave labour was underway, the rising power of Virginia's slaveholding class was threatened by a spectacular uprising of white settlers. Nathaniel Bacon, a "well-born" English planter, raised an army of several hundred landowners, traders, and freed indentured servants and overthrew the Virginia government. His success was short-lived, however, and the rebellion crumbled when a large royal force intervened. Bacon's "revolutionary" objective was far from seeking egalitarian reform in Virginia. Rather, he and his followers hoped to limit the influence of the larger planters who were allotting increasingly large parcels of land to themselves and moving rapidly to import larger numbers of slaves. Bacon wanted to remove natives, for example, so that their lands to the west could be open to more white settlement, allowing for newcomers such as Bacon himself to participate in the colony's politics and influence its economic development. Historians see Bacon's rebellion as defining the future of Virginia because its failure reinforced the economic and political power of the slaveholding Virginia hierarchy.[8]

John Rolfe, the white husband of Princess Matoaka (Pocahontas), is credited with introducing commercial tobacco to the struggling Virginia settlement sometime around 1612. One version of the story alleges that Rolfe simply turned the plants used in native ceremony and recreation into a marketable variety, the so-called sot weed.[9] Perhaps he did. But it is likely that Rolfe also had some Spanish seed from the Caribbean. Whatever its source, it sparked a revolution in the colony's economy. It also demanded a great deal of labour. Tobacco's grueling year-round schedule was an intense and wearying process from seeding to harvesting to curing and shipping. In the Chesapeake, beds were prepared and seeded in January with stooped labour using hand tools such as hoes and even bare hands. After some necessary spring rains, the seedlings were gathered and carefully transplanted. Daily hoeing kept the soil from hardening. Weeding, the cutting of excessive top growth, and the removal of worms and other pests went on through the spring and summer. The process hurried to intensity in the fall when each stalk had to be sliced and the leaves made limp, then picked, hung, dried, and cured in sheds. The tobacco was packed, not in bales, but in large barrels for the weeks-long trip to Europe. Some of the larger barrels, "hogsheads," contained as much as 500 pounds of compressed tobacco leaf and came with an axle and rollers for ease of transport to the nearest wharf for shipping. On small holdings, a planter and one or two servants or slaves might constitute the entire workforce.

After Rolfe's initiatives, Virginia tobacco was marketed aggressively. By 1700, demand in Europe accelerated, and investment in Virginia and Maryland rose with it. Planters were shipping 30 million imperial tons of cured tobacco annually, a remarkable volume that amounted to 340 imperial tons per capita for every man, woman, and child, slave or free, in the Chesapeake. Those numbers and the slaves who produced them would multiply steadily into the nineteenth century. At the same time, south of the Chesapeake another portentous development was underway.

In 1663, a proprietary charter to be called Carolina was issued to favourites of the Stuart monarch for a great swathe of land located south of the

Chesapeake and running to Spanish Florida. The huge grant was ready-made for slavery, and when the original scheme to attract aspiring gentry to huge blocks of land failed, the way was then open to enterprising slaveholders from the Chesapeake and Barbados. The area was split in stages into north and south jurisdictions, and by 1729 fully separate governing entities were in place. South Carolina matured with a black majority that would persist to the Civil War. By 1700, only 5,704 people lived in South Carolina, but 47 per cent of them were black. By 1770, blacks, almost all of them in bondage, represented 60 per cent of the province's population of 124,244. North Carolina had a substantial slave population in its coastal plantation zone but also attracted great numbers of white settlers to its backcountry. In fact, on the eve of the Revolution, North Carolina was the fastest growing North American colony, characterized by a tidewater slave-based cash crop tobacco economy and a backcountry small white family farm culture.[10]

Rice propelled semi-tropical South Carolina into a major slave society. As with most staples, one crop of rice took the best part of a year to mature and be processed, and cultivation benefitted from the expertise of slaves who had been familiar with it in Africa. The rudimentary engineering for raising dikes for low-lying swampy fields required strenuous labour with hand tools. Sluices for flooding the seeded fields and then draining them during the rice growing cycle were often flawed and needed constant repair and realignment. When ready, the rice had to be cut with sickles, then threshed, and the rice kernel separated from the grass and screened to remove imperfections before being packed and shipped.

Indigo was also important to the early South Carolina economy. This blue blooming plant was a superb dye source and much admired in Britain where it was already a major import from India. The commercial viability of the plant in Carolina was serendipitous, the result of the experiments of Elizabeth Pinckney (1722–93) on her father's estate. The plant produced a blue flower that required constant attention as it grew; it then had to be pulled by hand, soaked, fermented, and mixed with limewater, pounded by paddles, fermented again, and then formed into the paste that made it an ideal dyestuff. The last part of the production was as important as any. As sugar was prepared in a special way for storage and transport, so too in its own way was every New World staple: tobacco in hogsheads or rice in barrels, cotton in bales, and indigo dye paste in cubes. At every point along the way in the sunrise to sunset routines of the fields, for at least 300 days each year, from the seeding to the shipping, slaves made it possible.

By the early eighteenth century, North America's slave societies began abruptly south of where the Pennsylvania and Delaware borders touched

Virginia and Maryland—the "Mason-Dixon Line," named after 1760 for the English surveyors Charles Mason and Jeremiah Dixon. South of the line there was little of the white ethnic pluralism of the middle colonies or the white homogeneity of rural New England. A traveller arriving from the North in the eighteenth century saw what appeared to be another country. No northern colonist or European newcomer was unaware of slavery, but the sight of tobacco fields, slave quarters, and sometimes gangs of black slaves were proof of stark regional differences.

By the first half of the eighteenth century, about 2.5 per cent of New England's population was black, a figure that actually declined during the Revolution. The figures were slightly larger in the middle colonies, and at the Mason-Dixon line, the contrast was striking: Delaware's black population was 5.2 per cent of the whole and Pennsylvania's 2.4 per cent, but just across the colony lines, Maryland's population was 31.5 per cent black and Virginia's 42 per cent with only a tiny percentage of them free. In the South, as in Brazil, a significant minority of slaves were employed in raising edible crops and livestock.

Much of the Chesapeake and the South was an untidy mix of cultivated fields and vacant wastelands, thickets and woods, small farms, scattered hamlets, and plantations. The landscape bore little resemblance to the order and symmetry of the family farm communities of southern New England or the middle colonies' Hudson and Delaware River valleys to the north. In the Chesapeake, the heavy demands of single crop cultivation exhausted soils in some areas, and plantations were vacated or turned over to small holdings or to pasture. The large plantations in the southern British colonies had their own slave blacksmiths, tanners, millers, carpenters, carters, child care women, full time cooks, and laundrywomen. The planters convened around county courthouses for business, politics, and socializing and ruled the vestry of the established Church of England (Anglican). Some of the older plantations were on navigable rivers where crops could be shipped from private docks. Where native populations had once thronged, their remnants had been pushed to the social and economic margins. They were barely visible in older settled parts of the Chesapeake and the South.

Not Fit For Freedom: Racial Determinism in North America

Regardless of how slavery came to be codified, by the 1770s, it fixed blacks as worthy only of bondage. Practice and observation confirmed the codes. Slaves seemed to whites to be incompetent and utterly dependent, or rude and sometimes dangerous, and even those recognized as skilled were despised as a consequence of race. In all capacities, as field hands, domestics, drivers, or craftsmen, whether newly arrived or born into the system, young or old, male or female, slaves were perceived to be docile, testy, or lazy. Others were seen as untrustworthy and even cunning. Some of the amateur behaviourists among slaveholders and other observers saw positive habits or traits, but race-based slavery allowed little room for fairness. Freed blacks, always few in number, were seen as either a menace or a nuisance and were mostly segregated. If sociology or theoretical determinism did not justify slavery, then any moral hesitation could be allayed by scripture, as in the "curse of Ham." According to Genesis 9 and 10 in the 1611 King James Version of the Bible, Ham (or Cham), the son of Noah, had seen his father drunk and naked after the flood. Ham's son Canaan was then cursed by Noah to be a "servant of servants" to Ham's brothers. How that story made the leap from servitude to slavery and then to African slavery and the degradation of blacks is convoluted and never entirely clear. Clarity did not matter, though, if a curse through Noah, who had been blessed by God, was intended to apply to Africans and their progeny.[11] Scripture, as it was understood, made the African and the African American a pariah, and the civil law agreed.

The slave was subject to calculated oral degradation in day-to-day relations with white masters, overseers, or white servants and lived in fear of sale or separation from spouse and children, since the intimacy of family or the camaraderie of the slave quarters could be interrupted without warning. For some time now, historians have studied the other side of laws, court cases, deeds, wills, planters' accounts, diaries, and a variety of statistics attempting to see the world through the eyes of slaves. What we find is that regardless of the psychological and physical assaults on their privacy and person, slaves did aspire to social and emotional self-respect. Many played a tactical role in mitigating and even determining some of the conditions of their bondage, not by direct negotiation, really, but by day-to-day action. Planters recorded slave torpor and indifference, sometimes as natural traits. They understood that illness could be feigned or the hoe deliberately broken; they understood that the lackadaisical habits of slaves were very often calculated ways of testing the limits of what masters would tolerate.[12]

As we shall see in Chapter Six, the slave family along with music, religion, hope, collective solidarity, and remnants of African roots did much to conceal or muffle despair. Some revisionist historiography argues that slavery in North America was sustained by slaves' calculated accommodation to it. Slaves were routinely rewarded with a vegetable patch, a harvest pig roast, and occasional celebrations of dancing and singing that mostly amused slaveholders but that allowed for a spirit of independent identity among slaves. Complaints of slave inefficiency, ignorance, or chronic laziness clearly hint at a form of slave resistance. However, most of the obvious behaviours were tolerated by masters and overseers who believed that there were limits to the slaves' productivity. Violence and the threat of it were used, but slaves were as likely to respond to masters' favours. Slave marriage went with other perks and was allowed and even encouraged by some planters as a brake on restlessness. Over time, Christianity took hold among American-born slaves, but in many ways it was cynically encouraged by masters as a mechanism, like marriage, to soften the edges of bondage and keep the peace. Well into the nineteenth century, white preachers presented the scriptures to slaves mostly to proselytize the rightness of their lot. By then, however, black preachers were circulating with their own carefully presented emphasis on slave spiritual worth. But most whites believed that even if slaves adopted Christianity, it did not lead to moral equality or, in a peculiar twist, access to a white hereafter. As part of the separation of souls, marriages among slaves could not be sanctioned in ecclesiastical terms and were usually conducted informally, as social but no less serious and solemnized affairs for the slaves involved.[13]

By the time of the Revolution, a majority of slaves in the Chesapeake were American-born, allowing for a reasonable use of the term African American. By the start of the nineteenth century, on larger plantations more and more slaves were being born, raised, married, and living out their lives in the same setting. The majority of rural slaves, however, were held on estates of about 20 slaves, and the very large populations so often depicted in popular images were the exception. Indeed, even the larger North American plantations were on average smaller than the large operations in Brazil and the Caribbean. Just as there was no composite New World slave, so too was there no single undifferentiated slave setting or experience.[14]

The legal rights of masters were applied with racial bias; the slave needed to be defined by whites as permanently inferior. Views of the African as the heathen "other," a bestial offshoot, had long circulated among the English and were folded into the doctrine of white superiority, as the earlier anti-miscegenation codes made heredity the central definition of status. Paradoxically, while the slave was property, he or she was capable of volition, a sideways recognition of the slave's humanity. So the law recognized the slave's potential for resistance and set a graduated set of corporal punishments where severity was tied to the seriousness of offences. The scarring, flogging, chaining, and mutilation of slaves was certainly more common in the plantation societies than in New England, for example, but all slaveholders had the "right" to punish any slave in specific ways. No white servant was ever castrated for being a repeat runaway.

Urban slaves in the northern mainland colonies could be rented out to earn money for their own use, but there is little evidence of self-purchase in North America. The looser rhythms of race relations in the port cities ultimately fostered fears and resentments in New York City, the site of the largest concentration of slaves and free blacks in the North. Rumours of conspiracies and criminality cropped up from time to time there and resulted in barbaric attacks on "suspicious" blacks in 1712 and again in 1741, discussed below in this chapter. In the southern plantation societies, the threat to public order was constrained by planters, local white farmers, and the constant patrols that hunted runaways and deterred others, but whites did fear interplantation conspiracies. It was certainly easy in the plantation zones to spot or detain individual persons of colour "abroad" without a pass, yet information and ideas did get from one plantation to another. The Stono Rebellion of 1739 forced white Carolinians to recognize that not only did slaves have the potential to conspire but more to the point were eager for revenge, rape, pillage, and murder. Thus, whites in the southern colonies lived with an obvious dilemma, a sublime paradox, really, where slaves could accept bondage and be controlled in part because of presumed inferior intelligence and yet be capable of leadership, planning, concerted action, and clear objectives.

By the end of the eighteenth century, there were about 1 million slaves in Brazil and roughly 700,000 free coloured peoples. The British American numbers at that time show a slave population of 575,000 and a paltry 32,000 free blacks. The French and Dutch islands had similar ratios, and only in the Spanish islands were there substantial numbers of free coloured people. The relatively closed system meant that by 1860, after 200 years, free blacks comprised only a little over 6 per cent of black people in North America. Even if their fortunes failed or if they died without heirs, very few Virginia or Carolina planters considered freeing their slaves. In either event, slaves could be sold or disposed of by the authorities. The records show some repentant slaveholders on their deathbeds freeing slaves, all too often into a hostile environment.[15] Revolutionary ideologues such as George Washington and Thomas Jefferson freed their slaves as sincere gestures to the rhetoric of "liberty" but could do nothing to prevent the inclusion of slavery as a property right in the US Constitution, because when it was composed in 1787 ending slavery was as impracticable as it was undesirable.

The image of the stooped slave with hoe or scythe or cotton sack in hand sends a disturbing message of the weary chattel, and we should respect that. That was certainly not the lot of every slave in every setting, and even the most abused field hand was rarely if ever worked to counterproductive exhaustion, let alone death. There was no logic in that. In the nineteenth century, slavery looked terribly inefficient to critics. But in the South it was not only a fixed part of the social structure but was praised as an efficient labour model, and it is unlikely that any southern planter doubted the efficiency of slave labour and its role in his own and the South's wealth.[16] Large plantation owners balanced their production projections and accommodated the deliberate limits slaves would work to. Efficiency could be had with the so-called task system. This alternative to gang work assigned specific jobs in rotation to individual slaves, allowing the slave to relax after completing an assigned task, much as it did in the larger Brazilian *engenhos*. In other cases, opportunities existed for slaves to become carpenters or blacksmiths. Slaves on smaller holdings were often conventional farm workers, "husbandmen," and in many cases general handymen. Women fit every labour category and, as noted earlier, over time appeared on larger holdings as wet nurses, house domestics, seamstresses, full-time washerwomen, or mammies. Some operations were in fact a set of physically separate plantations or farms spread over a neighbourhood, a county, and across county lines.

Making the System Work

In the early eighteenth century, Robert "King" Carter (1662–1732) became one of the largest planters in Virginia, with 390 slaves on 48 different sites of various sizes, producing everything from tobacco to wheat to cattle. Fifty years later his successors, several extended family groups, had used his estate to aggregate 2,000 slaves distributed on many holdings over a large swathe of Virginia. Families such as the Carters were at the top end of Virginia's family dynasties. Thomas Jefferson was hardly the largest slaveholder in revolutionary Virginia, but he was in the highest rank. He worked 45 slaves at Monticello, his grand residence, and owned 140 more slaves on six other holdings. Jonathan Bryan amassed about 32,000 acres of land and 250 slaves on properties in Georgia and South Carolina. North American planters tended to feed and clothe their worn-out, sick, old, or infirm slaves when they were no longer productive. Retired slaves showed up in the records as supported by either younger slaves or masters in the rural South, and in the urban almshouses of the North, older "retired" slaves were cared for as public welfare cases.

The paucity of personal accounts makes direct evidence of the slaves' inner worlds difficult to assemble. For a start, and largely because of laws banning formal education, the vast majority of slaves were illiterate. Freed or escaped slaves did produce some autobiography, reflection, and commentary, but those are mostly for the 1830–60 antebellum period and have been used to good effect by historians.[17] Oral ex-slave testimonies collected after the Civil War and as late as the 1930s are useful but reveal the perils of expecting complete accuracy from geriatric reminiscence.[18] And even when there are contemporary accounts from inside the system, we are still left with only a few individual experiences from which we cannot always generalize with confidence. On many estates, large or small, females mingled with males, children with adults, and young with old. Africans met third-generation American-born slaves. There were bright slaves and dull slaves. In the nineteenth century in wealthy Brazilian households and on many southern US plantations, white children played with black children, and black wet nurses gave milk to white babies. The love of a white child for a black mammy could not be sustained when the child became a slaveholder or wife of a slaveholder. The evidence from slaves themselves is usually what was filtered through the screen of white observation or court testimony.

Exceptions are rare, especially for anything before the middle of the nineteenth century, but an important and celebrated account is Oloudah Equiano's *Life* (1789). Equiano claimed to be an African nobleman, and his vividly recalled experiences cannot be seen as typical of the millions of forlorn captives who crossed the Atlantic. Although the authenticity of the authorship and the factual detail have each been questioned, there is drama in the evocation of the cruelty and humiliation that went with slavery and in a narrative that reads like the picaresque adventures so popular in English-language literature in the eighteenth century. Still, evidence from white observers corresponds to much of what the Equiano biography describes.[19] Frederick Douglass's compelling *Narrative* (1845) is a reliable, eloquent account of the slave experience and has clear application to the late eighteenth century. Douglass was a rare witness to the institution, literate (taught by a benevolent master) and free, or rather escaped, and encouraged to write and publish in the New England abolitionist community. The point to remember about these accounts is their undeniable propaganda value in the late eighteenth and early nineteenth centuries in the heat of white abolitionist activity.[20]

Most of what we have from the slave perspective is really what was inferred by planters, traders, and travellers and shaped, of course, by the subjective framework of the observer. For example, the botanist William Bartram, travelling through Georgia in the 1770s, recorded a group of male slaves cutting down trees and noted:

> The regular heavy strokes of their gleaming axes re-echoed in the deep forests; at the same time, the sooty sons of Africa, forgetting their bondage, in chorus sang the virtues and beneficence of their master in songs of their own composition.[21]

What exactly did Bartram witness? Did he really believe that the "sooty sons of Africa" forgot they were slaves? Were they truly happy to be working for a "beneficent" master, or might they know that they were chopping down trees for a tyrant? Was the singing genuinely joyful or was it escapism? For Bartram, these slaves were contented. Bartram's intuition tended to the model of the "kindly master" and some harmony between the slave and the owner. Other observers were more realistic. For example, a German Lutheran minister in Georgia in the 1750s, Johann Martin Bolzius, responded to a set of questions including one asking if slaves were as "false, malicious, and terrible as they are described." Bolzius had recently seen slavery introduced to Georgia, and his comprehensive report catches some of the psychology of master-slave relations while hinting at slave behaviour and character as being less inherent than conditioned by the power relationship:

> A faithful and sincere Negro [by which he meant slave] is a very rare thing, but they do exist, particularly with masters who know how to treat them reasonably and in a Christian way. Foolish masters sometimes *make* disloyal and malicious Negroes. Nearly all like to lie and steal, and if they gain the upper hand in a rebellion they give no mercy, but treat the whites very cruelly. Eternal slavery to them as to all people is an unbearable yoke, and very harsh treatment as regards food and work exacerbates them greatly. New [slaves] therefore must be treated very carefully, for they frequently take their own lives out of desperation, with the hope of resurrection in their homeland, and of rejoining their people. [Emphasis added.]

Bolzius's theme throughout is that slavery was an artificial relationship marked by distrust, hostility, force, and revenge. If he saw that rebellious slaves gave no mercy and treated whites "very cruelly," he also noted that the "agitators of rebellion are punished in a ... nearly (sic) inhuman way (which is generally not the way of the English), for example, slowly roasted at the fire."[22]

Slaves certainly understood the relationship from experience or anecdotal gossip. They witnessed routine punishments and broken families. They were certainly made aware of laws such as the 1712 South Carolina code that determined that if a slave threatened or struck a "Christian or white person," he could be whipped, branded for a second offence, and put to death for a third assault. If a white person was injured or maimed by a slave, the slave was to be killed immediately with impunity. Captured escapees were also subject to incremental punishments for repeated offences: whipping, then branding, then ears cut off for a third offence, and castration for a fourth. If the slave were to die as a result of the castration, the slaveholder was to be compensated for the loss by the colonial government. If owners did not punish the miscreants, they could be fined. For a fifth escape, the slave was to be sentenced by two justices and have "the cord of one of [his] legs to be cut off above the heel" or sentenced to death.[23] The rules were not always adhered to, but they had legal force, and even if they were not followed to the letter, slaves were aware of them. On the other hand, there were also laws that restrained masters from arbitrary or unprovoked violence against slaves, but slaves were prevented from petitioning the courts. Female runaways were rare.

From the planters' perspective, discipline and order were the paramount means to profit and ultimately the objectives of the estate. William Byrd II (1674–1744) of Virginia was among the most prolific diarists and correspondents of his generation. He was a powerful man in an elite society of powerful men. Like others of his class, he inherited an estate with slaves and a status that had been forged generations earlier by the so-called first gentlemen of Virginia. He was educated in England, read Greek and Hebrew daily for his intellectual nourishment, and "danced" for exercise. He ate a wholesome diet and took his social, political, Christian, and marital responsibilities very seriously. He took pains to properly manage his "people," which included his white servants, who were more "hirelings" than long-term indentures, and his slaves. He demanded in return more than token faithfulness. The absolute candour even in his incidental jottings shows that he could be irascible and peevish, as well as affable, generous, and conscientious. He was supremely paternalistic and did not tolerate "stubborn" or morally loose slaves whom he felt betrayed his trust. Minor infractions provoked him to anger, and he often browbeat slaves publicly. Yet he saw all of that as duty, not only to his interests of course but also to the benefit of an ordered society at home and in the broader world of Virginia. In a telling admission, he, like others later in the century, came to see that the slave trade was an abomination, and he shuddered at the thought of Virginia becoming "not unlike Jamaica." He had no wish to end slavery and assumed its permanence and his responsibility for it. But he believed that it could best be controlled with home-raised slaves as a minority in the overall population. He disdained the work habits of white servants and the attitudes of poor non-slaveholding whites who saw menial labour as being fit only for slaves. As he saw it, that attitude bred a dangerous sloth in the white lower classes, and while those poor whites deferred to local plantation grandees, they also saw their own colour as raising them above the slave. Byrd did not doubt that slavery made possible the glamour and prestige of his position, his finery, and his cultural ostentation. Yet he believed in his role as providing a positive good for his slaves. Historian Eugene Genovese's memorable phrase "the world the slaves made" from *Roll, Jordan, Roll* referred primarily to the way accommodation shaped power relations in the closed system. However, slaves also affected the moral outlines and behaviour of whites in every slave society.[24]

Planters such as Byrd, indeed all whites in all slave societies, lived in a state of apprehension, fearing a breakdown of the system and, in the worst of all scenarios, slave uprising. Yet some of the most violent slave or free black disturbances in North America during the colonial period occurred not in the plantation South but in New York City. In 1712, when an angry organized protest seemed to authorities to threaten riot, 21 blacks were murdered by white vigilantes. In 1741, an outbreak of arsons and rumours of a plot by free blacks and white labourers to take over the government resulted in an official response that was applied with little justice and a great deal of conspicuous violence. Eighteen blacks and four whites were hanged, and thirteen blacks were burned alive. Anticipation of unrest made for paranoia and obliged whites to use informers. There was a policy of vicious, preemptive action to rumours of trouble. The Charleston "plot" of 1740 led to the hanging of 50 blacks suspected of planning a large-scale insurrection. This was in the wake of the Stono Rebellion of 1739, the most frightening collective action by slaves in the colonial period. Several dozen escaped slaves were intercepted by militia, and 30 whites and 44 blacks were killed in the ensuing fights. South Carolina's already stringent slave codes were tightened immediately.

Virginia families such as the Byrds and Carters were rich, of course, but the South Carolina and Georgia "low country" (coastal) elites were on average even richer. In Virginia, some 30 per cent of slaveholders owned 20 or more slaves; in South Carolina, nearly 75 per cent did, and over 50 per cent of that class owned 50 or more slaves. The political leadership that fired the revolutionary movement came from the Chesapeake's intellectuals and political activists, who blended self-interested Lockean "natural right to property" and the inherited commitment to public affairs and political office. South Carolina's elites produced the revolutionary Pinckneys, Rutledges, and Laurens, but Virginia produced Thomas Jefferson, who crafted the penultimate draft of the Declaration of Independence. James Madison (1751–1836), a principal shaper of the US Constitution, was another notable Virginian and a member of a decisive political cadre that included George Washington, Richard Henry Lee, Patrick Henry, James Monroe, George Mason, and Edmund Randolph, among a galaxy of "founders." What made its way into national politics began locally and prepared a political class in the intricacies of village and farm life and vestry politics. In New England, by the same token, local politics inspired John Adams, a farmer and lawyer in Massachusetts whose wealth was insignificant compared to the great slaveholders. Radicals such as Samuel Adams and Paul Revere came from a highly politicized New England society that had no slave base. Revolutionary leadership in Pennsylvania included Benjamin Franklin and John Dickinson. Still, four of the first five presidents of the United States were Virginia slaveholders.[25]

By the time of the Revolution, South Carolina had begun to show signs of its future as an economic powerhouse in the South. Its centre of gravity was Charleston, which was something of an aberration in a sea of plantations and rural hamlets. Its 10,000 residents made it the only urban centre south of Philadelphia. It was South Carolina's cultural, political, judicial, and financial centre. It retained a social connection with Barbados and hummed with its own commerce. It was the gateway into the South for thousands of slaves each year and served the South somewhat in the way Rio de Janeiro served southern Brazil, without the latter's large free black and mixed coloured population. It was home to theatre, visiting lecturers, conspicuous wealth, and regular slave auctions. There was little civic infrastructure and no courthouses beyond Charleston and the coastal plantation zone. Charleston's planters built fine homes and imported fine clothes, expensive furniture, and wines to create a pocket of refined urbanity. As the lower South's hub of politics and wealth, it exercised a form of regional imperialism. It was not Recife or Kingston, Jamaica, even if it shared some of the opulence at one end and visceral human degradation at the other, but it was not Virginia either, and it certainly was not Pennsylvania or New England. It was the administrative and economic engine of a bona fide slave society in what would be the powerful "lower South" in the nineteenth century. In South Carolina, as in the

Chesapeake, slavery helped shape a distinctive ruling class of white planters, and the slave system they maintained worked to elevate not only their status but their presumptions of rights, authority, and privilege.

Of the 3 million slaves in all the Americas at the end of the eighteenth century, fewer than 800,000 (about 25 per cent of the hemisphere's total) were in North America in the new United States. By 1860, however, there were 6 million slaves in the Americas, and nearly 4 million of them were in the United States (about 65 per cent). The reasons for that remarkable trend are many and include the abolition of slavery in the French, Dutch, and British Caribbean; the continued rise in Brazil's free coloured population despite increases in slave imports; and the end of slavery in the newly independent states of mainland Spanish America while Cuba and Puerto Rico remained in the Empire. More to the point, during the three generations between the American Revolution and the Civil War, the territorial range of slavery created the cotton kingdom that stretched west to the Mississippi River and Texas and a slave population that doubled every 20 or so years almost entirely from domestic births. By then, the state of Mississippi had joined South Carolina with a black majority. The nation that came into being with the American Revolution would consist of two historically developed sections, separated socially, culturally, and economically.

Notes

1   Jordan, *White Over Black*, 72.

2   For Anthony Johnson, see Lindsay, *Captives as Commodities*, 41–43; Thomas C. Holt and Elsa Barkley Brown, *Major Problems in African American History*, Volume I (Boston: Houghton-Mifflin, 2000), 85. See also A. Leon Higginbotham Jr., "The Ancestry of Inferiority, 1619–1662," in Edward Countryman, ed., *How Did American Slavery Begin* (Boston: Bedford/St. Martin's, 1999), 87–98; and Vaughan, "The Origins Debate."

3   Cited in Nancy Cott, ed., *Root of Bitterness: Documents of the Social History of American Women* (Boston: Northeastern University Press, 1996), 29–30.

4   Robert Beverley, "The History and Present State of Virginia" in Greene, *Settlement to Society*, 284–86.

5   Lyle N. McAlister, *Spain and Portugal in the New World, 1492–1700* (Minneapolis: University of Minnesota Press, 1984), 344.

6   Edmund Morgan, *American Slavery, American Freedom: The Ordeal of Colonial Virginia* (New York: Norton, 2003 [1975]) is a comprehensive and sophisticated history of colonial Virginia. See also James Horn, *Adapting to a New World: English Society in the Seventeenth Century Chesapeake* (Chapel Hill: University of North Carolina Press, 1994), 141ff.

7   Alan Gallay, *Colonial America and the American Revolution: Text and Documents* (Upper Saddle River: Prentice Hall, 2011), 148ff. See also Gallay, *Indian Slavery in Colonial America*.

8   Stephen Webb, *1676: The End of American Independence*, repr. (Syracuse: Syracuse University Press, 1995).

9 Morgan, *American Slavery, American Freedom*, 90.

10 See the brief overview in Nellis, *An Empire of Regions*, 247–56.

11 Book of Genesis, Chapter 9, verses 21–25; see also the repeated references to bondage and servitude in the Book of Leviticus, Chapter 25. David Brion Davis, *Inhuman Bondage: The Rise and Fall of Slavery in the New World* (New York: Oxford University Press, 2006), Chapter 3.

12 Two notable books on the subject of slave agency are Eugene Genovese, *Roll, Jordan, Roll* and John W. Blassingame, *The Slave Community*. Ira Berlin, *Many Thousands Gone: The First Two Centuries of Slavery in North America* (Cambridge, MA: Belknap, 1998) identifies the way slave culture was influenced by regional differences, for example, New York to South Carolina.

13 Genovese, *Roll, Jordan, Roll*, 203–79.

14 See Schwartz, *Sugar Plantations*, 464, on slaveholding comparisons; Berlin, *Many Thousands Gone*, for regional differences in North America.

15 Alan Watson, *Slave Law in the Americas* (Athens: University of Georgia Press, 1989), Chapter 4.

16 Robert W. Fogel, *The Slavery Debates, 1952–1990* (Baton Rouge: Louisiana State University, 2003), 24–48.

17 Blassingame, *Slave Community*, "Critical Essay on Sources."

18 Rawick, *The American Slave*. See note number 33 in Chapter Three above. For a cautionary note on the ex-slave oral testimonies, see James West Davidson and Mark Hamilton Lytle, "The View from the Bottom Rail," in their book *After the Fact: The Art of Historical Detection*, 5th ed. (Boston: McGraw Hill, 2004), 177–209.

19 See Costanzo, *The Interesting Narrative of the Life of Olaudah Equiano*, Introduction and Appendix A.

20 William L. Andrews and William S. McFeely, eds., *Narrative of the Life of Frederick Douglass, An American Slave, Written by Himself* (New York: Norton, 1997). See the useful selection in Henry Louis Gates Jr., *The Classic Slave Narratives* (New York: Penguin [Signet], 2002).

21 William Bartram, *Travels of William Bartram* (New York: Dover, 1928), 257.

22 From *William and Mary Quarterly*, 3d Series, 14 (1957) cited in Karen Ordahl Kupperman, ed., *Major Problems in American Colonial History*, 2nd ed. (Boston: Houghton-Mifflin, 2000), 298–301.

23 Watson, *Slave Law in the Americas*, 69–70.

24 Byrd's diary and other writings are available in various editions. See the references in Kenneth Lockridge, *The Diary and Life of William Byrd II of Virginia 1674–1744* (Chapel Hill: University of North Carolina Press, 1987). On "the world the slaves made" see Genovese, *Roll, Jordan, Roll*, 75–86.

25 Joseph Ellis, *Founding Brothers: The Revolutionary Generation* (New York: Vintage, 2000), 81–119; Paul Finkelman, *Slavery and the Founders: Race and Liberty in the Age of Jefferson* (Armonk: M.E. Sharpe, 2001). William Freehling, "The Founding Fathers and Slavery," *American Historical Review* 77 (1972): 81–93 remains the clearest short analysis of the Founders' approaches to the contradictions in slavery and revolutionary "liberty."

6 The Slave as Person: Women, Children, Family, and Culture

"Whoever would like to buy a black woman with milk, who can also wash and cook should go to Rua dos Senhor dos Passos, No 35 ... "
    —*O Diario do Rio de Janeiro*, December 17, 1821[1]

Historians and Slave Culture

In the great sweep of time that bracketed slavery in the Americas, new plantations were started while others failed, changed hands, or just disappeared with changing times and prospects. Moreover, slaves were found in every economic environment in the Americas, from a few in some places to majorities in others. Masters died, and new ones appeared with inherited or acquired status. Slaves were born into slavery or came to it from Africa. They lived and died, some prematurely and others of old age, without leaving their birthplace; or they were sold, freed, or escaped. While it was difficult for slaves in many settings to achieve domestic stability, significant numbers did form and sustain families and find cultural meaning and emotional comfort in them. For all peoples, as a nuclear unit or kinship cluster, the family is most often a person's first point of social reference. The slave family, where it was allowed or encouraged, was a curious blend of fragility and strength, often subject to interference and dissolution as slaves were sold or separated, sometimes for punishment. The slave family was always under scrutiny, and for new slaves African polygamy had to give way to European monogamy. Male to female slave ratios were often unbalanced, and slaveholders differed in their views on the value of the slave family to their own interests. As for the family's independent authority, in slavery's mature phase in the first half of the nineteenth century in the United States, for example, it was not unusual for a slaveholder to consider his slaves, both married and single, especially those born into his ownership, as part of his extended "family" with no concern for the defective morality of that view.[2]

Despite the impediments, the slave family was a refuge and a major force in the formation and survival of Afro-Brazilian, African American, and Caribbean culture. Over time, when taken together with the shared identity that came from status and colour, slaves in families, in slave quarters, on urban street corners, or other meeting places created a set of cultural norms that were not entirely defined by white standards or the persistent oversight of masters and overseers. Music, dialect, and religious practices were forged and sustained, in part, in family settings. Monogamous slave families were often encouraged for reasons that ran from an owner's strategic approach to peace, stability, and co-operation to deliberate policies of procreation. Quite often, masters simply sought to temper sexual looseness or just as piously respect a slave marriage as a moral imperative. In any event, the slave family was a sanctuary of self-regard, normal intimacies, and opportunities for personal and social dignity and responsibility. What follows in this chapter is a broad discussion of family, gender issues, and the cultural outcomes of the social world of the slave. We need to keep in mind the absence of the composite slave and that there was no typical family or setting for the family. There was always the force of change over time and the demands of the system. Nevertheless, in hundreds of recent case studies, the slave family has been brought to life from sometimes scattered records, perhaps from a single Brazilian *engenho* or a Virginia tobacco, Cuban coffee, or Jamaican sugar plantation.[3]

As mid-twentieth-century scholars, especially historians, social scientists, and activists, began to look at the role of the slave family in the formation of slave culture, questions were raised about the effects of slavery on individual slaves and their personalities and psychological development. What kind of legacy might slavery have passed on to post-emancipation coloured peoples? In the United States, for example, in order to explain the lowly status of African Americans in contemporary societies, some scholars traced the problem to the damages inflicted on them by slavery. The so-called damage thesis drew on white accounts of slave behaviour. It suggested that slaves in North America were conditioned to an abject dependency that led to failed and flawed personalities. As noted earlier, slaves were seen as "types": the docile and even obsequious "Sambo" or the clever and manipulative "Jack" or the dangerous "Nat," as historian Stanley Elkins in *Slavery: A Problem in American Institutional and Intellectual*

Life famously characterized slave personality types. The most commonly perceived slave personality, in most accounts, was Sambo, a cartoon image in popular white depictions of coloured Americans well into the twentieth century. According to Elkins's social science models, Sambo was damaged by slavery into a form of neotony, a childishness that was internalized and passed on in the wake of emancipation.

The simplistic reductionism of that picture has been aggressively challenged and rejected by three generations of historians, most of whom stand the damage theory on its head. Oppression does bring out defensive and coping strategies in the victim and also distorts the view of the oppressor. In that way, racism not only survived emancipation but also settled into modified stereotypes to explain the manners, condition, and roles of freed African Americans. Long after emancipation in the United States, evidence shows that African Americans were subject to a persistent exclusionism and oppression. Claims of prolonged damage were countered by historians who demonstrated that slavery had, in fact, produced a resilient culture that resisted bondage with religion, music, storytelling, and an optimistic hope for redemption. Thus, the plight of the emancipated slave was not because of an inherent inferiority distilled and passed on as "damage" but because of official, legal, and popular race-based exclusion and segregation after slavery had ended.[4]

A serious revision began in 1944 when the Nobel Prize winning Swedish economist Gunnar Myrdal published an exhaustively researched study of race relations 80 years after abolition. In *An American Dilemma: The Negro Problem and Democracy*, Myrdal claimed that "*White prejudice and discrimination* keep the Negro low in standards of living, health, manners and morals. This in turn [reinforces] white prejudice" [emphasis added]. At the same time, historian Herbert Aptheker published his landmark *American Negro Slave Revolts* (1943) and demonstrated from hard evidence the degree to which North American slaves had resisted their condition. The revolts against the system, examples of which are included in this book, were mostly instigated by the slaves themselves, rather than inspired by free coloured agitators. His contribution to subsequent studies of slave defiance, resistance, and self-awareness is inestimable. His promotion of an assertive and resilient slave culture was picked up by generations of African American historians such as John Hope Franklin (1915–2009) and John Blassingame (1940–2000), along with two generations of white scholars who viewed slave and freed black culture from a different angle. They and many others provided alternative ways of looking at slave culture, women, and families. Today's scholars now take very seriously the work of earlier, previously ignored, black historians such as W.E.B. Du Bois (1868–1963) and Carter Woodson (1875–1950). Du Bois and Woodson and other African American scholars were also social and political activists. So much evidence of resistance, however it was manifest, blunted the damage thesis and left scholars to study the effects of the repression of African Americans after emancipation. In the end, one might rather accept the nineteenth-century abolitionists' view, which inverted the damage thesis to argue that slavery had in fact damaged the moral bearings of slaveholders and of whites in general.[5]

Slaves and their progeny in each slave society experienced distinct conditions and outcomes. Black scholars in the Caribbean looked at slavery with the kinds of subjective reality that had informed Du Bois and Woodson. For example, Haiti's troubled post-independence history, as we shall see, started with the way its revolution led to autocracy but was exacerbated by the economic ostracism by Europe and the United States. C.L.R. James (1901–89), a declared Leninist whose 1938 study of Toussaint L'Ouverture and the Haitian Revolution is still in print, offered a unique perspective on slave assertiveness. Eric Williams (1911–81) shaped the debate on the role of economics in British abolitionism and was a long-time prime minister of independent Trinidad and Tobago. In contrast to legal racial segregation in the United States, no such laws were enacted in post-abolition Brazil. Gilberto Freyre had argued that miscegenation was a positive measure of Brazilian slavery's legacy. But where he saw a blending of races, earlier critics of Brazil's miscegenation and manumission rates saw slavery as creating what Louis Agassiz's wife, in 1868, is alleged to have called a "mongrel, nondescript type." In any case, nothing as reductionist as Elkins's damage theory emerged in Caribbean or Brazilian historiography to explain slavery's effects or race relations.[6]

As slave personality came under the microscope, so too did the slave family and the experiences of slave women. While tacitly acknowledging the obvious—that slavery for women was not what it was for men—serious attention to the female slave had been negligible before the 1970s. Family and gender studies opened up a refreshing, if often troubling avenue to provide a better picture of day-to-day relationships in the world of the slave. For example, scholars found that in Brazil large mixed and free coloured populations in the proximity of *engenho* slave populations influenced marriage patterns and the formation of kinship groups. In the North American slave societies, that external free coloured population was missing, and the more confined slave family became a major lynchpin in the development of African American culture. But any comparison prompts the question of variables, including the important one of sex ratios and the reproduction rates of slaves in North America against the lower rates in Brazil and the Caribbean. No survey of family and womanhood can reduce the complexity of time, place, and circumstance to a universal pattern. However, some qualified outlines can be drawn from a review of what we do know about slave women, families, and children in the Americas.

Slave Women, Children, and Families in Brazil

In Brazil, women suffered all of slavery's common tribulations: fatigue, erratic diets, threats of physical punishment, and the emotional burden of captivity. Most female slaves were brought to Brazil as healthy specimens to be consigned to the fields. Slave women had the nominal protection from sexual exploitation afforded by the law, the Church, and the master's ostensible paternalism. None of that fully prevented coerced sex with masters and white overseers or afforded protection against unwanted attention from particular male slaves. In any event, where marriage was encouraged, the female slave was the axis around which the family revolved.[7]

In the *engenhos*, especially the larger ones, women were likely confined to fieldwork and driven for 12 to 16 hours a day, often malnourished and poorly clothed. Female domestic servants may have been spared the hoe, but sewing, cooking, tending vegetable patches, hauling water, and raising children went on from daybreak to dark. All women in rural Brazil coped with the inevitable burdens of pregnancy in often squalid conditions. The absence of any routine medical care and deficient hygiene standards increased the risk of puerperal infections and postpartum illnesses that made most pregnancies unpleasant and dangerous. Such were the perils of pregnancy for all women in rural colonial Brazil. We may be sure that secure white mothers led healthier lives as the wives of wealthy planters or in the urban households of merchants, politicians, bureaucrats, and others of the white upper classes. Even there, however, pregnancies could end in disaster for mother or baby or both. All women, including whites and mixed free coloured women, were at risk. It was simply worse for slave women. If mother and baby did survive, then the strain of work and the threat of the sale of the child made motherhood a constant test of emotional and physical resilience.

Brazilian slaves produced far fewer pregnancies than slave women in North America. They had longer lactation periods, and the presence of large numbers of African-born slaves and the African custom of avoiding sexual intercourse during lactation meant that they simply produced fewer babies than North American slave women. Average intervals between pregnancies were twice as long in Brazil as in the United States. Limited birth rates were compounded by a lower marriage frequency in the Brazilian slave population, and that translated into a phenomenon that we might call the Brazilian slave trade cycle. The cycle can be understood in the following way: the peasant class of free coloured peoples increased as more slaves were freed, which meant that they would have to be replaced by new African arrivals. The combination of manumissions, low slave birth rates, and normal mortality rates failed to provide a rate of natural increase to satisfy demand. The cycle was pushed to the point where the free coloured population of Brazil outnumbered the slave population by three to one by the 1860s even as African slaves poured into Brazil.[8]

The illegitimate rate was about one-third of total slave births, roughly the same as the rate for free blacks, mixed coloured, and whites. Children born to slave mothers became the property of the mother's master, regardless of the father's identity or status. Manumissions, sales, and runaways meant that serial marriages or cohabitations were not uncommon. There were trial slave "marriages" that produced one or even two children before being recognized formally.[9] In her discussion of "slave unions" and the "sexual lives of slaves" in Brazil, historian Katia Mattoso claims that "African polygamy" gave way to "a succession of brief encounters" as the prevalent model for slave relations. In a sweeping summary, she writes that "Brazilian slaves had so few children because slaves were not always free to choose permanent mates." She continues:

> Many [female slaves] sought abortion rather than bear a child into slavery, and men practiced coitus interruptus. Sexuality for slaves was a response to physical needs, not a means of procreation. On the plantations the men's dormitories were separate from the women's, and even legally married couples had to resort to furtive encounters. The masters' policy was to make sexual liaisons difficult but not impossible.[10]

This is a tantalizing summation. It is far too reductionist to be applied everywhere because not all masters and not all plantations in all regions of Brazil at all times fit this thesis. We can never know if a majority of men practiced coitus interruptus, but we can be certain that affection, physical need, promiscuity, or attraction could lead to sexual relations for the vast majority of unmarried men and women, free or slave, white or coloured.

There was nothing unique in the urges of unmarried Brazilian slaves, most of whom were in their prime. However, in all Christian societies, sexual intercourse for all unmarried couples was frowned upon, even illegal, regardless of class, and did lead to "furtive encounters." Mattoso's blanket review has merit in defining what clearly went on in much of the plantation culture and, we can be sure, in most other environments. There is evidence that planters and merchants preferred to buy African or Creole slaves rather than pay to raise a child to adulthood. Her comments warrant comparison with the unwritten policy in North America of encouraging or at least supporting slave procreation.

As for children born into slavery, an often unhappy fate awaited them. A carefree and usually integrated childhood ended abruptly with a work assignment that took the eight- or ten-year-old child to the cane or cotton fields. Parents, or often a mother alone, might educate the child to its fate, but it remains a peculiar feature of slavery throughout the Americas that a black girl might play easily with a white master's children for years only to be taken away and introduced to a very harsh new experience. The other side of that coin was the child care for white children provided by female slaves or the constant demand on lactating slave women to nurse white owners' babies.

An especially striking feature of slave marriage in Brazil was the practice in impoverished neighbourhoods of free coloured (*pardos*) or manumitted blacks (*pretos forros*) marrying slaves to secure food and clothing.[11] These relationships forged a linkage between slaves and the ever expanding free coloured community in the eighteenth and nineteenth centuries into a growing rural underclass that historian Stuart Schwartz in *Slaves, Peasants and Rebels* describes as a coloured "peasantry." The practice of reaching out to slaves at times for support is evidence of need among ostensibly "free" coloured peoples. The slave population was generally ill-fed, ill-clothed, and poorly housed. Basic fodder, ramshackle dwellings, and rags are terms commonly cited in descriptions of Brazil's rural slave population, and the cases of free peoples seeking help from the slave population shows that, at least at some times and in some places, being coloured and free was no guarantee of security.[12] The free coloured population was not an amorphous mass. Lighter skinned people were more likely to link with each other. Marriage and the intersection of free and enslaved people and the ever more nuanced divisions of colour made Brazil racially complex in ways that were unique. The African slave population remained the darkest patch in the racial quilt.[13]

Brazil's laws allowed masters to leave substantial estates to their slaves. While that practice was not unique to Brazil, it was generally far more difficult to do elsewhere. Moreover, the Catholic Church required that all slaves be baptized in a Brazilian version of "godparentage." Given the importance of the protocol, the status of the godparents (*compadre* and *comadre*) could influence the slaves' future prospects. For newly arrived Africans, the godparent(s) could be chosen from any source for convenience. In most cases, members of the free coloured community were solicited by the slave or chosen by the master. A slave with a master who was also a godparent acquired some lustre and perhaps a secure future. Sincere and respectable mixed coloured godparents were also sought, and all godparents were obliged to tend to the spiritual needs of the child and later could be enlisted to represent the grown slave in legal matters. On the other hand, godparents expected respect, deference, and favours from their charges.[14]

Kinship groups flourished. Regional vernacular language took shape where various residual African dialects fused with Portuguese and Portuguese-Brazilian colloquialisms that even included residual native Brazilian words and phrases. Nominally Catholic practices gave way often to syncretic blends of Christianity and African spiritualism, superstition, and myths. Priests often competed with local shamans who were often important underground mystic prophets and medical fixers. Music, dancing, and storytelling took on local flavours, again influenced by the steady arrival of new slaves. As late as the 1840s, tens of thousands of Africans arrived in Brazil each year, adding linguistic variety, customs, and spirituality to the habits and language patterns of older acculturated slaves, mixed coloured Afro-Brazilians, and the white population. The characteristics of modern Brazilian society were being shaped in the constant mixing of European, African, and residual native peoples, their manners, and cultural assets. At the same time, a clear racially defined social and political ladder was formed under a white ruling class.[15]

Of the 4.8 million African slaves who were landed in Brazil, some 1.5 million of them were female. They were identified as being from Benguela or Mina or Angola, for example, and a great many arrived as frightened, emaciated teenagers. They may have been whipped or raped en route. They were destined for the cane fields or the laundry or kitchen. Some ended up as important members of a slaveholder household, but most were pawns at the mercy of owners and were bought, sold, and resold. Because of Brazil's manumission rates, many ended up being liberated into poverty. They appeared in every niche in the Brazilian economy and all of Brazil's neighbourhoods. To try to reduce it all to the "slave woman" would be folly, but as mothers one finds a common thread. The "oil of media-tion" that Gilberto Freyre claimed to be Africa's decisive contribution to the miscegenation that underlay Brazil's national character was perhaps the slave woman's greatest legacy. But the slave woman was too often the target of contempt, and the "oil of mediation" did not sit well with racially biased views. A Brazilian Jesuit's eighteenth-century warning to white masters to restrain themselves, referring to African slaves as "brutish" people, com-bined a demand for moral responsibility with a lurid view of slave women: "How many masters are there who are married to [white] women gifted with honor and beauty who leave them, perhaps for some enormous, wicked, and vile slave woman?" One of the solutions to the temptations of the lascivious African female offered by this Jesuit was for masters to encourage slave marriages to curb the natural licentiousness of Afro-Brazilians and to have fewer "wicked and vile" slave women running loose.[16]

Slave Women, Children, and Families in the Caribbean

A great deal of what faced female slaves in Brazil also faced slave women in the Caribbean: sexual exploitation and the combined burdens of work and child rearing. The female slave was the backbone of the plantation economy, providing close to half the fieldworkers on most estates, yet their status was lower than that of the males whose resale value was usually higher. Although there were some important seaports with the trappings of minor urban culture, the islands were dominated by plantations and farms, and the image of the female as a domestic is largely a distortion. Examples from the late seventeenth century to the late eighteenth century in the British Caribbean show that up to 75 per cent of women were field hands compared to about 60 per cent for males. Any suggestion that the majority of female slaves were settled in nuclear, monogamous households caring for their children needs to be tempered. Female slaves in all the islands were restrained by planter strategy and physical limitation from having anything near the successful pregnancies one found in white European communi-ties or in the slave families of North America. Before the sustained attack on the slave trade, there was a disproportionate ratio of African to Creole slaves in Brazil and the French and British West Indies. African women in the Caribbean attempted to avoid sexual intercourse while lactating with taboos similar to those found in Brazil. The practice was an effective brake on pregnancies despite a nearby community of sexually deprived males. Reproduction rates were reduced further by the obvious physical limitations placed on female slaves by heavy work, poor diets that at times bordered on malnourishment, and the inevitable irregularities in menstruation, including some evidence of premature menopause. It is estimated that about half of female slaves in the Caribbean never had children.[17]

Where monogamous slave relationships occurred in the French and British Caribbean, they did not guarantee permanent, secure nuclear families. If planters sanctioned connubial relations among slaves, they did so usually for the sake of keeping the peace rather than for any humane concern. Still, some unions survived, and when metropolitan governments responded to growing abolitionist agitation, there was an upsurge in the number of nuclear family arrangements as owners made concessions under pressure from late eighteenth-century imperial reforms.[18] Even under the reforms, in the latter phase of British Caribbean slavery, we need to be cautious about assuming too much security and privacy in slave marriages. Mary Prince (ca. 1788–1833), whose important autobiography contributed directly to the British abolitionist movement in the 1820s, has left us with a lively female perspective on the tenuous nature and often demeaning conditions of slave marriage. As a domestic slave in Antigua, she met a free black man at a Moravian church mission. She notes that:

> We were joined in marriage about Christmas 1826 by the Rev. Mr Olufsen. We could not be married in the English Church…. English [Church] marriage is not allowed for slaves; and no free man can marry a slave woman. When Mr Wood [her master] heard of my marriage he flew into a great rage,… Mrs Wood was [even] more vexed … but stirred Mr Wood to flog me dreadfully with his horsewhip. She said that she would not have nigger men about the … premises, or allow a niggerman's clothes in the same tub where hers were washed. I had not much happiness in my marriage owing to my being a slave.

She and her husband were kept apart a great deal of the time, and the husband, a free man, had to endure the knowledge and often the sight of his wife being beaten or orally abused.[19]

Slave children came into life as slaves, and loving mothers wrestled with the frustrations that went with prospects of permanent separation. The tendency was for masters or overseers on larger estates to segregate the children as the mother worked and then sell or assign the child at a certain age. Slave mothers coped with a painful dichotomy that did not weaken the spirit of motherhood. For children chores began at an early age with simple things like picking up loose leaves in the fields or fetching water for workers. That same expectation might also have applied to family farm white children in New England or Pennsylvania, but in those places the work was meant to instill the virtues of collaborative and family-related needs and self-sufficiency. For slave children, on the other hand, work was conditioning for a future of obligatory enforced labour. In a French Caribbean example, slave women were used directly in the indoctrination of the children of other slave mothers to a future of slavery. The Marquis Poyen de Sainte Marie employed women on his Guadalupe estate as "drivers" to supervise children's "duties":

> The primary task of the female driver of the child gang must be the preservation of the children's health. She must monitor them constantly … teach them how to perform all their duties well … and conform … to obey orders without question…. As nothing accounts more for laziness among blacks than [chigger, a biting mite] infection … she must inspect, clear and remove [chiggers] from their feet daily. At a young age, children are very receptive. Thus much depends on authority figures who mold them into either good or bad subjects. Those [slave female drivers] who execute their task well merit much from their masters … those who neglect their tasks and shatter the planters' confidence are guilty.[20]

Sugar, coffee, and tobacco economies and the societies they spawned resembled each other from island to island, but each system's legal principles affected the way each society evolved. As noted, the French *Code Noir*, the Spanish *Siete Pardidos*, and the British charter systems each shaped their respective societies. Both the French and Spanish codes mandated Christian identity for slaves. The more liberal *Siete Pardidos* went beyond the *Code Noir* by allowing regular manumissions and more liberal terms for slave marriage and godparentage. In fact, the Spanish, like the Portuguese, had a set of colour gradations, at least 25 of them for the free coloured population, unlike the usually generic "negro" or "coloured" used in the British and French islands. Slave marriages and family networks in the French and British systems were shaped by the serious imbalances of male to female ratios of the seventeenth and early eighteenth centuries. These conditions were being corrected by the time of British abolition in the 1830s when small female slave majorities appeared on most islands.[21] Notwithstanding the impediments they faced, something akin to normal family relations were possible for slaves on the larger British and French holdings. The trend over the eighteenth century had been to better housing and perquisites such as access to small plots of land for family use. We need to understand the planter's compensatory designs here—a bit of self-sufficiency was likely good for slave morale as well as the planter's account ledgers.[22]

Despite the limits to natural increase, by the start of the nineteenth century the British and French islands had developed huge slave majorities. Jamaica, for example, with a population of 340,000, was 88 per cent slave in 1800; tiny Anguilla's 1819 population of 3,080 was 77 per cent slave. Similar ranges existed in the French islands, from the Caribbean's most heavily populated colony, Saint Domingue, with 520,000 people (87 per cent slave) to the island of Saintes and its population of 1,139 in the 1830s. Saint Domingue was the western part of the island of Hispaniola, and across the mountains from it was the Spanish colony of Santo Domingo with 125,000 people and, in contrast to the British and French ratios, only 15,000 slaves. In Jamaica, the white population constituted a mere 4.4 per cent and the free coloured population only 7.4 per cent of the whole. Similar ratios prevailed in the French islands. Not until the great early nineteenth-century boom would the Spanish islands, especially Cuba, trend heavily to slave-based plantation cash crops. By the 'late eighteenth century, there were substantial numbers of whites and mixed free coloured in the Spanish islands, a fact that persisted in Cuba far into the nineteenth century. For example, as several hundred thousand slaves were brought in, the white and free mixed coloured populations also rose.[23]

Slave Women, Children, and Families in British North America and the Antebellum United States

It bears repeating that fewer than 6 per cent of all coloured peoples in the United States at the time of the American Revolution were free. As the use of "coloured" took hold in the nineteenth century, it embraced a cluster of terms like "negro" or "mulatto" or "quadroon" and, in informal usage, "darky," all usually denoting "slave." In *The Souls of Black Folk* (1903) W.E.B. Du Bois described coloured persons as "brown and dull" or "brown and yellow" or as having a "smooth black face" or a "golden face" and, tellingly, as a "midnight beauty."[24] Still, to most white observers, they were all "negroes."

Even as large numbers of slaves were being imported into British North America after 1750, by the time of the American Revolution a slight majority of slaves had by then been born into the institution. High rates of natural increase meant that two or three generations of slaves could be found on some large estates owned by three generations of the same family. It was common in North America for the planter to be resident or to have members of his family in charge. Over time and certainly by the early decades of the nineteenth century, many planters assumed paternalistic roles for themselves.[25] In those circumstances, slaves were obliged to find their identities in two families. The slave's attachment to a spouse and offspring was balanced awkwardly with the expectation of a white master of loyalty and obedience to his version of "family." For children, that might have seemed feasible, according to testimony such as the following, given in the late 1930s by an aged former slave who remembered that:

> Old Massa, he used to come to de plantation drivin' his rockaway en my Lord a mercy, we chillum did love to run en meet him…. "Massa comin'! Massa comin'!" En he would come ridin' through de big gate and say, "Yonder my little niggers! How my little niggers? Come here and tell me how you all!"[26]

The kindly fatherly tone of the master in that account may be accurate and sincere or it might be exaggerated or distorted by a 70-year-old recollection, but what teases the reader is the plausible joy of children witnessing the spectacle of the master, a figure of authority, potency, and security—a paterfamilias. We can guess that perhaps as children, these innocents were being groomed for slavery without knowing exactly what awaited them. Children in all slave societies enjoyed some innocence and "freedom." The planter mentality, *vis à vis* a self-interest that was couched in tones of care and protection, can be seen in the rules laid down by the important southern slaveholder and proslavery theorist James Hammond. The following, intended for nursing slave mothers, the old, and the infirm, was written during the mature phase of antebellum slavery:

> Sucklers are not required to leave their houses until sun-rise, when they leave their children at the children's house [a form of day care] before going to the field. The period of suckling is 12 mos. Their work lies always within [a half mile] of the [slave] quarters. It is the duty of the nurse to see that none are heated when nursing…. They are allowed 45 minutes at each morning to be with their children. They return 3 times a day until their infants are 8 mos old…. On weaning, the child is removed entirely from its Mother for 2 weeks [placed] in charge of some careful woman without a child, during which time the Mother is not to nurse at all. The amount of work done by a suckler is about three-fifths of … a full hand. Old and Infirm … who from age and infirmities are unable to keep up with the prime hands are put in the Suckler's gang. Pregnant women, at 5 mos … no plowing or lifting must be required of them. [All of the above] receive the same allowances [food and clothing] as full-work hands.[27]

As for masters, they might be benign or cruel, efficient or careless, but the institution was secure, confirmed in law and practice; in the unshakable judgement of most whites, coloured peoples were fit for slavery and little else. The plantation was really a curious kind of biracial community. The interplay of slaves with white masters and overseers brought them together in a series of contacts marked by role and status in day-to-day interactions. We can be sure that many slaves adopted the roles in what masters defined as a "family" and demonstrated loyalty to it. But it was, in the end, a designed relationship based on power and subordination and hardly a natural one. Thus, any display of loyalty to it by slaves was not as deep as most planters believed. And it is stretching logic to assume that otherwise intelligent slaveholders would delude themselves into thinking that well-behaved adult slaves were displaying sincere gratitude for the protection of the presumptive paterfamilias. So, the system's historically etched race relations really represented a bizarre and false integration. A conscious and functional separation was enforced by status. What is of note, however, is that slavery's rules and black-white relationships were not a bit like the intense physical and violent segregation that came after slavery was ended.

Slowly over time, the slave family, as distinct from the presumptive planters' plantation "family," consolidated itself, as slavery took a deeper and broader hold in the South and as the slave population rose by 600 per cent between the American Revolution and the Civil War. By the first half of the nineteenth century, slavery had crossed the Appalachians and established itself in the great cotton belt that ran south of the Ohio River and all the way to the Mississippi River and the Gulf of Mexico. A steady, profitable domestic slave trade went with it, as did all the legal codes. The demand for slaves after the end of the slave trade to the United States in 1808 put pressure on slaveholders to increase their slave populations by natural increase.

The majority of slaveholders owned 20 or fewer slaves, yet a slight majority of slaves lived on plantations with more than 50 slaves. That statistical anomaly nevertheless tells us that slaves' lives were spent in relatively small slave communities. When the figures are analyzed further, they suggest that the southern planter elite were few. On the eve of the Civil War, only about 20 per cent (fewer than 400,000) of white southern families owned slaves, and 88 per cent of them owned fewer than 20. Only 10,000 of 400,000 slaveholding families were considered large slaveholders, and only 3,000 families counted their land in thousands of acres and hundreds of slaves. That minority represents the southern political and economic ruling class and two-thirds of the richest Americans on the eve of the Civil War. The book value of the South's 4 million slaves in 1860 represented the largest portion of the South's total assessed property value.[28]

By that time, monogamy had come to define most slave relationships. In some cases, slaves were pushed together by masters, in others by a natural or spontaneous encounter or work relationship. By the early nineteenth century, the majority of slave marriages were sanctioned by either black or white Protestant ministers. Marriage on large holdings was arranged usually between two slaves owned by the plantation owner. On smaller holdings, slaves were often linked to slaves from adjacent or nearby farms or estates. Slaves who did have choice had to cope with the normal social and personal issues of courtship and marriage while dealing with unpredictable owners. Testimony by ex-slaves in the 1930s about slave courtship and marriage, however clouded by memory, remind us of universal patterns of romance and decorum. For example, one former female slave recalled poignantly:

> I walk with Jim to de gate and stood under the honeysuckle dat was smelling so sweet. I heard de big ol' bullfrogs a' croakin' by de river and de whippoor-wills a' hollerin' in de woods. Dere was a big yellow moon ... [Jim] asked me to marry him and he squeezed my hand. He ain't kissed me yet but he asked my Mammy for me ... and dere in de moonlight he kisses me right before my Mammy who am a' cryin.' [This was oral testimony and the phonetics are recorded in the Federal Writers' Project interviews.][29]

Perhaps a more common theme in the slave narratives about marriage suggests that there were convenient and spontaneous nuptials. The evidence also emphasizes the fragile nature of slave unions. As one testimonial notes, slaves

> just takes one anoder—we asks de white folks' leave and den take one anoder. Some folks dey's married by de book; but den, what's de use? Dere's my fust husband we'se married by de book, and he sold off to Florida, and I's here. Dey do what dey please wid us, so we just make money for dem.

The legendary "tradition" of newly married slaves jumping "over the broomstick together" as a marriage contract was not as common as the preferred but segregated Christian sanctioned marriage.[30]

Premarital and extramarital sex occurred in ways that ostensibly troubled posturing masters who just as often accepted this "promiscuity" as evidence of the lower moral character of slaves. This is another extraordinary example of a hypocritical double standard, given the conspicuous evidence of extramarital sex between masters and slaves, usually coerced in one way or another. There are examples of women having several children of several fathers, some of whom were white.[31] Roughly one-third to one-half of slave marriages failed and made serial marriages inevitable but persistently monogamous. A tradition emerged that provided a semblance of comfort, warmth, and emotional security in an otherwise unpredictable and uncomfortable world where everyone in the family was property. The major risks to matrimonial permanence lay in simple economics and planter mobility. Plantations and farms failed and slaves were sold, not always as a nuclear unit but as separate commodities to satisfy specific buyer needs. Planters sometimes moved to greener pastures, perhaps from Virginia to Mississippi, or bequeathed slaves to offspring to open new estates. There is some evidence that male slaves preferred to marry outside their home plantation as they did in the West Indies, so as not to witness the potential abuses wives might suffer from the routine punishments that went with plantation life. The movement of slaves, the selling of young adults, and the apparent fragility of the family was simply a terrible fact of life, as was the assumed right of owners to intrude on the private lives of married slaves.

Slaves everywhere in the South adapted the English language to their distinctive perceptions, interactions, and coded meanings. Colloquialisms, accents, and patterns of storytelling, with parables and references to Africa, could be found everywhere in the slave societies. Unlike the syncretic blends of African and Christian spirituality found in Brazil and much of the Caribbean, slaves in the North American South found affinities with Baptist and Methodist practices. As with any Christian protocol, individual salvation merged with family and communal values. Slave hymns were often original and took on a particular tone of redemption and hope, and sacred music was less solemn and more uplifting in tempo than white interpretations. They were woven around rhythms and cadences found in what comes to us as "gospel" music. There was secular music to go with the sacred. New sounds and rhythms found their way into all the places in the Americas where slavery was dominant, from Rio to Jamaica to New Orleans and Mississippi. Music served to link generations. Melodies and lyrics were not written and had to be passed on by word of mouth from parents to children and from elders to young people. As in Brazil and in the Caribbean, slaves in the North American South fashioned instruments with African provenance, such as the drum and the stringed precursor to the banjo, improvised from the gourd. The "call and shout" vocals of field hands were a distinctive slave improvisation that led to a rich tradition. In black music, the work songs and their variants call to mind the image of toil and struggle, both physical and spiritual.[32] Sadly, whites in blackface in the first half of the nineteenth century parodied slave music and mocked slave behaviour in the minstrel show phenomenon that was fashioned to amuse white audiences.

Here, it should be stressed that as Christian identity was allowed for slaves, white preachers were often used to reinforce the inevitability of the slaves' status, emphasizing Christian imperatives for obedience. But black preachers, either slave or free, raised a great tradition in metaphor and straightforward alternatives to the doctrine of submission, not advocating revolt or mayhem but rather suggesting a spiritual rejection of the white belief in the rightness of slavery. The fact of the afterlife for slaves as "freedom" was not a melancholy surrender to the rigidity of slavery but a deeply spiritual reassurance of self-worth. However, there was a segment of the slave population that saw an end to slavery as possible, and the northern states, which had gradually ended slavery after the Revolution, did offer hope, especially as the abolitionist movement became more active after 1830. Yet one of the depressing realities of slavery was the way slaveholders and their political representatives tightened the system as it came under fire. As Chapter Seven notes, slaveholders went to war in 1861 to preserve the institution.

A commonly recorded slave memory emphasized the harshness, injustice, and apparently indelible nature of bondage, with an occasional nod to a happy social memory or a benevolent master. Whites recorded their roles as either something of a burden or simply as a right. As they did, they stereotyped slaves in diaries, letters, and memoirs. What masters thought of their slaves reveals the rooted nature of the institution. While the minstrel show portrays a common white perception, perhaps a more enduring stereotype was the African as sexually promiscuous, wanton, and potent. The image applied to both males and females, and the white perception of African carnal imperatives had become an *idée fixe* by the nineteenth century. In the United States, the African American was for the most part seen as a modified version of the male African with the same potential for extravagant sexuality. Africans were seen not only as sexually overactive and indiscriminate but were also understood to possess genitalia larger than those of whites. The centuries-old European caricatures of Africans copulating with apes had not entirely lapsed. By the early nineteenth century, Charles White's 1799 anatomical discourse was being widely circulated in the English-speaking world. When he announced that "... the penis of the African is larger than that of an European," he was adding "scientific" cachet to popular assumption.[33] He was also reflecting earlier sixteenth- and seventeenth-century assumptions that spoke of "large propagators" of "extraordinary greatness."[34] The anatomical and behavioural package included the assumed sexual aggressiveness of African women, and all of it maintained the notion of the "bestial" African, the slave as the unredemptive primitive in contrast to the refined delicacy of white women and the manners and moral restraint of white men. In the case of a great many white males, the racial bias here was contrary to the obvious evidence in the miscegenation rates and the modesty that white males must have seen in their female slaves.

The fear of slave revolts in the South brought along specific fears for the safety of white women. Slave marriage perhaps satisfied white male fears of rampaging, frustrated, lustful, and vengeful male slaves; from the perspective of white women, slave marriage helped constrain the presumed sexual urges of slave women and lessen infidelity among white husbands and temptations for their sons. In fact, it almost certainly did not restrain white males. And the sexual exploitation of slave women by masters, overseers, and the male children of slaveholders produced a substantial mulatto population in the slave quarters. While much of that exploitation was occasional rather than sustained, there were master-slave relationships that went on for years and produced several children. The most notorious long-term example is that of Thomas Jefferson and Sally Hemmings, an affair that was clearly known to many of Jefferson's contemporaries, including his political enemies, and obviously was known in the neighbourhood of Jefferson's plantation. Sailors exploited female slaves in the middle passage. Some slaveholders sold female slaves into prostitution, and others sold them to other planters to avoid domestic conflict. The subject is a complex and troubling one that conjures up its own stereotype of antebellum whites. Historian Deborah Gray White uses a useful planter binary to summarize the female slave in white minds. She contrasts the "jezebel" image, a sexual temptress, with the "mammy" image, the benign stereotype of the faithful mature housekeeper and interracial confidante. Deborah White and other historians have demolished the simple bifurcation of these types but nevertheless leave us with much evidence of relationships built on power. She notes that young slave women were sometimes made to strip for whippings or other kinds of punishments in what can only be seen as staged pornography in demonstrations of white male authority intended to frighten female slaves and humiliate male slave onlookers.[35] These events were clear examples of the calculated displays of power and submission that attended the culture's basic racial template.

Notes

1 Cited in Conrad, *Children of God's Fire*, 112.

2 There is a large and growing literature on the slave family. For a comprehensive North American study, see Herbert G. Gutman, *Black Family in Slavery and Freedom, 1750–1925* (New York: Vintage, 1976). For useful introductions, see Blassingame, *The Slave Community*, Chapter 4; Deborah Gray White, *Ar'nt I A Woman? Female Slaves in the Plantation South* (New York: Norton, 1985), Chapter 5. For Brazil, see Mattoso, *To Be A Slave*, 105–14; Schwartz, *Slaves, Peasants and Rebels*, Chapter 5; and Russell-Wood, *Slavery and Freedom*, Chapter 9. For the British Caribbean, see Richard Dunn, "A Tale of Two Plantations: Slave Life at Mesopotamia in Jamaica and Mount Airy in Virginia, 1799–1828," *William and Mary Quarterly* 34.1 (1977): 32. For the Caribbean generally, see Engerman and Higman, "The Demographic Structure of the Caribbean Slave"; and Michael Craton, "Changing Patterns of the Slave Family in the British West Indies," in Heuman and Walvin, *The Slavery Reader*, 274–99. For the French Caribbean, see Bernard Moitt, *Women and Slavery in the French Antilles, 1635–1848* (Bloomington: University of Indiana Press, 2001). On paternalism, see Genovese, *Roll, Jordan, Roll*, Book One, parts 1 and 2. The relevant chapters in Klein and Vinson, *African Slavery*, and in Berlin, *Many Thousands*, should be consulted.

3 For a good example of the comparative case study, see Dunn, "A Tale of Two Plantations." See also Craton, "Changing Patterns."

4 On the "damage thesis," see Stanley Elkins, *Slavery: A Problem in American Institutional and Intellectual Life*, 3rd ed. (Chicago: University of Chicago Press, 1976 [1959]). On the controversy it sparked, see Ann J. Lane, *The Debate over Slavery: Stanley Elkins and His Critics* (Urbana: University of Illinois Press, 1971). A useful review of the 1950s to 1970s literature for North America is Littlefield, "From Phillips to Genovese." See also Fogel, *The Slavery Debates, 1952–1990*. For Brazil, see Cleary, "Race, Nationalism and Social Theory"; and Schwartz, *Slaves, Peasants and Rebels*, Chapter 1; see the 40-page historiographical essay in Russell-Wood, *Slavery and Freedom*, xiii–liii; for the Caribbean, see Knight, *The Caribbean*, 350–55. Few historians accept Elkins's theory, and his plantation slavery-Nazi concentration camp analogy has been roundly criticized.

5 Gunnar Myrdal, *An American Dilemma: The Negro Problem and Modern Democracy* (New York: Harper, 1944); Aptheker, *American Negro Slave Revolts*; Eric Williams, *Capitalism and Slavery* (Chapel Hill: University of North Carolina Press, 1994 [1944]).

6 C.L.R. James, *The Black Jacobins: Toussaint L'Ouverture and the Saint Domingue Revolution* (London: Allison and Busby, 1980 [1938]). On the Brazil debate, see Cleary, "Race, Nationalism and Social Theory."

7 Conrad, *Children of God's Fire*, 56–57 and 65–70, has some interesting notes on the ways slaves were seen as exploited labour. Klein and Luna, *Slavery in Brazil*, Chapter 8 offers an accessible and enlightening survey of slave marriage as does Russell-Wood, *Slavery and Freedom*, Chapter 9.

8 Klein and Luna, *Slavery in Brazil*, 78; Bergad, *Comparative Histories*, 123 and Chapter 4.

9 Jennifer L. Morgan, *Laboring Women: Reproduction and Gender in New World Slavery* (Philadelphia: University of Pennsylvania Press, 2004), Chapter 4. For a North American-Caribbean comparison, see Dunn, "A Tale of Two Plantations."

10 Mattoso, *To Be A Slave*, 105–14, quote on 110–11; see also Conrad, *Children of God's Fire*, 57, 60, 100, 133–40.

11 Schwartz, *Sugar Plantations*, Chapter 14; and Schwartz, "Peasants and Slavery: Feeding Brazil in the Late Colonial Period" in *Slaves, Peasants and Rebels*, 65–101.

12 Conrad, *Children of God's Fire*, 317ff; Mattoso, *To Be A Slave*, Chapter 9.

13 Schwartz, *Slaves, Peasants and Rebels*, Chapter 5.

14 Klein and Luna, *Slavery in Brazil*, Chapter 8. Genovese, *Roll, Jordan, Roll*, 168–83 offers a brief comparison of Brazil, the United States, and the British Caribbean.

15 Klein and Luna, *Slavery in Brazil*, Chapter 8.

16 Conrad, *Children of God's Fire*, 175. On "oil of mediation" see Freyre, *The Masters and the Slaves*, 256.

17 Rhoda E. Reddock, "Women and Slavery in the Caribbean: A Feminist Perspective," *Latin American Perspective* 12 (1985): 63–80; Dunn, "A Tale of Two Plantations." See also Barbara Bush, *Slave Women in Caribbean Society, 1650–1838* (Bloomington: Indiana University Press, 1990), Chapter 7. On the slave family see Bush, 83–119.

18 Reddock, "Women and Slavery"; and see Chapter Seven in the present text.

19 Moira Ferguson, ed., *The History of Mary Prince, a West Indian Slave Related by Herself*, rev. ed. (Ann Arbor: University of Michigan Press, 2000), 84–85.

20 Moitt, *Women and Slavery in the French Antilles*, 43.

21 Knight, *The Caribbean*, 131.

22 See Dunn, "A Tale of Two Plantations."

23 Engerman and Higman, "Demographic Structure"; and Knight, *Slave Society*, 3–24.

24 W.E.B. Du Bois, *The Souls of Black Folks*, Chapter IV. See the examples in Rawick, *The American Slave*; and in Genovese, *Roll, Jordan, Roll*, Book Three, parts 1 and 2.

25 Genovese, *Roll, Jordan, Roll*, 3–7; Patterson, *Slavery and Social Death*, 94–97.

26 Genovese, *Roll, Jordan, Roll*, 512; for a comment on "black English" see Genovese, *Roll, Jordan, Roll*, 437–41; and Rawick, *The American Slave*, 178.

27 See the Hammond reference in Phillips, *American Negro Slavery*, 264–65.

28 Kenneth Stampp, *Peculiar Institution: Slavery in the Ante-bellum South* (New York: Knopf, 1956), 29–31.

29 Dorothy Sterling, *We Are Your Sisters: Black Women in the Nineteenth Century* (New York: Norton, 1984), 33–34. (From the Federal Writers' Project documents.)

30 Sterling, *We Are Your Sisters*.

31 Blassingame, *The Slave Community*, 154.

32 Blassingame, *The Slave Community*, Chapters 1–3 (see especially figures 13 and 14). See the excellent commentary on black music in Du Bois, *The Souls of Black Folk*, Chapter XV.

33 Jordan, *White over Black*, 501.

34 Jordan, *White over Black*, 34–35 for the anatomical references. For the public or popular stereotyping of African Americans, see William L. Van Deburg, *Slavery and Race in American Popular Culture* (Madison: University of Wisconsin Press, 1984). See, for example, Van Deburg's discussion of the white minstrel phenomenon, 39ff.

35 White, *Ar'nt I A Woman*, Chapter 1 (especially page 33).

7 | The Apogee: Revolutions, Abolitionism, Persistence

"Whereas divers Persons are holden in Slavery within divers of His Majesty's Colonies, and it is just and expedient that all such Persons should be manumitted and set free ..."

—1833 Chapter 73, 3 and 4 William IV

(The Emancipation Bill of the British Parliament of 1833, which freed all remaining slaves in the British Empire as of 1834, compensated the owners, and transferred the slaves' status to a six-year apprenticeship.)

"No bill of attainder, ex post facto law, or law denying or impairing the right of property in negro slaves shall be passed."

—The "Bill of Rights" in the Constitution of the Confederate States of America, 1861

During the last century of the slave trade, the rising world consumption of sugar, cotton, coffee, and other American commodities resulted in the transfer of 7.5 million Africans to the Americas, some 60 per cent of the total number for the entire 350 years of the trade. At the same time, slavery came under serious and sustained attack from secular intellectuals and ecclesiastical leaders, mostly in Britain, in what became an outpouring of treatises and public campaigns attacking slavery and arousing public support for abolitionism.[1] The language of equal civil and political rights for whites in the American and French Revolutions often skirted the question of ordinary human rights for slaves. The sheer tenacity of the slaveholding classes, their political weight, and the deeply entrenched legality of slavery for the most part confined the rights issue to whites. The limited abolitionist constituency even at its busiest was more vigorous and effective in places where there was little or no slavery—in the British Isles, the northern United States, and continental France. In the hollow application of equal rights in the US Constitution, property rights, including the right to own slaves, were made a fundamental and protected right of citizenship in 1791 in the revered first Ten Amendments, the "Bill of Rights." It was protected all the way to the Thirteenth Amendment of 1865. The universal rights trumpeted by the French revolutionaries ebbed and flowed as the revolution itself changed direction.

Christian organizations such as the British Methodists, American Unitarians, and Quakers played up the increasingly well-publicized horrors of the slave trade and saw the slave traders as parasites. But slavery was an undeniable fact of life in the Americas. It had always "been there." It would not go easily regardless of human rights advocates even as the seeds of abolitionism, sown in the seventeenth and eighteenth century, bloomed in the "age of revolutions."[2] On the face of it, the abolitionists' assumption that the slaveholding class could be swayed by moral argument was illogical. Slaveholders categorically could hardly be expected to attack the source of their and their successors' wealth and status. Otherwise, there were few serious official initiatives until the early nineteenth century when the voices of private individuals and groups did begin to play on the ears of politicians throughout the Atlantic.

The Early Abolitionists

The Marquis de Pombal, an Enlightenment reformer, had outlawed slavery in Portugal in the 1760s, a not unimportant act considering the numbers of slaves in Portugal at that time. However, Pombal's economic and trade policies for the Portuguese Empire actually streamlined and consolidated slavery in Brazil. He belonged to a generation of European bureaucrats and planners who were purveyors of rational inquiry and models of efficiency and competitiveness. He purged the Jesuits, blunting their influence in the colony even as he removed the excesses of the heretic-hunting Inquisition in Portugal. But he made sure that slavery would fuel Portugal's imperial strategies and economic prospects.

In Britain, the Somerset Decision in 1772 (an appeal by a slave that his enslavement in England was unlawful) seemed to ban slavery in England, and a case in Scotland appeared to do the same there, even though there were fewer than 15,000 slaves in Britain at that point.[3] In truth, in the immediate term, the British slave trade continued apace, and slavery grew in Britain's North American and Caribbean colonies even as the Somerset case was being argued. British military strategy during the American Revolution (1775–83) encouraged slaves in Virginia to defect with promises of freedom, a strategy that cannot be seen as an example or harbinger of reformed British imperial policy. The Somerset case did, however, arouse Granville Sharp (1735–1813), a former government clerk, to correspond with the French-born Pennsylvania Quaker Anthony Benezet (1713–84) regarding the prospects for action against slavery. Meanwhile, a racially specific edict of Louis XVI in 1777 banned the importation into France of blacks and mixed coloureds regardless of status. While this put an end to any growth in the small French slave population, it was clear that even free blacks were not welcome in European France. At the same time, while abolitionism was not on any official agenda, it began to crystalize privately in Britain and France in particular and in some North American quarters.[4]

Granville Sharp had published an incendiary rebuke of slavery in 1769, and in 1770, the French philosopher Abbé Raynal, in what was treasonable language, called for a "Black Spartacus" to rise up and destroy slavery in the French colonies. In North America, the charge of "theft" was used by the Mennonite Daniel Francis Pastorius as early as 1688, and John Woolman in a 1754 essay agreed that the denial of "self" was theft. He scolded his fellow Pennsylvania Quakers for keeping slaves and warned that merchants who had no slaves but who made money from the slave trade were party to the crime.[5] By the time of the American Revolution, there were legal actions, many of them initiated by African Americans, to end slavery in the northern independent states where, it should be emphasized, there were negligible numbers of slaves and hardly a culture or economy that needed slavery.[6] Indeed, in 1777, Vermont came into being as an independent state and banned slavery in its constitution. When it became the fourteenth state in the United States in 1791, it was the only one to have a constitutional prohibition on slavery. Yet as antislavery sentiment took root in the North, especially among New England intellectuals, religious leaders, and freed blacks, the percentage of freed blacks actually declined in the South, despite the gestures of some revolutionary southerners.[7]

By the 1780s, the European reading public was routinely exposed to graphic accounts of the middle passage, embellished by anecdote and the formal commentaries of ship's captains and officers, including medical officers.[8] When British abolitionists needed a more focused approach, they found it in the work of the indefatigable William Wilberforce (1759–1833), a Member of Parliament and an evangelical Christian whose campaigns rejected any moral basis for slavery. If Christianity could be called upon to endorse slavery as a moral obligation for owners, then for Wilberforce and other Christian abolitionists such as the reformed ex-slaver John Newton, the same God could be called upon to condemn slavery. Wilberforce's proposals in and out of Parliament endured repeated disappointments between 1791 and 1805, often stalled or circumvented by procedural issues and by the opposition of slaveholding and slave trading interests. The busy Granville Sharp had publicized the grotesque case of the Liverpool-registered slave ship *Zong* and the insurance claim in 1781 for the 133 slaves whose owners claimed had been lost at sea. The case made clear that sick and malnourished slaves had lost resale value and had been thrown overboard in what became known as the *Zong* massacre.[9]

Sharp's exposé added inestimable propaganda value to the campaigns that were coalescing around Wilberforce, Sharp, Thomas Clarkson (1760–1846), and the Quaker-dominated Society for Effecting the Abolition of the Slave Trade of 1787. Parliament eventually yielded to coalitions of parliamentary agitators and zealous public factions and banned the trade in 1807. The British slave trade ban did not, of course, signal an immediate end to slavery in the British Empire; that would take until 1833–34. However, the process had begun. Meanwhile in the new United States, the slave trade was ended not on humanitarian grounds but for political reasons; more to the point, the end of the trade did not retard the growth of slavery, which quickened and became more firmly entrenched in the South. Slave reproduction rates continued to rise.

The Expansion of Slavery in the United States and the Politics of Sectionalism

In the 12 years between the Declaration of Independence of 1776 and the making of the Constitution in 1787, the 13 contiguous North American mainland colonies fought a bloody war with Britain, left the Empire, and established a federated republic. A major cause of independence was the preservation of political and economic rights that had been threatened by British imperial reforms after 1763. After independence was secured, the older colonial slave codes were simply transferred into the newly minted constitutions of the South and were then absorbed into the Constitution of the United States. The language of rights and liberties that rolled off the revolutionary leaders' tongues and flowed from the pamphleteers' pens spoke only of the civil and political rights of white men, including the rights of slaveholders.[10]

The United States began by designing a modern republican state lodged in the rule of law. It also began as a divided confederation, with divergent social, cultural, and economic sections. The original 13 states grew to 33 by 1860, and 15 of them had state constitutions protecting the rights of whites to hold slaves as permanent property. There was no political will to end slavery and compelling economic imperatives to maintain it, with no abolitionist movement in the South to speak of. Freeing slaves might have been manageable in the northern states, but turning hundreds of thousands of slaves loose into the rigid racial hierarchies of the South was not feasible. When emancipation was forced on the South after the Civil War, it opened the way for a century of resentment, hostility, violence, and rigidly applied racial segregation.[11] (See Table 7.1 for population figures in colonial British America and the United States.)

In the summer of 1787, the revolutionary Continental Congress passed the third Northwest Ordinance. It decreed that the area north of the Ohio River and west from the older colonial boundaries in the Appalachians to the edge of Spanish territory to the west would be divided into three or five territories that would be admitted as states when populations warranted it. It included a ban on slavery in all of the territory, and whites in the North would now be able to establish family farms in an agricultural zone rich in soils, water, and timber resources. This was not so much an attack on slavery but an implicit compromise. The Ordinance said nothing of the area south of the Ohio River. There, slaveholders would be free to expand into a vast territory that was suitable for cash crops.

When the US Constitution was ratified, it assumed the legality of the Northwest Ordinance and added three clauses that guaranteed the legal right to slaveholding. The most controversial clause counted the slave population in each state as an additional three-fifths for assigning seats in the national House of Representatives. It did not mean to suggest that slaves were each now measured as three-fifths of a person, nor did it advance the possibility of any new rights for slaves. Northern states understood that slavery had to be accepted if a national union was to be made, and they conceded the representation issue on the basis of tax revenues (slaves were assets and taxed as such). A second compromise conceded African slave imports until 1808 when the trade was to be reassessed. The reassessment blocked slave imports from further enhancing southern representation in the national government. This concession was less important than it seems because of the rates of natural increase in the slave population. The third constitutional reference to slavery was the "fugitive slave clause": for example, if a Virginia slave ran off to

TABLE 7.1 Selected Population Figures, Colonial British America and the United States

	Total Population	White Population	Black Population (% of whole)	Free Coloured and as (%) of Total Black Population
Colonial British America				
1700	250,888	223,071	27,871 (11)	
1750	1,170,670	934,340	236,420 (20)	
1770	2,148,076	1,688,254	459,822 (21)	
Southern British Colonies				
1700	104,558	82,112	22,476 (21)	
1750	514,290	309,588	204,702 (39)	
1770	994,434	587,604	406,827 (41)	
United States (includes non-slave states)				
1790	3,929,214	3,172,006	757,208 (19)	
1810	7,239,881	5,862,073	1,377,808 (19)	
1840	17,069,453	14,195,805	2,873,548 (16)	
1860	31,443,321	27,001,491	4,441,83 (14)	
Southern United States[a]				
1790	1,961,372	1,265,488	657,527 (33.5)	32,357 (4.7)
1810	3,094,228	2,208,785	1,005,296 (32.5)	108,265 (9.7)
1840	7,150,472	4,632,530	2,343,376 (32.8)	211,908 (8.3)
1860	12,315,373	8,097,463	3,953,696 (31.1)[a]	261,918 (6.2)

a   The South eventually consisted of two distinct regions, an "upper" South and a "lower" or "deep" South. In 1860, the percentage of slaves to the whole population in the lower South was 44.8 per cent, ranging from 25.5 per cent in Arkansas to 55.2 per cent in Mississippi and 57.2 per cent in South Carolina. The percentage of free coloured peoples in the total coloured, slave, and free population was 0.2 per cent in Mississippi and 2.4 per cent in South Carolina.

Adapted from *Historical Statistics of the United States from Colonial Times to 1970* (Washington, DC: Bureau of the Census, 1975), Part 2, Section Z, 1178ff.; Nellis, *An Empire of Regions*, 211–14, Cohen and Greene, *Neither Slave Nor Free*, 339; Kolchin, *American Slavery*, 254.

Pennsylvania where slavery was being outlawed, the Pennsylvania authorities would be legally obliged to return the "property" to the owner.

If existing laws and geographic opportunity spelled a healthy future for slavery in the United States, so did technology and the market economy. In 1794, Eli Whitney of Connecticut patented the "Cotton *Gin*" ("en*gine*") for separating seeds from the cotton boll. The original, rather simple hand-cranked device freed hands for more fieldwork and more raw cotton.[12] As steam-powered mills in Europe and North America began to mass produce finished fabrics for expanding markets, cotton became the crop of choice for planters south of the Ohio River who were moving west to congenial space and conditions. The great "Cotton Kingdom" was born within a generation of independence in territory that later formed the states of Mississippi, Louisiana, and Alabama. In 1803, the territory of Louisiana, under the control of Napoleon's France, was sold to the United States in one of the great real estate bargains in history. The territory, stretching from the Mississippi River to the Rocky Mountains and to British territory to the northwest, doubled the size of the United States and sent Americans across the Mississippi River. The question then was how the tidy division between slave and non-slave states along the Ohio River could be accommodated in the new lands. A compromise in 1821 established Missouri as a slave state, and Maine was admitted as a free state. This kept the number of free and slave states at 12 each, a balance that was actually maintained into the 1850s.

After 1830, canals, railroads, and the telegraph spurred industrial and capitalist investment that complemented the traditional small farm culture of northern families. More to the point, trade, communication, and settlement in the North, even when it was linked to investment and agriculture in the South, was increasingly pointing to the west in a corridor that ran from the Atlantic to beyond the Mississippi River. The South, and in particular the new cotton-growing regions, grew and prospered on the conservative principles of the older cash crop agrarianism and a hierarchy with a fixed dependency on slavery. What helped bind the union in this period was economic growth driven in part by common attachments to the dominant Democratic Party and by northern investment in transportation and northern cotton mills dependent on raw cotton.[13]

If the South had seemed foreign to a New England or Pennsylvania visitor in 1750, by 1850 it had become even more exotic and distant. In turn, the southern political and intellectual leadership saw the North as equally foreign. Factories and cities dotted the northeast and continued as far west as the Great Lakes, and Irish and Catholic immigrants appeared in numbers.

On the eve of the Civil War, 18 states had banned slavery by law. On the other side of the divide, 40 per cent of the population in the other 15 states was black and in permanent bondage. In South Carolina and Mississippi, close to 60 per cent of the population was enslaved.

Sectional politics hurried along the fate of slavery in the United States. Southerners found their way into Texas, a part of newly independent Mexico where American slaveholders ignored the prohibition of slavery in the 1829 Mexican Constitution, rebelled against Mexican authority, and established the Texas republic in 1836. In 1845, Texas was annexed to the United States as a slave state at a time when continental expansionism and the cry of "Manifest Destiny" filled the political air. A war between the United States and Mexico (1846–48) was ostensibly over a border dispute but was clearly driven by territorial ambition. It led to Mexico's cession of its North America territory from the Rio Grande to the British boundaries to the north and west to the Pacific and completed the continental reach of the United States. To deal with the slavery issue in the new territories, Congress attempted compromises in 1850 and in 1854 passed the Kansas Nebraska Act. The Missouri Act of 1821 had banned slavery north of the 36 degrees 30 minutes north latitude, but it was revoked in 1854 and replaced with the principle of "popular sovereignty" whereby settlers would decide the issue of whether or not slavery would be legalized in the newly created states. War broke out in Kansas in 1855–56 between slave and antislavery forces over the proposed constitution for the new state.[14]

The popular sovereignty approach failed, and in 1856 sectional tensions resulted in one of the more memorable events of the era when the abolitionist Senator Charles Sumner of Massachusetts was beaten nearly to death on the floor of the Senate by Preston Brooks, a Congressman from South Carolina. Then, in 1857, the long-running Dred Scott case was decided in dramatic fashion. Scott, a slave, had sued for his freedom after being taken in the 1830s to Wisconsin Territory where slavery was prohibited under the Missouri Act, which was then still in effect. In a decision that raised the stakes in the slave state–free state crisis, the Supreme Court ruled that the Missouri Act had violated the property rights clause in the Bill of Rights by depriving slave owners of their property without due process. What the decision meant, in effect, was that the federal government and the states could not legislate against slavery. Every ban on slavery from the Northwest Ordinance to the Missouri Act to the various state constitutions and statutes, and presumably any future acts, might be invalid. The South had been vindicated by Dred Scott's failed attempt for freedom, but the first reaction to the decision was apprehension—the northern states would not stand for its implications.[15] As for abolitionism, it was no nearer to influencing southerners than it had been in 1830. In fact, the northern abolitionist movement made southerners more than ever committed to the institution.

The intractable defenders of slavery explained, mostly to themselves, a sociological defence for slavery's utility. Slavery had confirmed slaves' inability to function in a free, competitive economy. Theories of biological inferiority still applied, but slavery in practice had now confirmed it. Southerners were unapologetic and argued forcefully that slave labour was also more efficient than wage labour.[16] Therefore, slavery spoke to an economic reality and was a "positive good" for the slaves themselves. We need to note that popular opposition to slavery in the North in this period was generally opposed to slavery's expansion rather than its existence in the South. Apart from the abolitionist community, the majority of northerners shared some of the same prejudices as southerners and allowed for the historical and social reality of the South's "peculiar institution." Even prominent progressive leaders spoke of black inferiority, as had Thomas Jefferson and, two generations later, Abraham Lincoln. While each deplored the institution as an affront to national principles, neither could concede that blacks, by nature or condition, could be made equal to whites, have sufficient competency to vote or hold office, or in Lincoln's stated view be allowed to intermarry with whites.[17] Still, by the middle of the nineteenth century, the territorial expansion of slavery was a political concern, and the abolitionist movement, however limited its constituency, convinced southerners that there was a great potential for increased support for antislavery. To southerners, all attacks on slavery were deeply misguided. Moreover, and this was central to slaveholders' deeply held beliefs, any attack on slavery undermined their Constitutional rights. The issue was compounded by what appeared to be a rise in slave resistance and the potential for social disorder. (See Map 7.1 for the division of free and slave states within the United States in 1860.)

Slave Revolts

The shocking violence of the Haitian Revolution and its remarkable outcome in 1804 (see below in this chapter) sent tremors through the Caribbean, the United States, and Europe. It evoked some uneasy visions in the US South. What was its propaganda value to slaves? Could it possibly incite slave populations in the South to rise up, collectively, running rampant and

MAP 7.1 The United States, 1860

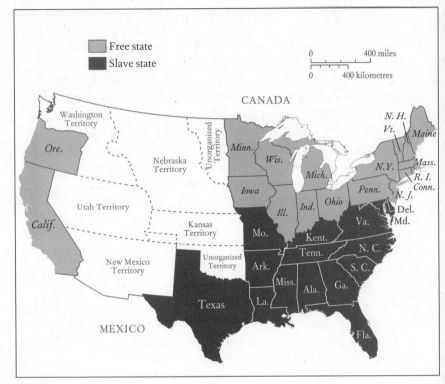

slaughtering whites? With Haiti in mind, southern planters and politicians reacted to slave disturbances or conspiracies much as they had in the eighteenth century with swift and deadly responses. Gabriel Prosser in Virginia in 1801 and Denmark Vesey in 1822 in South Carolina plotted local uprisings that were crushed mercilessly. Some estimates claim that 35 plotters were lynched after Gabriel Prosser's plan fell apart, and 37 were executed after the Vesey plot was uncovered. The most frightening of all to southerners, Nat Turner's Virginia rebellion of 1831, panicked an already paranoid white population. Turner's following consisted of a core of fewer than 100 slaves, but they killed 57 whites. Again, the reprisals were savage. One hundred blacks were killed in the extensive manhunt that followed the outbreak, and a further 22, including Turner, were executed after trials that tended to amplify planter resolve. While the masses of slaves in the South were not capable of rising up and violently overthrowing the regime, let alone their local authorities, the frequency of revolts and the rising numbers of runaways (though this was more a nuisance and a symbolic problem than a threat to the regime) persuaded southerners that their assumptions of slave docility and even contentment were not guaranteed. Slaves continued to resist their condition as they always had. But it now seemed that their leadership was more resourceful. Prosser, Vesey, and Turner were intelligent, dedicated, and focused men. Turner, in particular, represented an especially dangerous type, as he was a literate slave preacher.[18]

The Limits to Abolitionism in the United States

The well-organized American Anti-Slavery Society, founded in 1833 and directed by William Lloyd Garrison (1805–79) attracted a galaxy of New England religious and secular worthies. It raised the banner of reform and thus put the South on the defensive. The Society's pamphlets and its newspaper the *Liberator* were seized in southern post offices. In the North, its members were as likely to be attacked by anti-abolitionists as they were to convert a public majority to the cause. Indeed, in Alston, Illinois in 1837, an anti-abolitionist mob murdered the abolitionist publisher Elijah P. Lovejoy. The eloquence and example of the escaped slave Frederick Douglass, the popularity of Harriet Beecher Stowe's heartrending *Uncle Tom's Cabin* (1852), and the tireless campaigning of Garrison and his supporters, including legions of activist women such as Maria Weston Chapman, kept the issue alive. Chapman was a key organizer of a trans-Atlantic network of women whose annual Anti-Slavery Bazaar in Boston provided significant funds for the abolitionist cause while spreading the abolitionist message. The activities of women in the abolitionist campaigns on both sides of the Atlantic dovetailed with other issues such as temperance and women's legal and political rights. While many female abolitionists adopted and reflected the views of their husbands or fathers, many others, such as Maria Chapman, were completely independent actors. A well-known example is the career of the Grimke sisters, Sarah (1792–1873) and Angelina (1805–79). These South Carolina women were raised in the slave environment but found purpose in the North, attracting large crowds to their lectures and meetings. The Grimkes combined an advocacy of women's rights with antislavery and did so in the face of criticism and even hostility because they defied the era's assumptions of feminine passivity.

But the abolitionist literature that called for extreme strategies often infuriated northern moderates as much as it aroused bitterness in the South.

Angelina Grimke's *Appeal to the Christian Women of the South* was burned in public in South Carolina. What the southerners wanted most was a reduction in the already tiny freed slave population, and some joined with a briefly popular northern movement that idealistically sought to offer freed blacks even greater freedom by sending them "back" to Africa. The American Colonization Society was founded in 1817; by the time it was disbanded in 1867, it had relocated a paltry 6,000 freedmen to what was called Liberia, established by the Society in 1821. The organization's objectives say nothing about abolition and a great deal about the unwanted free coloured person, whose numbers were so small to begin with. As historian Peter Kolchin points out, the numbers of freed blacks who left over several decades was the equivalent of the number of slaves being born every two months in the United States in the 1820s.[19]

In 1829, David Walker (1785–1830), a free black in Boston, published *Appeal to the Coloured Citizens of the World* and called for slaves in the South to rise up *en masse*. He warned slaveholders that unless they repented, they would face the wrath of God. The circulation of the *Appeal* as the Nat Turner rebellion was underway in Virginia was evidence that the South's social and cultural survival was under siege. The Fugitive Slave Act of 1850 was offensive to many northern editorialists and was routinely violated by the "underground railroad" for escaped slaves, which created a hero in Harriet Tubman (1820–1913) and a haven in slave-free Canada. This was a symbolic chapter in the history of slave resistance. Fewer than 50,000 of the millions in bondage made their way along the trail of safe houses and facilitators. To southerners, those abetting the escapes were violating their constitutional rights under the Fugitive Slave Clause. The issue came to a head in 1859 when the notorious radical abolitionist John Brown (1800–59) crossed into Virginia with a force that included blacks. He seized a federal arsenal and called for a full-blown insurrection and violent cleansing of the South. He was captured, and in an effort to appease southern fears, he was quickly convicted of treason, a national crime, and hanged within weeks. Lincoln won the presidential election of 1860 without southern support, and he, and the recently formed "free soil" Republican Party, controlled Congress and the presidency. The national government was now a northern government.

War, Freedom, Segregation, and Lynch Law

Within weeks of Lincoln's election, South Carolina seceded and took 10 other slaveholding states out of the union with it over the next few months.

The United States never recognized the Confederate States of America as a "nation"; Lincoln denied the legitimacy of any state's "right" to secede and obliged the South to defend its decision with force. The war that followed would be treated, officially, as a "rebellion." The Confederacy saw the conflict differently, as a war to secure the independence it had declared, a war to preserve its heritage and character. But in rushing to secure slavery, secession brought on slavery's demise. As historian Peter Kolchin succinctly puts it, "by going to war for the preservation of slavery, [the South] took the only action that could foreseeably have led to its speedy and complete abolition."[20] Lincoln's Emancipation Proclamation of January 1863 declared that all slaves in Confederate territory were free. It was a tactical device to disrupt the Confederate economy and in fact did not free any slaves who remained within the Confederacy. But it served as a deliberate prelude to ending slavery in the United States. To defeat the South and restore the Union, slavery had to go, and it was ended, constitutionally, with the Thirteenth Amendment of 1865. Over 600,000 mostly white men were killed in the war, a sobering toll that stunned the nation. For a time between the Emancipation Proclamation and the end of southern reconstruction in the 1870s, there was a tendency to see the war as a moral crusade to free millions of slaves and restore the nation's integrity as a republic of rights. In a sudden end to generations of legal race-based slavery, nearly 4 million slaves were freed but then neglected by the national government and left to cope with an embittered white South and a somewhat indifferent nation.

Slavery was abruptly ended, without compensation. The suddenness of its end with no historic pattern of manumissions and no substantial free coloured rural class to absorb them freed slaves into a hostile world that was not prepared for them. They became the South's coloured rural underclass, free and oppressed at the same time, and marked in freedom the way colour had defined them in bondage. There would be little room after 1865 for a status based on gradations of tone, shade, and previous condition. In the United States, there was a simple divide—black and white—and in the South, a clear definition of class was based on that division. Before the Civil War John Calhoun, in his "Speech on the Oregon Bill" (1848), had remarked that:

> With us [the South] the two great divisions of society are not the rich and poor, but white and black; and all the former, the poor as well as the rich belong to the upper class, and are respected and treated as equals, if honest and industrious, and hence have a position and pride of character of which neither poverty nor misfortune can deprive them.

That sentiment would be as relevant to southerners in 1868 and 1898 as it had been in 1848. The poor white southern agricultural classes operated as they always had—as superior to blacks exactly as Calhoun had suggested. The majority of freed slaves drifted back into the roles they had as slaves but as a sharecropping class.[21] They were marginalized, segregated, and slowly denied the rights of civil equality lodged in the Fourteenth Amendment (1868) and the voting rights in the Fifteenth (1870). With the end of the Civil War and the destruction of the South's infrastructure came the loss to the South, without compensation, of its major asset, $3.5 billion (in 1865 values) worth of slaves, a figure worth more than the assessed value of all the farms in the South and three times the capital invested in business and industrial property. And with it went the loss to the South of its international cotton markets. The South was not "reconstructed" but rather adapted itself to the end of slavery by perpetuating its rural mien with modified economic policies and revised and stringent race relations. At the core of the southern adjustment were state-sanctioned segregation laws.[22]

In 1890, the Louisiana state legislature passed the "Separate Car Act," which legalized the segregation that was already being practised. It mandated separate passenger rail cars for whites and blacks. In 1892, Homer Plessy, an "octoroon," under the direction of local black anti-segregationists, boarded a whites-only rail passenger coach. He was removed. He sued and appealed all the way to the United States Supreme Court, which, in a landmark decision in 1896, determined that the Louisiana act was constitutional. It declared that the principle of "separate but equal" was preferred to any enforcement of integration. The decision claimed that "If one race be inferior to the other socially, the Constitution of the United States cannot put them on the same plane."[23] The guarantee of "equal protection" (in effect, the mark of US citizenship) could only be assured by separating the races. In a revealing reflection of the racial tensions of the age, the Supreme Court went so far as to suggest that forced integration would lead to levels of violence by whites and that formal "separate but equal" conditions would help ensure African American safety. But as the principle was vigorously applied at the state level in the South, it inspired not only communal separation, economic discrimination, exploitation, and exclusion but violence against any perceived breach by blacks of the "separate but equal" doctrine.

The catch-all term "lynching" refers to the murdering of a suspected felon in organized or spontaneous vigilante and extralegal attacks, mostly by mobs. It is worth noting that lynch mobs attacked whites as well as blacks, and before 1890 whites more likely were the targets of lynching. But after

1890, the ratios changed dramatically to where blacks were being lynched at a 10 to 1 ratio over whites per capita. Indeed, as the vigilante killing of whites almost disappeared after 1900, it rose for blacks. In one important contemporary study, the reforming African American Ida B. Wells produced sobering, harrowing records of the terror.[24] In the period from 1880 to 1920 as many as 3,000 African Americans were mutilated, tortured, and then hanged or burned alive in spectacles that drew hundreds of spectators, including men, women, and children. In one year, 1892, 160 blacks were murdered by mobs.

There is really nothing in the history of the various slave regimes to compare with the lynching craze in the United States. To be sure, in Brazil there were countless individual acts of homicide by masters and overseers and reprisals against slaves involved in insurrections and conspiracies. Even after emancipation in Brazil, there were racially motivated crimes of violence. But lynching in the United States is a very troubling example of clearly discriminate terror by one powerful class against another specified class of free citizens in a republic of laws. Its scale and frequency still shocks and more than anything underlines the vengeful, fearsome racism of the era and the inability of the South to cope with free blacks as anything other than dangerous and unworthy cohabitants. Any mild breach, or perceived breach, of the segregation edicts and practices could put any black person in mortal jeopardy. Racial discrimination, forms of segregation, and exploitation certainly occurred in other former slave societies but there was nothing to match what occurred in the United States after emancipation.[25] By 1900, the black euphoria of 1865 was gone, and legal segregation was being entrenched in the general national indifference to its conditions. The sinister term "Jim Crow," stemming from the laws separating blacks from whites, is now used to define the long era of constitutional segregation and the open violence that went with it. As a reference to blacks, "Jim Crow" had been coined in 1838 by a white minstrel show actor in blackface. His theatrical suggestion of black simplicity was nothing compared to the post-emancipation mockery of black civil rights.

The Civil War has been called the American "Iliad," the great national epic. The carnage, destruction, and elevated rhetoric of sacrifice remain vibrant reminders of the nation's survival and renewal. The Civil War saved the nation and ended slavery. If the latter was a necessary outcome of the Union's triumph and folded into the cause as a moral imperative, its importance receded in the decades afterwards. As historian David Blight reminds us in a telling anecdote, during the fiftieth anniversary of the Battle of Gettysburg in 1913, over 50,000 geriatric white ex-Confederate and ex-Union soldiers were feted at the battle site. In his commemorative speech, President Woodrow Wilson spoke about how the veterans represented the nation's unity as "brothers and comrades ... the quarrel forgotten ... the splendid valor, the manly devotion of the men then arrayed against each other, now grasping hands and smiling into each other's eyes." Wilson made no mention of the Emancipation Proclamation or the fact that some 200,000 African Americans fought for the Union. For African Americans, the 1913 reunion meant employment: blacks helped construct the vast site, delivered supplies to the attendees, and cleaned latrines.[26] The Civil Rights Acts of 1866 and 1875 would need to be reapplied with the 1964 Civil Rights Act and the 1965 Voting Rights Act before slavery and freedom, race and racism were addressed more honestly.

France and the Haitian Revolution

The overthrow of France's *ancien régime* in 1789 and the revolutionary movement that followed remains one of the most important events in modern history. It was accompanied by theories of rights and stoked by anger over the material, legal, and political deprivations of the masses of Europe's largest population. The French Revolution, an assault by the masses on generations of aristocratic privilege, overthrew the Bourbon monarchy, and the stirring "Declaration of the Rights of Man and the Citizen" of 1789, which resembled the 1776 "Virginia Bill of Rights," promised equality and the end of ranks, classes, and discrimination—lofty sentiments, indeed. The remnants of feudal order were shattered, and the vast French peasantry acquired equal rights, a boon as it turned out later to the enthusiasm required for Napoleon's citizen armies. The early heady days gave way to constitutional experiment, factionalism, extremism, and chaos. It led to the execution of King Louis XVI in 1793 along with thousands of aristocrats and assorted royalists in Jacobin purges, called the "Terror." France was drawn into war with a coalition of nations including Spain, the Netherlands, and Britain who judged what they saw in France to be potentially infectious. The Directory of 1795 to 1799 settled some of the revolution's excesses and introduced Napoleon Bonaparte as France's military saviour *par excellence*. The *coup d'état* of 1799 created the Consulate and elevated Napoleon to autocratic First Consul and then to his coronation in 1804 as Emperor of the French. The "République" was now the "Empire." Napoleon's rise to power curbed the revolution's ideological collectivism but made the new state a formidable threat to the peace of Europe. His armies reached Russia and Egypt and occupied parts of Italy and Spain before their collapse in 1815 at Waterloo. Although Napoleon's imperial vision bankrupted the country, a reformed France did emerge from the strife. The events of 1789–99 struck · hard at hereditary privilege in France. It also struck chords in the Caribbean.

At the time of the revolution, Saint Domingue was the largest sugar producer in the Americas. Its slave population had reached 434,000 and its white population a small but potent 31,000. A smaller but important part of the colony's economy came from hundreds of coffee estates, many of them run by free coloured owners, part of a tiny minority of 25,000 free coloured who happened to be the wealthiest non-white community in the Americas. Saint Domingue's sugar accounted for over one-third of France's overseas trade. The colony had developed a distinctive character, and Creole dialects were important identity markers for the coloured population. The integration of African with Caribbean-born slaves made for unique local language patterns.[27]

Christian, African, and other Afro-Caribbean cults and superstitions merged with folk medicine, various cultural novelties, and adaptations to shape a black Franco-Caribbean culture. Voudon (*vodu* in French; voodoo in English) was one of the extraordinary inventions of French Caribbean slaves. It took fractured bits and pieces from French, African, and colonial cultures and from African and Christian symbols and iconography and created new deities and spiritual identities. It became a common bond of identity, almost an ideology among the slaves who destroyed French Saint Domingue and created Haiti.

As in Brazil, Saint Domingue's slave culture was infused with contributions from the steady and heavy stream of Africans including the quarter million who arrived between 1781 and 1791. As the political ripples from Paris reached the Caribbean, every segment of the population understood that very important changes were in the air. Rumours spread easily through the colony's oral networks. If slaves were not entirely familiar with the agitations of the *Société des Amis des Noirs* or Raynal's decades-old call for freedom or of the many other antislavery declarations, they were quickly made aware of the "Declaration of the Rights of Man" if for no other reason than the white planter class began to debate it with passion. Colonial royalists and republicans quarrelled with each other over the possibility of a general emancipation while the emotive rhetoric coming from France raised spirits among the slave population. The fact that whites constituted only 6 per cent of the colony's population made the system vulnerable to the aroused slave reaction to the news from France. In that confused atmosphere, slaves gathered to exchange hopes and fears. In 1790, a brief uprising of free coloured men demanding citizenship was crushed and their leader, Vincent Oge, was tortured and executed. The general agitation took a decisive turn in 1791 on the colony's Northern Plain when a wave of rebel slaves began killing planters, burning their houses, and laying waste to their estates in a desperate prelude to a full-fledged, colony-wide uprising.

Within months, 80,000 slaves were on the move. This was an angry, vengeful, and spiritually driven movement fuelled by the cultural solidarity of the enslaved and the power of voudon. Within months, 2,000 whites and as many as 10,000 slaves were killed. The violence and subsequent destruction of crops and buildings were the opening acts of a decade of bloody conflict and a long descent into racial warfare. The ravaged landscape was stark evidence of the uprising's anarchy and brutality. The sugar industry, civil authority, the planters, and the rest of the white population were now under constant assault from armies of slaves. In 1792, the revolutionary French Legislature decreed that all free coloured people everywhere in the French Empire were to be made full citizens of France. Adding to the whirl of factional confusion, in 1793 Britain and Spain invaded Saint Domingue as a strategic corollary to the European war. At the same time, one of the most dynamic personalities of the age, the free black Toussaint L'Ouverture (1743–1803) appeared. He first allied himself and his revolutionary movement with the Spanish invaders in hopes of defeating the French military in the colony. But when, in 1794, the Revolutionary Convention in Paris banned slavery in all the French colonies, Toussaint turned his military and political skills and his resources against the British as well as the Spanish, seeing them now as intruders threatening his ambitions for black sovereignty. Conversely, the planters saw in the British a way to hold on to their slaves and defy the radical Paris government and its emancipation decree.

Toussaint raised large forces, armed in some cases by abolitionists in the United States. By 1797, his army was inflicting heavy casualties on a wavering British army that gave up and left in 1798. British losses in this and other Caribbean campaigns amounted to as many as 25,000 deaths from combat and diseases. The death rates, driven by reprisal and torture, turned Saint Domingue into a charnel house. As the news of the uprising circulated throughout the Atlantic world, it became clear that Toussaint's movement was a profoundly revolutionary one, and as alliances shifted and blood flowed, Saint Domingue crumbled. Napoleon sent in a large first-class army to try to restore the status quo of 1789. But a renewed war with Britain limited support for the French military on the island, and steady attrition from disease and relentless guerrilla warfare ate away at the French. At one point, as the movements fractured, each of six separate groups was at war with one or several of the others. In 1802, after promises of a settlement, Toussaint was betrayed, captured, and sent to France where he died in prison. His legacy as the de facto spark to Haitian independence is secure. But his end was a pathetic reflection of a confused bloodbath, the idealistic ambitions of all the factions notwithstanding.

Slavery was formally restored in the other French Caribbean colonies in 1803 and was maintained even after the high-minded liberalism of the Napoleonic Civil Code of 1804. The planters in Martinique and Guadalupe enjoyed newly defined civil rights including the renewed right to own slaves. But Napoleon's recovery policy failed in Saint Domingue, and his decimated, demoralized army finally surrendered to the British. Jean Jacques Dessalines (1758–1806), Toussaint's former chief lieutenant, declared the independent Republic of Haiti in January 1804. Approximately 500,000 slaves had freed themselves and were now full-blown citizens of the world's first black republic, a republic that ironically elevated Dessalines to the position of "Emperor Jacques."

The Haitian Revolution, seen by many as a shocking event, raised alarm bells in the rest of the Caribbean and the southern United States even as it brought joy to many abolitionists. Its bloody events reinforced a widespread white view that blacks were especially brutish when loosed on whites. Reports of decapitations, torture, pillage, and the systematic destruction of property had accompanied the 10 years of war. It mattered not that the French themselves suspended even the rudimentary ethics of military conduct and behaved with equal or greater savagery. In other slave societies, the lesson of Haiti led to fears of imitation and to tighter controls over slaves. Years later, the Aponte uprising in Cuba, the Nat Turner rebellion, the Jamaican uprising of 1831, and the near civil war that came with the 1835 Muslim slave revolt in Bahia were all ruthlessly stifled. Yet the strain of maintaining slavery against a backdrop of ideologically motivated black leaders and the always bubbling abolitionist movements pulled the Haitian drama into sharp focus. The war destroyed the colony's plantations, crops, refineries, and homesteads. Haiti had been made a wasteland. It made no difference to detractors that most total wars among whites did much the same thing.[28]

Independent Haiti soon became a byword for the perils of black rule. The economic impact was immediate and disastrous, and the failure of Haiti to recover a viable economy is a tragic coda to its war for independence. Statistics tell part of the story: in 1789 Saint Domingue produced 70 million imperial tons of sugar for export, but in 1820 Haiti produced a meagre 1,260 imperial tons, and in 1840 the reported commercial yield was less than one ton. The amazing disappearance of the sugar economy ran parallel to the disappearance of slavery. The planters and the cane fields, the mills and transportation system were also gone. No effective black planter class or servant class remained, and no white investors came to restore sugar production. Coffee production fell from 38,000 imperial tons to 17,500 tons, and cotton dropped from 3,500 to 173 imperial tons between 1789 and 1820. The production of indigo disappeared entirely.[29] Tobacco and dyewood exports and local food production seemed to be all that was left for Haiti's impoverished hundreds of thousands of liberated slaves. Their misfortune was ascribed by opponents to black inferiority, with little notice of the calculated boycotts or the fact that neither Europeans nor North Americans saw any value in supporting Haiti's independence by helping it to rebuild. On the contrary, Haiti's troubles were compounded by the global market's need to replace the lost sugar production. The supply side of the sugar economy abandoned Haiti and shifted to Spanish Cuba and the rest of the Caribbean. A great irony followed Haiti's independence as African slaves now arrived in spectacular numbers in Cuba, adding more slaves to the Caribbean than had been freed in Haiti. Haiti's ill-considered and failed attempts after 1822 to annex Spanish Santo Domingo further isolated it from the international community.

After the loss of Saint Domingue, France made weak efforts to restrict the slave trade and improve the lot of slaves in its other colonies. Napoleon went into exile in 1814. When he returned to France for the "100 days" that ended at Waterloo, he decreed an end to the slave trade, as did the restored Bourbon royalty. These were largely gestures to appease the British who were now aggressively extending their 1807 ban on the maritime slave trade by intervening in the trade of all nations off the west coast of Africa. After the fall of the Bourbons in the revolution of 1830, reformers in France pressed more forcefully for abolitionism, and in 1834 the French *Amis des Noirs* was replaced by the more specific *Société Française pour l'Abolition de l'esclavage*. Slavery was abolished in France in 1836 and, finally, in the French Caribbean in 1848 during the reform movements and political upheavals that swept Europe that year. Sweden in 1846, Denmark in 1848, and the Dutch, belatedly, in 1863 ended slavery in their overseas possessions. Compensation was an issue, of course, but so was the matter of transition.

There was no smooth exit from centuries of entrenched institutionalized racial practices.

Great Britain, the Slave Trade, and Emancipation

By the end of the second decade of the nineteenth century, the end of slavery in the British Empire was imminent. The tiny population of British whites in the Caribbean was often transient, and the planters were never more than a marginal if noisy force in Parliament. In a direct contrast with slavery in the United States where the decision makers were the resident slaveholders, the decision makers in the British Empire were in London, far away from the slaves. In Britain, the Wilberforce coalitions applied near constant pressure on Parliament to enact legislation to end slavery; boycotts of slave-produced sugar captured public attention and tapped into the era's mood of "progress" and "reform." There was popular agitation for change, and the Reform Act of 1832 began a decades-long trek that led eventually to universal male suffrage and industrial, civic, and public health improvements. A series of factory acts brought the state more directly into industrial, social, and economic regulation. While much of this reform was aimed at efficiency, trade unions were politicized and active, and changes were made to buffer the misery that had come with industrialization, slums, dim factories, 12-hour workdays, low pay, poor health, and political exclusion. That is not to say that a democratic revolution was underway in Britain—far from it. Rather, the mood of reform and improvement pulled antislavery into the mix.

The important southern apologist John Calhoun defended slavery in the United States as a brake on what he saw as the evils of wage labour and attacked the notion that wage labour might be more productive and more flexible than slave labour. There can be no doubt that abolitionists influenced the ending of slavery in the British Caribbean. Indeed, historians such as David Brion Davis and Seymour Drescher have argued persuasively against the theory that failed economic models, including the use of slave labour, were no longer profitable in the British Caribbean and therefore a serious reason for abolition's success. Certainly, many Jamaican plantations were in financial trouble before the slave trade ended; and while the tobacco and cotton economies in the US South were efficient and profitable, there might have been some inefficiency in the British Caribbean sugar economy in what was a highly competitive sugar market. Moreover, the social structure of the British Caribbean rested on a weak foundation before 1834. As noted, no large permanent white population existed, and there was little residential commitment. On a more important level, the British Empire was changing its shape and redefining its economies. Sugar, coffee, cotton, and the raw materials that fed the home industries could be had from other, cheaper sources in and out of the imperial system. In the end, however, one must acknowledge the enormous public pressure in Britain to end slavery in the Empire. Reformist Methodists were preaching liberty at home and in the islands, and no one wanted another Haiti. In any case, a major event in the history of slavery had occurred.

The slave trade ban in the United States corresponded to and encouraged policies of rising rates of slave reproduction and therefore did not presage in the slightest way any potential end to slavery in the South. The British ban, on the other hand, starved the planters of supplies of new slaves, given the relatively low rates of natural increase. Thus, the banning of the slave trade was clearly a first step toward abolition powered by activists, the press, and the public. The Jamaican slave revolt of 1831–32 and fears of unrest throughout the British Caribbean were taken as signs of an impatient expectation of abolition among the enslaved. An estimated 60,000 slaves (about 20 per cent of the slave population) were involved in the 10-day uprising led by a Baptist preacher. The movement was easily suppressed by British troops, but the news of harsh reprisals by planters further illuminated the public perception of the institution's inhumanity. By this point, abolition was a matter of "when" not "if," and the Abolition of Slavery Act of 1833 (effective in 1834) confirmed the expectation. Without any clear precedent, the British government ordered the end of a 200-year-old practice in the Caribbean. They defied an albeit small but wealthy and vocal proslavery opposition and freed 700,000 British slaves quickly with the force of law.[30]

It should be noted that in 1834 when this took place, slavery in Brazil, the United States, and Cuba was expanding. Historian Seymour Drescher argues that the end of slave labour in the British Caribbean was in the short term an act of "econocide" for Britain's Atlantic enterprises and so allows for a significant role for the abolitionists in the ending of British slavery.[31] Planters were compensated with graduated amounts of money, and the act mandated a six-year "apprenticeship" transition, a status barely removed from bondage. It was roundly resisted by the "apprentices" and abandoned. The ex-slave was now the British Caribbean's paid working class, and freed slaves were encouraged to enter commerce, politics, law, and education and to establish farms and free communities on available land. The islands remained under an imperial authority that curbed some of the excesses of the local white ruling minority. But the majority of former slaves saw few economic improvements in the short term. British sugar production actually increased in the wake of abolition. As it declined in Jamaica and Barbados, it moved to Trinidad, acquired from Spain in 1797, and British Guyana on the South American coast. Indentured labour from India was used extensively in the transition, inaugurating a new system of servitude in the service of sugar production.

Independence and Abolition in Spanish America and the Caribbean Exception

Revolution and independence came to Spanish America a generation after the American and French Revolutions, and most of today's 18 Spanish-speaking Latin American republics emerged between 1810 and 1830 as the Vice Royalties were dissolved and new nations emerged where the old imperial subdivisions had been. However, a combination of geography, economy, ideology, factions, and localism doomed any coherent union of the liberated parts of the Empire. The names of Spanish America's revolutionary leaders such as Simon Bolivar (1783–1830), José de San Martin (1778–1856), and Bernardo O'Higgins (1778–1842) resonate to the present as the heroes of independence and architects of the republics. But the failures to harmonize the interests of various groups and communities and the rise of the *caudillos* (local and usually powerful leaders) and their authoritarianism led to decades of conflict.[32] In Spanish America, the struggles of the lower classes and the repeated attempts to find satisfactory constitutions for most of the new nations were in part a legacy of the Empire's administrative and preferential model. Still, out of the smoke and confusion came an end to slavery.

The break-up of the Spanish Empire in Central and South America had little to do with slavery as a cause or concern. Broadly speaking, the independence movements began in the shadow of the French control of Spain (1808–13) under Napoleon. Nascent problems with Spanish imperial authority stimulated the aspirations of interest groups, ideologues, and local autocrats. The various components of the Empire, from the grand administrative Vice Royalties down to the *cabildos* (municipalities), had by the start of the nineteenth century produced local, American-born political classes and tensions between white *criolos* and the Spanish-born *peninsulares*. Mixed free coloured populations were prominent in some regions and *mestizo* majorities in others. In a total Spanish American population of about 12 million, excluding the Caribbean, the slave population constituted less than 5 per cent of the whole and was concentrated in Peru, New Granada,

Venezuela, Colombia, and Panama. Even then, the numbers of free blacks and mixed coloured peoples outnumbered slaves by wide margins. In Mexico in 1800, for example, in a population of nearly 6 million, 10 per cent were *afromestizos* (African mixture), and the vast majority were *mestizos*. A mere 10,000 slaves were recorded as living in Mexico.[33]

The Caribbean's whites proved to be an exception to the bourgeois leaders of the revolutions in mainland Spanish America. There, local planters in Puerto Rico, Santo Domingo (under Haitian control from 1822 to 1844), and Cuba stayed with the Empire, bolstered by the wealth they enjoyed from sugar, coffee, and tobacco exports. White Cubans were fearful of Haiti's influence and rightly so as it turned out. Early in 1812, an unusual coalition of slaves, free coloureds, and some whites, organized by the free black José Antonio Aponte, an officer in a black militia unit, rose against the Cuban plantocracy. The rebels flew the Haitian flag, and many adopted the hats associated with Haitian rebels. In two separate uprisings, the rebels murdered white planters and overseers, destroyed property, and terrified the white population. The rebellion was short-lived and ferociously suppressed by local and imperial forces; as a deterrent, 30 conspirators and participants were executed publicly, while hundreds were jailed, lashed, or tortured. In the tradition of deterrence, Aponte was hanged, then decapitated, and his head displayed prominently. The Aponte episode fits a pattern of resistance, revolt, and plotting that swelled everywhere in the Americas during and in the immediate wake of the Haitian Revolution. A sense of restlessness among slaves and anxiety among colonists underlay race relations in the Spanish Caribbean. But the Aponte uprising pales in contrast to the Haitian Revolution, and the failure of the revolt in Cuba revealed the regime's power. It showed that a large free coloured and white population could deflect and smother a potential Cuban version of Haiti.[34]

In 1774, Cuba's population was 56 per cent white, 23 per cent slave, and 21 per cent free coloured. In 1827, the slave population reached a peak of 44 per cent of the whole, declining to 27 per cent of the whole in 1860. During that time, the island's population rose spectacularly, nearly tenfold to 1,389,214. The growth in the white population was as great as in any comparable space in the Americas, yet over 400,000 slaves were imported between 1827 and 1860, a number greater than was counted in 1860[35] (see Table 7.2). Where did the slaves go? Mortality rates account for part of the disparity, but the numbers of manumissions rose, and the free coloured population doubled during that time. Cuban planters repeated a practice common in particular in Brazil by discouraging female slave imports and

TABLE 7.2 Selected Population Figures, Cuba

Cuban Population 1774–1860

	Total	White	Percentage of Total	Slave	Percentage of Total	Free Coloured	Percentage of Total
1774	171,420	96,440	56	38,679	23	36,301	21
1827	704,487	311,051	44	286,942	41	106,494	15
1860	1,389,880	793,484	57	370,553	27	225,843	16

Adapted from Cohen and Greene, *Neither Slave nor Free*, 339.

slave marriages and the associated costs of feeding plantation children. The island had achieved a healthy balance of trade with Europe by the middle of the nineteenth century, and the belated slave and sugar boom meant that its investors benefitted from the efficiencies brought about by railways and steam-powered refining so that, by the 1840s, large parts of the island had new sugar operations. While free coloured peoples featured as small land owners, whites still sat at the top of a political, economic, and racial pecking order. A great many whites in Cuba were engaged in mixed farming, cattle ranching, and small cash crop operations. But power lay with the relatively small numbers of large-scale slaveholding whites. It made for a very narrow concentration of wealth and power in Cuba. By mid-century, the richest Cuban planters owned larger numbers of slaves on average than those in Brazil or the United States.[36]

After 1840, serious British naval interference began to affect the flow of slaves into the Spanish Caribbean and Brazil. Although the imperial government routinely ignored its treaties with Britain with respect to the slave trade, by the 1850s there was growing abolitionist sentiment in Spain. At the same time, there were rising colonial-metropolitan tensions involving small planters, independence advocates, abolitionists, and free coloured farmers with protests against taxes, privilege, and what appeared to be an over-intrusive state. Criticisms in Cuba also arose about the way Spain supported local elites and appointed government favourites to positions of influence. In 1868, the so-called Ten Years' War broke out. This was a politically driven civil war that ended with a badly damaged infrastructure of the smaller, older sugar plantation and mill complexes (*ingenios*). Wealth became even more concentrated in the western part of the island as many small landowners planted cane to sell to the ever more efficient and larger *ingenios*. But the future viability of slavery was now uncertain.

In 1870, during the Ten Years' War, Spain yielded to British and American pressures and passed the Moret Law. This was a major breakthrough that managed to satisfy the relatively small abolitionist movement in Spain. The law was based on a process of gradual emancipation and is remembered as the "free birth" law. All children of slaves born after 1870 were to be completely free at age 22, after being held in apprenticeship programs to that age. Compensation was paid by the state to slave owners, but as is often the way with compromise, none of the parties was completely satisfied.[37] Nevertheless, in 1880, a stricter version of the Moret Law was passed to hurry along the end of the institution. This allowed for an eight-year apprenticeship period for released slaves, and in 1886, with only 30,000 full-time slaves remaining, slavery formally ended in Cuba. Here again, in what was a common pattern throughout the Americas, freed slaves and the large free coloured populations were then dragged into dependent roles in the new class-ridden and racially laddered Cuba. As the century ended, investors from the United States began to buy into Cuba's agricultural economy. Spain's feeble hold on the island was strained even further, and it struggled to contain a broad-based liberation movement in the 1890s. The "instability" that followed encouraged US intervention. In 1898, the United States went to war with Spain, ending with the loss of Cuba and Puerto Rico. The great Spanish Empire in America was ended.

Brazil: Weaving along the Road to Abolition, 1822–1888

When Brazil achieved independence as a constitutional monarchy in 1822, the economic centre of gravity was firmly set in the south in the coffee growing regions of Sao Paulo and Rio de Janeiro. British efforts to quash the slave trade did not block the arrival in Brazil of new Africans, and a great boom in slave importation was underway. Half of all the slaves ever landed in Brazil came in the half-century between 1800 and 1850.[38] At the same time, rising numbers of free blacks, a growing mixed coloured population, shifting economic models, steam technology, more complex global markets, and a generation of Brazilian liberals who shared the ideals of international abolitionism made for a dynamic flux. Brazil's elites had installed themselves as the local political authorities by the 1820s and transferred their aggregate local powers into the new national government of 1822.

The Sao Paulo liberal intellectual, José Bonifacio (1763–1838), after three decades in Europe, returned to become the first prime minister of independent Brazil. In 1823, he issued a long and passionate proposal to the new Constituent Assembly calling for the gradual abolition of slavery. As he put it, "How can there exist a liberal and lasting Constitution in a country constantly inhabited by a huge multitude of brutalized and hostile slaves?"[39] The question sailed past the slaveholders who were bent on importing as many slaves as they could by defying the treaties Britain had made with Portugal. Shortly after Bonifacio's appeal, the Assembly passed Brazil's first Constitution and a bill of equal rights for all—except slaves and former slaves. Brazil's small, largely impotent white abolitionist movement was deflected by government and marginalized by a powerful proslavery faction. As in North America, antislavery talk gave rise to an active proslavery counter movement that reached deep into government. Bonifacio's speech was translated into several languages and published as an abolitionist treatise over the following 25 years while at the same time another million slaves were imported into Brazil. Britain's Aberdeen Act of 1845 authorized Royal Navy seizure of Brazilian slave ships, and, in 1850, under growing British diplomatic and naval pressure, Brazil formally and effectively banned the slave trade. Then, owing to the costs of a war with neighbouring Paraguay in the 1860s, Brazil became heavily indebted to Britain for loans, which added leverage to the British campaign against Brazilian slavery.[40]

In the decades before the end of slavery, slave defiance was continued in the steady pattern of running away and the communities that arose from it, the *quilombo*. By the early nineteenth century, slave resistance was often political, ideological, and collectivist. In one remarkable revolt in 1805–06, a large component of a 300-slave *engenho* in Bahia ran off to the forests, without any violence. Then, in response to the master's call for an end to their actions, the slaves' leadership sent in a list of demands for a negotiated amelioration of their working conditions. This was an extraordinarily telling event. The flamboyant tone of the demands included such things as having "Friday and Saturday to work for ourselves" to allow slaves to sell and transport their surpluses, as well as limiting the amount of manioc they were to plant and reducing "the daily quota of sugar cane." The bold tone noted that the "present overseers we do not want, [you will] choose others with our approval." As to the sugar fields and the mill, the resisters were specific in their grasp of the sugar producing process:

> We will go to work the cane field of Jabiru this time and then it must remain a pasture for we cannot cut cane in a swamp.... At the milling rollers there must be four women to feed in the cane, two pulleys and a [woman to sweep up and do other chores].... At each cauldron there must be one who tends the fire and in each series of kettles the same, and on Saturday ... work stoppage at the mill.

Then the rebels finish with a flourish:

> We shall be able to plant our rice wherever we wish, and in any marsh, without asking permission for this, and each person [slave] can cut jacaranda or any other wood without having to account for this. Accepting all the above articles and allowing us to remain always in possession of the hardware, we are ready to serve you as before because we do not want to continue the bad customs of the other *engenhos*. We shall be able to play, relax, and sing any time we wish without your hindrance nor will permission be needed.[41]

This is negotiated slavery of a kind that does not appear anywhere else in the documented history of slavery in Brazil, and we cannot say it was common. We also lack similar slave inspired material for the times before the nineteenth century, so we have no way of seeing slaves' outlook in a longer historical pattern. But the tone of this group's preference for accommodated servitude rather than the perils of being hunted down or enduring the strain of *quilombo* life perhaps says something about the hardships of life in Brazil beyond the institution. And, equally important, the writer describes the *engenho* from the slaves' perspective. It is a teasing bit of evidence, reminding us of the way white workers negotiated their working conditions in industrial societies. The tone of reason in the slaves' appeal (or demands) stands in contrast to what existed for most slave resisters, the resort to violence by slaves and masters. Yet slaves did push for freedom in a rising tide of organized conspiracies and revolts. Prime Minister Bonifacio's remark about "hostile slaves" was on the mark, and several serious uprisings, in rural and urban settings, from north to south, occurred in the first few decades of the century.

While none of these was of the scale, scope, or duration of the Haitian Revolution, they confirmed the racial and status tensions in the nation. Most threats were aborted as conspiracies were uncovered and quashed. This included the most serious slave uprising of the period, indeed in Brazil's history, the Muslim-led revolt in Bahia in 1835 (known as the *Male* revolt after the Yoruba word for Muslim). The plot was uncovered, but the rebels launched their campaign anyway and caused a great panic in the city of Salvador da Bahia before it was eventually crushed. Its full potential was not lost on the authorities who noted the fusion of several religious groups among the rebels, presumably inspired and led by literate and influential African Muslims. Even more than 30 years after the Haitian Revolution, some of the participants in the riots wore Haitian decorations. The scale of the uprising was not especially great, but the cultural, ideological, and symbolic trappings of the leadership were serious enough to frighten authorities. Four leaders were executed and dozens were jailed or flogged. Some of the floggings were levied in the hundreds of lashings and meted out in regular doses over several weeks, invariably with the prospect of a fatal end. Many participants were also deported to Portuguese outposts in Africa.[42] As in all slave uprisings everywhere in the Americas, the Bahia episode was answered by the theatre of public executions and then by the inevitable draconian tightening of laws, curfews, and restrictions on move-ment and behaviour. There were no major uprisings in Brazil after 1835. Yet the nation's problems were visible everywhere, not only in the continuance of slavery but in the conditions of the rural coloured peasantry living in environments that were often violent and impoverished. Crime haunted many slave and free coloured communities whether in the streets of Rio or in the coffee or sugar fields of Sao Paulo or Bahia.

Finally, in 1871, Brazil enacted the Rio Branco Law, the so-called law of the free womb, similar to Cuba's, in which all children born to slaves after that date were born free—but with conditions attached. By the early 1880s, many local authorities banned slavery outright, and in 1888 all slavery was ended in Brazil without compensation. By then 700,000 slaves remained in bondage. This had dropped from the 1872 census figure of 1.5 million. But the final emancipation released a significant population of free labour into what was now an open economy. They joined the slaves who had already begun to leave their masters in droves. They returned to work for pay in the coffee and other agricultural industries, if they returned at all. Slaves had taken part in the final chipping away of slavery to join the mass of free coloured in the rural stretches and cities of Brazil.

The outlines of post-emancipation Brazil were already taking shape long before abolition was completed. The Brazilian census of 1872 listed a popu-lation of 9.9 million including 1.5 million slaves. The free mixed coloured population stood at 43 per cent of the whole and included a large *caboclo* (white-native) population. The steadily rising white population comprised 42 per cent of the whole. After that the volume of white immigration to Brazil soared and included hundreds of thousands of Italians, many of them migrant farm workers destined for the coffee plantations formerly worked by slaves. Brazil's post-abolition working classes also included smaller numbers of South and East Asians who joined the masses of poor southern European immigrants and the existing and newly freed peoples of African ancestry.

Brazil was declared a republic in 1889, and the 1891 Constitution included a citizenship clause that trumpeted the country's racial democracy.

That nominal corrective to centuries of graduated racialized class structures did not change the ranking or conditions of Brazil's castes and classes, nor did freedom blunt racist attitudes and behaviour. There was not a Brazilian version of the US Jim Crow "rule of descent" nor of its constitutional segregation, but race mattered in economic, political, and social relations. In response, coloured men formed "brotherhoods" that helped promote and support some entrepreneurship, and many individuals succeeded in moving into the ranks of the emerging middle classes. Abolition did not, however, change Brazil's political or economic structure; power continued to lie with whites at most levels. The majority of former slaves became sharecroppers or wage labourers and subject to a graduated, preferential hierarchy of light to dark colouration in Brazil's institutional and social structures. In the nation's fields, villages, mines, or cities, freed slaves were now subject to the prejudices that had defined Brazil's free coloured population over many generations.[43]

All over the Americas, freed slaves were assigned particular status and roles, by practice everywhere and in law in the United States. Slavery created classes and castes of coloured peoples in Brazil. When slavery ended in the protracted, episodic way it did, most African slaves and their descendants carried their colour into the legal freedom of the late nineteenth century; freedom did not remove the liability of the rule of descent. That was as true in Brazil as it was in the United States, the Caribbean, and in any part of Spanish America that was shaped by slavery.

Notes

1 Davis, *Problem of Slavery*. This is an eloquent and comprehensive treatment of the struggle to end slavery and the institutional, cultural, and economic obstacles to abolition in the British and US systems. For a recent comment on abolition in Cuba and Brazil, see Bergad, *Comparative Histories*, Chapter 8.

2 Davis, *Problem of Slavery*; Bergad, *Comparative Histories*.

3 Dabydeen et al., *The Oxford Companion to Black British History*, 457–58.

4 Davis, *Inhuman Bondage*, Chapter 12.

5 On Raynal see Davis, *Inhuman Bondage*, 47 (n. 55); on Sharp, see Dabydeen et al., *The Oxford Companion to Black British History*, 440 and Davis, *Inhuman Bondage*, Chapter 12. See also John Woolman, *Some Considerations on the Keeping of Negroes* (1754). For Pastorius, see *American National Biography* (New York: Oxford University Press, 1999–2002).

6 See "Negro Petitions for Freedom" cited in Cynthia Kierner, *Revolutionary America, 1750–1815, Sources and Interpretation* (Upper Saddle River: Prentice Hall, 2000), 221–23.

7 David W. Cohen and Jack P. Greene, eds., *Neither Slave Nor Free* (Baltimore: Johns Hopkins, 1972), 339 (table).

8 Klein, *The Atlantic Slave Trade*, 184–87 is a good starting point. See the relevant chapters in Robin Blackburn, *The Overthrow of Colonial Slavery, 1776–1848* (London: Verso,

1988) and Davis, *The Problem of Slavery*. Aguet's *La Traite Des Nègres* is a collection of graphic images of the trade.

9 Dabydeen *et al.*, *The Oxford Companion to Black British History*, 534–35.

10 Morgan, *American Slavery, American Freedom*, Book IV. This original approach offers a convincing analysis of the way the absence of freedom in slaves contributed to the ideology of freedom in slaveholders.

11 Leon F. Litwack, *Been in the Storm So Long: The Aftermath of Slavery* (New York: Knopf, 1979); C. Vann Woodward, *The Strange Career of Jim Crow*, 3rd rev. ed. (New York: Oxford University Press, 1974 [1955]).

12 On Whitney and his "gin," see http://www.history.com/topics/cotton-gin-and-eli-whitney; for a brief review of growth and consolidation, see Peter Kolchin, *American Slavery, 1607–1877*, rev. ed. (New York: Hill and Wang, 2003), Chapter 4. See also Finkelman, *Slavery and the Founders*.

13 William Freehling, *The Road to Disunion*, Volumes 1 and 2 (Oxford: Oxford University Press, 1990 and 2007) is the most comprehensive recent treatment of the sectional crisis.

14 Freehling, *The Road to Disunion*.

15 The principle of "popular sovereignty" was a way to let settlers in any territory applying for statehood to be free to decide by majority for or against legalized slavery. See also Paul Finkelman, *Dred Scott v. Sandford: A Brief History with Documents* (Boston: Bedford/St. Martin's, 1997).

16 Fogel, *The Slavery Debates*, is a welcome discussion on the economics of slavery. See also the essays by Elizabeth B. Field Hendrey and Lee A. Craig, and James R. Irvin in Eltis, *et al.*, *Slavery in the Development of the Americas*, 236–87.

17 See the debate for August 21, 1858 in Rodney O. Davis and Douglas L. Wilson, eds., *The Lincoln-Douglas Debates* (Urbana: University of Illinois Press, 2008).

18 Kolchin, *American Slavery*, 155ff and the bibliographical review, 295–98.

19 Kolchin, *American Slavery*, 185. On Chapman, see Alice Taylor, "Fashion Has Extended Her Influence to the Cause of Humanity: The Transatlantic Female Economy of the Boston Antislavery Bazaar," in Beverly Lemire, ed., *The Force of Fashion in Politics and Society* (Aldershot: Ashgate, 2010), 115–42; on the Grimkes, see Kathryn Kish Sklar, *Women's Rights Emerges within the Antislavery Movement, 1830–1870* (Boston: Bedford/St. Martin's, 2000). See also Julie Roy Jeffrey, *The Great Silent Army of Abolitionism: Women in the Anti-Slavery Movement* (Chapel Hill: University of North Carolina Press, 1998).

20 Kolchin, *American Slavery*, 199.

21 Sharecropping was a system of leasing a plot of land in which the lessee paid for the use of the land by "sharing" the crop with the landowner. Many poor white farmers also sharecropped. The system required a family unit in most cases and in many cases an extended family. See Kolchin, *American Slavery*, 217–20 and Leon Litwack, *Trouble in Mind: Black Southerners in the Age of Jim Crow* (New York: Knopf, 1998), Chapter 3.

22 Comprehensive treatments of the post-Civil War problems of southern blacks are Litwack, *Been in the Storm So Long* and the same author's *Trouble in Mind*. See especially the chapter "Hellhounds" in the latter. For an accessible review and commentary on the Plessy case, see Brook Thomas, *Plessy versus Ferguson: A Brief History with Documents* (Boston: Bedford/St. Martin's, 1997).

23 From the majority decision of the United States Supreme Court in *Plessy versus Ferguson*, 1896.

24 Jacqeline Jones Royster, ed., *Southern Horrors and Other Writings: The Anti-Lynching Campaign of Ida B. Wells, 1892–1900* (Boston: Bedford/St. Martin's, 1997); Orlando Patterson, *Rituals of Blood: Consequences of Slavery in Two American Centuries* (Washington, DC:

Civitas/Counterpoint, 1998), especially Chapter 2; *Historical Statistics of the United States, Colonial Times to the Present* (Washington, DC: US Bureau of the Census, 1975), 422.

25 Thomas, *Plessy versus Ferguson.*

26 See David W. Blight, *Race and Reunion: The Civil War in American Memory* (Cambridge, MA: Belknap/Harvard, 2001) and the references in Davis, *Inhuman Bondage*, 305–06.

27 Albert Valdman, "Creole, the Language of Slavery," in Doris Y. Kadish, ed., *Slavery in the Caribbean Francophone World: Distant Voices, Forgotten Acts, Forged Identities*, 2nd ed. (Bloomington: Indiana University Press, 2011), 143–163.

28 David Geggus and Norman Fiering, eds., *The World of the Haitian Revolution* (Bloomington: Indiana University Press, 2009) offers a comprehensive set of essays on the Haitian Revolution.

29 Knight, *The Caribbean*, 184 and 370 (table).

30 On the controversial thesis that economic factors brought down British slavery in the Caribbean, see Williams, *Capitalism and Slavery*; Fogel, *Slavery Debates*; Davis, *Inhuman Bondage*, 241–49. The questions raised by Seymour Drescher, *Capitalism and Anti-Slavery: British Mobilization in Comparative Perspective* (Oxford: Oxford University Press, 1987) continues to attract scholars to the issue. The same author continues to publish significant studies on that and related issues. See the Bibliography below. See also Knight, *The Caribbean*, Chapter 6.

31 Seymour Drescher, *Econocide: British Slavery in the Age of Abolition*, 2nd ed. (Cambridge: Cambridge University Press, 2010).

32 Jay Kinsbruner, *Independence in Spanish America: Civil Wars, Revolutions and Underdevelopment* (Albuquerque: University of New Mexico Press, 2000); Bakewell, *A History of Latin America*, Chapter 14.

33 Frederick Bowser, "Colonial Spanish America," in Cohen and Greene, *Neither Slave Nor Free*, 19–58.

34 Matt D. Childs, *The 1812 Aponte Rebellion in Cuba and the Struggle against Atlantic Slavery* (Chapel Hill: University of North Carolina Press, 2006). See the brief note on other hemispheric revolts in his conclusion.

35 Cohen and Greene, *Neither Slave Nor Free*, 339.

36 Klein and Vinson, *Slavery in Latin America and the Caribbean*, 92ff.

37 Klein and Vinson, *Slavery in Latin America and the Caribbean*, 234.

38 Eltis and Richardson, *Atlas*, Table 6.

39 Conrad, *Children of God's Fire*, 418–19.

40 Fausto, *A Concise History of Brazil*, 120–26.

41 Stuart Schwartz, "Resistance and Accommodation in Eighteenth Century Brazil: The Slaves' View of Slavery," *Hispanic American Historical Review* 57 (1977), 69–81, cited in Conrad, *Children of God's Fire*, 397–406. See the contemporary notes on *engenho* slaves in Schwartz, *Early Brazil*, 224–28.

42 See Schwartz, *Sugar Plantations*, 472–88 for a commentary on the context of the revolts.

43 Russell-Wood, *Slavery and Freedom*, Chapter 10; Klein and Luna, *Children of God's Fire*, 319 and Chapters 9 and 10.

8 | Conclusion

Before Columbus set sail to the west, the Iberians had been trading with Africans for African slaves for decades, and the models for African slavery in the New World were already being practised in Iberia, the Azores, Madeira, and other Atlantic islands. The legal and moral principles that defined the slave by race were in place well before the 1490s. By the time slavery was ended in the Americas in the late nineteenth century, it had been adopted by every Western European colonizing nation from Portugal to Sweden. Slavery as an institution took varied forms over three centuries as it helped shape the colonies and later independent nations of Portuguese Brazil, Spanish America, North America, and the French, British, and Dutch Caribbean.

No part of the Americas was spared the European onslaught in the sixteenth to nineteenth centuries, and few regions were completely unaffected by African slavery. It was present in places such as New England and the adjacent northern colonies and states but did not define those places as "slave societies." Likewise, it was present in most of the mainland Spanish Empire although it was not a major factor in shaping the histories of Argentina or Mexico, for example. We have identified those places as "slaveholding societies" to distinguish them from Brazil's northeast, Mississippi, and Haiti, to name only a few of the fully developed "slave societies." Where slavery mattered most as a social, economic, and political determinant was in tropical and subtropical America. Thus, the few slaves on Boston's or Philadelphia's docks did not shape the societies around them, except to say that the vast white majorities in those places accepted the racial determinant in slavery, even if the true slave societies existed only in neighbouring states. Yet slavery became a politically divisive issue in the United States and was a catalyst that drew the northern population into a civil war with their southern neighbours and countrymen. Slavery's place in the history of the United States is an indelible one. Slavery's role in every other colonial and national history in the Americas is tangible even if it is not as dramatic or bloody as the American Civil War or the great black war of independence in Haiti.

In the wake of Columbus, slavery created hierarchies of wealth and politics and classes and castes unique to the Americas. Africans and Europeans and their progenies erased most of the pre-Columbian social and cultural and even physical landscapes as millions arrived and reproduced in the Americas and as millions of American natives disappeared. The nature and scale of the transportation of millions of slaves—that is, the slave trade— remains one of history's great exercises in cruelty and shame. At the same time, it created wealth for an international class of merchants, intermediaries, insurers, and shipping interests. The great Atlantic commodities economy that slavery sustained provided capital for Europe's industrial and market expansion in the eighteenth and nineteenth centuries.

Sugar was the engine that sustained the colonial slave societies in Brazil and the Caribbean, but eventually every cash crop from tobacco to cocoa and coffee to cotton consolidated the slave economies in the tropics and subtropics. In colonial British North America and its successor, the United States, tobacco and rice gave way by the nineteenth century to cotton. In Brazil and Spanish America, slaves provided urban labour and crafts and worked in commercial cattle ranching and in mines and aboard ships. Slave women worked the fields, tended the households, wet nursed white babies, and helped sustain families.

The range and variety of slave systems and conditions is too great to reduce to a few consistencies. But some important factors were common to all jurisdictions at all times. All slaves in all slave systems were defined as legal, permanent property; they were human property under laws that were enforced by governments and force of arms. Even in the more fluid Latin American systems where slave owners had more freedom of disposal of their human property than was the case in the British and French systems, the state guaranteed that right of disposal and determined in law the slave's inferior status. A second common condition in New World slavery was that the slave was explicitly African or of African descent. Native slavery did exist in some places at various times, especially in the early phases of settlement, but it was not a significant variation on the African model. Racial attitudes and codes did keep a minority of native slaves in bondage in various systems such as the mining industries in Spanish America. A third common variation was that bondage was surely a bitter experience for all slaves, at all times, in all places and circumstances. As demoralizing and physically wearing as it was, it was resisted by slaves who for the most part rejected their lot as just and denied the inevitability of it. They forged positive identities individually, in families and in kinship groups, thus creating a cultural solidarity and in doing so shaped more than the economies and politics of the New World. African and Afro-Brazilian or Caribbean or African American cultural innovations were decisive to the shaping of Euro-American societies.

In Brazil, slavery was marked by a gradual spread from the early northeast sugar economy to where it intruded into and shaped every other economic activity in the colony (the nation after 1822). In all of Latin America, the law allowed for high rates of manumission which, when tied to high rates of miscegenation, created wide-ranging racial shadings to create one of modern Brazil's most conspicuous demographic distinctions. Manumission rates created a constant flow of freed blacks into the community, and that meant that African slaves were constantly being imported to meet Brazil's labour demands. Indeed, although Brazil was the largest single importer of African slaves, its free mixed coloured populace passed the slave population in numbers by the first quarter of the nineteenth century. The fluid character of Brazil's slave system led to a consistently large African-born slave population, a complex mixed race peasantry, and a white economic, political, administrative, and professional community. Three hundred years of slavery left Brazil with layers of racially nuanced castes and classes that had persisted to and then continued beyond the full abolition of slavery in 1888.

Sugar and slavery drove the development of the Caribbean island colonies, always augmented by other tropical crops in a medley of European colonies and languages. Close to half of all the Africans sent to the Americas went to the Caribbean, so that now the Anglo-French Caribbean, from Haiti to Trinidad, is the most Afro-centric area in the world outside Africa. When slavery ended in the Caribbean, it did so not only in the violence of the black Haitian Revolution of 1804 but also in the orderly, legal processes of 1834 in the British slave colonies. But slavery still boomed to the 1850s and then lingered to the 1880s in Spanish Cuba and Puerto Rico. What makes the French, British, and Dutch Caribbean unique is the way tiny white minorities oversaw a near total black population in most of the Lesser Antilles. The Spanish Greater Antilles were an exception because the Spanish, like the Portuguese, offered accessible means to manumission, which encouraged the growth of a significant free coloured population. In sharp contrast to the absence of free white immigration to the French, British, and Dutch islands, white Spanish immigration to the Greater Antilles was significant throughout the eighteenth and nineteenth century.

When the United States was formed from the British North American colonies as an independent republic, it inherited and maintained the most legally restrictive slave codes and practices in the Americas. The colonies and their successors, the southern states, discouraged manumission and allowed only a negligible number of freed slaves. Being black meant being in bondage. Slavery in the United States was distinguished very dramatically in the way slave states and slave-free states sat next to each other, each section with serious and differing political ideas on how the nation should develop. The sectional impact on the United States was without parallel in Brazil or the Caribbean. Another distinction was in the phenomenal natural increase of the slave population in the United States. To put that statistical note in perspective, during the history of the slave trade, the British mainland colonies and the independent United States imported some 400,000 African slaves in total. In 1860, the number of slaves of African descent in the United States was 4,000,000. By contrast, Brazil imported some 4.8 million slaves over the course of the trade. In 1872, there were 5.7 million people of African descent including 1.5 million slaves in Brazil. The coloured population of the United States increased tenfold from its source, and the overwhelming majority of it was enslaved; the Brazilian coloured population rose by only about 20 per cent even as it became the majority. Also, up to 1861 when the Civil War broke down the sectional balance, the scale and territorial range of slavery was growing in the United States while it was beginning to level off or decline in Brazil and the Spanish Caribbean.

Ending slavery in the Americas took close to a century to complete, from the agitation of Wilberforce's generation to the final chapters in Cuba and Brazil. The difficulty in eradicating the enterprise lay in its deeply embedded economic, social, and political roots in New World societies. It ended in different ways in different places because African slavery was never a single American phenomenon. Moral pressure helped bring it down, often resisted by racist and economic interests. It was not ended because of slaveholder epiphanies of guilt or conscience. Rather, it took violence in some cases and attacks on entrenched ideas of human rights in an age of "progressive" reforms. The end of this long epoch of sorrow and pain for millions did not and could not end the racist and caste values that were developed during its existence.

Abolition came about in episodic fashion in Brazil, Cuba, and the French and Dutch systems. It was more direct and immediate in the British Caribbean. It was ended in spectacular violence in Saint Domingue by the slaves themselves and in the United States after the bloodiest war in its history. The transition from slavery to freedom created rural, largely impoverished peasantries in the areas of the Americas where slavery had flourished. Capital investment and industrial and urban development were slow in coming to those areas, if they came at all. The great waves of European migration to the Americas in the late nineteenth and early twentieth century went to the northern United States, southern Brazil, Argentina, Chile, and Canada but not to Bahia, Haiti, Jamaica, or Mississippi. In the United States, the social, cultural, and economic differences between Pennsylvania and Mississippi were probably more striking than any regional contrast in any other jurisdiction. At the same time, Haiti, as well as having a population uniformly of African descent was on its way to being the poorest place in the Western Hemisphere. In the British and French West Indies, the black and mixed coloured majorities had settled at about 90 per cent on most islands and, although liberated, failed to make any political gains in the short term. As it did in the places where slavery stamped its imprint throughout the Americas, the Caribbean's subsequent history has seen the descendants of slavery struggle for what should be their rightful place in the societies they helped create. The imprint remains everywhere and far beyond the racial demographics that remain. It has defined the national character of every former slave society in the Americas.

Select Bibliography

The most accessible brief surveys of the history of African slavery in the Americas are Kolchin, *American Slavery* for North America and Klein and Vinson, *African Slavery in Latin America and the Caribbean*. The most comprehensive comparative studies dealing with the Atlantic and New World systems can be found in the work of Robin Blackburn, Laird Bergad, and David Brion Davis. Blackburn's trilogy covers the themes and chronologies of the present book in nearly 1,500 pages. Given the enormous volume of research articles, critiques, reviews, and monographs, the bibliographies compiled by J.C. Miller are invaluable. His entries number roughly 14,000 titles dealing with slavery.

On the slave trade, the work of David Eltis and his collaborators has now become the benchmark for reference. See his *Atlas* (with David Richardson) and the database at http://www.slavevoyages.org/tast/index.faces; James Walvin's *Atlas*; and the compact, up-to-date survey by Herbert Klein, *The Atlantic Slave Trade*. Every historian of the slave trade owes a debt to Philip Curtin's *The Atlantic Slave Trade: A Census*. Gunnar Myrdal's *An American Dilemma* is a landmark multi-volume study that inspired a public and academic upsurge in race relations in the United States; so, too, did Woodward's *The Strange Career of Jim Crow*.

Very useful sources for the latest scholarship are various anthologies: Eltis and Engerman; Eltis, Lewis, and Sokoloff; Inkori and Engerman; Heuman and Walvin; Heuman and Burnard; Paquette and Smith; and Knight. These volumes collectively run to dozens of research essays on the most recent scholarship. Robert Conrad's *Children of God's Fire*, a collection of documents translated from Portuguese to English, is invaluable. See also Stuart Schwartz's edited and translated documents in *Early Brazil*. Accessible document collections for the slave trade are in Elizabeth Donnan's chronologically organized four-volume set. See also the Federal Writers Project oral histories (see the reference to Rawick in the bibliography). A dated but still useful collection of some 400 research articles is Paul Finkelman, ed., *Articles on American Slavery*. For surveys that provide historical context for the subject see the references to Bakewell and also Lockhart and Schwartz for Latin America, Knight for the Caribbean, and Eric Foner for colonial North America and the United States. *Slavery*, edited by Engerman, Drescher, and Paquette, contains 186 short excerpts, articles, and documents on the subject.

The recent works that have informed the themes in this book are those of Robin Blackburn, David Brion Davis, Herbert Klein, Stuart Schwartz, and the specialized studies by the contributors to the anthologies listed above. The references throughout to Gilberto Freyre, Eugene Genovese, Winthrop Jordan, Katia Mattoso, Orlando Patterson, Herbert Aptheker—still the best introduction to the subject and an important historiographical influence—and Frank Tannenbaum reflect the ongoing value of older seminal studies of slavery. All materials consulted were published in English or translated into English. The references that follow contain extensive bibliographies in various languages.

Abbott, Elizabeth. *Sugar, A Bittersweet History*. Toronto: Penguin, 2008.

Aguet, Isabelle. *La Traite Des Nègres*. Geneva: Editions Minerva, 1971.

Aljoe, Nicole N. *Creole Testimonies: Slave Narratives from the British West Indies, 1709–1838*. New York: Palgrave Macmillan, 2012.

Aptheker, Herbert. *American Negro Slave Revolts*. New York: International Publishers, 1974 [1943].

Baines, Dudley. *Emigration from Europe, 1815–1930*. Cambridge: Cambridge University Press, 1995.

Bakewell, Peter. *A History of Latin America*. 2nd ed. Malden: Blackwell, 2004.

Barraclough, Geoffrey, ed. *The Times Atlas of World History*. Rev. ed. London: Times Books, 1984.

Beckles, Hilary McD. *White Servitude and Black Slavery in Barbados, 1627–1715*. Knoxville: University of Tennessee Press, 1989.

Bergad, Laird. *Comparative Histories of Slavery in Brazil, Cuba and the United States*. Cambridge: Cambridge University Press, 2007.

Berlin, Ira. *Many Thousands Gone: The First Two Centuries of Slavery in North America*. Cambridge, MA: Belknap, 1998.

Berlin, Ira and Philip D. Morgan. *Cultivation and Culture: Labor and the Shaping of Slave Life in the Americas*. Charlottesville: University Press of Virginia, 1993.

Bethel, Leslie, ed. *Cambridge History of Latin America*. Vol. I and II. Cambridge: Cambridge University Press, 1984.

Binder, Wolfgang, ed. *Slavery in the Americas*. Wurzburg, Germany: Konigshausen, 1993.

Blackburn, Robin. *The American Crucible: Slavery, Emancipation and Human Rights*. London: Verso, 2011.

Blackburn, Robin. *The Making of New World Slavery: From the Baroque to the Modern, 1492–1800*. London: Verso, 1997.

Blackburn, Robin. *The Overthrow of Colonial Slavery, 1776–1848*. London: Verso, 1988.

Blassingame, John W. *The Slave Community: Plantation Life in the Antebellum South, Revised and Enlarged Edition*. New York: Oxford University Press, 1979.

Blesser, Carol. *In Joy and Sorrow: Women, Family and Marriage in the Victorian South, 1830–1900*. New York: Oxford University Press, 1991.

Blesser, Carol, ed. *Secret and Sacred: The Diaries of James Henry Hammond, a Southern Slaveholder*. New York: Oxford University Press, 1988.

Bowser, Frederick P. "The African in Colonial Spanish America: Reflections on Research Achievements and Priorities." *Latin American Research Review* 7 (1972): 77–94.

Blight, David W. *Race and Reunion: The Civil War in American Memory*. Cambridge, MA: Belknap/Harvard, 2001.

Burkholder, Mark A. and Lyman L. Johnson. *Colonial Latin America*. 3rd ed. New York: Oxford University Press, 1998.

Bush, Barbara. *Slave Women in Caribbean Society, 1650–1838*. Bloomington: Indiana University Press, 1990.

Bush, M.L. *Servitude in Modern Times*. Malden: Blackwell, 2000.

Bush, M.L., ed. *Serfdom and Slavery: Studies in Legal Bondage*. London: Longman, 1996.

Camp, Stephanie M.H. *Closer to Freedom: Enslaved Women and Everyday Resistance in the Plantation South*. Chapel Hill: University of North Carolina Press, 2004.

Canny, Nicholas, ed. *Europeans on the Move: Studies on European Migration, 1500–1800*. Oxford: Oxford University Press, 1994.

Carney, Judith A. and Richard Nicholas Rosomoff. *In the Shadow of Slavery: Africa's Botanical Legacy in the Atlantic World*. Berkeley: University of California Press, 2009.

Cevallos-Candau, Francisco *et al.*, eds. *Coded Encounters: Writing, Gender and Ethnicity in Colonial Latin America*. Amherst: University of Massachusetts Press, 1994.

Childs, Matt D. *The 1812 Aponte Rebellion in Cuba and the Struggle against Atlantic Slavery*. Chapel Hill: University of North Carolina Press, 2006.

Christopher, Emma. *Slave Ship Sailors and their Captive Cargoes, 1730–1807*. New York: Cambridge University Press, 2006.

Cleary, David, "Race, Nationalism and Social Theory in Brazil: Rethinking Gilberto Freyre." Cambridge, MA: Harvard University Center for Latin America Studies, n.d.

Cohen, David W. and Jack P. Greene, eds. *Neither Slave Nor Free*. Baltimore: Johns Hopkins, 1972.

Collier, Simon, Harold Blakemore and Thomas E. Skidmore, eds. *The Cambridge Encyclopedia of Latin America and the Caribbean*. Cambridge: Cambridge University Press, 1985.

Conrad, Robert. *Children of God's Fire: A Documentary History of Black Slavery in Brazil*. University Park: Pennsylvania State University Press, 1994.

Costanzo, Angelo, ed. *The Interesting Narrative of the Life of Olaudah Equinao, or Gustavas Vassa, the African, Written by Himself*. Peterborough, ON: Broadview Press, 2004.

Countryman, Edward, ed. *How Did American Slavery Begin?* Boston: Bedford/ St. Martin's, 1999.

Craton, Michael, James Walvin and David Wright. *Slavery, Abolition and Emancipation: Black Slaves and the British Empire*. London: Longman, 1976.

Crosby, Alfred. *Ecological Imperialism: The Biological Expansion of Europe, 900–1900*. 2nd ed. Cambridge: Cambridge University Press, 2004.

Curtin, Philip. *The Atlantic Slave Trade: A Census*. Madison: University of Wisconsin Press, 1969.

Curto, Jose C. and Paul E. Lovejoy, eds. *Enslaving Connections: Changing Cultures of Africa and Brazil During the Era of Slavery*. Amherst: Humanity Books, 2004.

Dabydeen, David, John Gilmore and Cecily Jones, eds. *The Oxford Companion to Black British History*. Oxford: Oxford University Press, 2007.

Davis, David Brion. *Inhuman Bondage: The Rise and Fall of Slavery in the New World*. New York: Oxford University Press, 2006.

Davis, David Brion. *The Problem of Slavery in the Age of Revolutions: 1770–1823*. Ithaca: Cornell University Press, 1975.

Davis, David Brion. *The Problem of Slavery in Western Culture*. Ithaca: Cornell University Press, 1966.

Davis, Ralph. *The Rise of the Atlantic Economies*. Ithaca: Cornell University Press, 1973.

Deerr, Noel, *The History of Sugar*. 2 vols. London: Chapman and Hall, 1949–50.

Denevan, William M. *The Native Population of the Americas in 1492*. 2nd ed. Madison: University of Wisconsin Press, 1992.

Donnan, Elizabeth. *Documents Illustrative of the History of the Slave Trade to America*. 4 vols. New York: Octagon Books, 1965 [1930–35].

Drescher, Seymour. *Econocide: British Slavery in the Age of Abolition*. 2nd ed. Chapel Hill: University of North Carolina Press, 2010.

Drescher, Seymour. *Abolition: A History of Slavery and Antislavery*. Cambridge: Cambridge University Press, 2009.

Drescher, Seymour. *Capitalism and AntiSlavery: British Mobilization in Comparative Perspective*. Oxford: Oxford University Press, 1987.

Du Bois, W.E.B. *The Souls of Black Folk*. Oxford: Oxford University Press, 2007 [1903].

Dunn, Richard S. *Sugar and Slaves: The Rise of the Planter Class in the English West Indies, 1624–1713*. Chapel Hill: University of North Carolina Press, 1972.

Elkins, Stanley M. *Slavery: A Problem in American Institutional and Intellectual Life*. 3rd rev. ed. Chicago: University of Chicago Press, 1976 [1959].

Elliott, J.H. *Empires of the Atlantic World: Britain and Spain in America, 1492–1830*. New Haven: Yale University Press, 2007.

Elliott, J.H. *Do the Americas Have a Common History?* Providence, RI: John Carter Brown Library, 1998.

Eltis, David and David Richardson. *Atlas of the Transatlantic Slave Trade*. New Haven: Yale University Press, 2010.

Eltis, David and Stanley L. Engerman, eds. *The Cambridge World History of Slavery*. Vol. 3. New York: Cambridge University Press, 2011. http://dx.doi.org/10.1017/CHOL9780521840682

Eltis, David, Frank D. Lewis and Kenneth L. Sokoloff, eds. *Slavery in the Development of the Americas*. Cambridge: Cambridge University Press, 2004. http://dx.doi.org/10.1017/CBO9780511512124

Engerman, Stanley, ed. *Terms of Labor: Slavery, Serfdom and Free Labor*. Stanford: Stanford University Press, 1999.

Engerman, Stanley, Seymour Drescher and Robert Paquette, eds. *Slavery*. Oxford: Oxford University Press, 2001.

Fausto, Boris. *A Concise History of Brazil*. New York: Cambridge University Press, 1999.

Ferguson, Moira, ed. *The History of Mary Prince: A West Indian Slave, related by Herself*. Rev. ed. Ann Arbor: University of Michigan Press, 1997.

Finkelman, Paul, ed. *Women and the Family in a Slave Society*. New York: Garland, 1989.

Finley, M.I., ed. *Classical Slavery*. London: Frank Cass, 1987.

Fogel, Robert W. *The Slavery Debates, 1952–1990*. Baton Rouge: Louisiana State University, 2003.

Fogel, Robert W. *Without Consent or Contract: The Rise and Fall of American Slavery*. New York: Norton, 1989.

Fogel, Robert W. and Stanley L. Engerman. *Time on the Cross*. Boston: Little Brown, 1974.

Foner, Eric. *Give Me Liberty: An American History*. New York: Norton, 2012.

Foner, Laura and Eugene Genovese, eds. *Slavery in the New World: A Reader in Comparative History*. Englewood Cliffs: Prentice-Hall, 1969.

Fredrickson, George M. *The Comparative Imagination: On the History of Racism, Nationalism and Social Movements*. Berkeley: University of California Press, 1997.

Freehling, William W. "The Founding Fathers and Slavery." *American Historical Review* 77, 1 (1972): 81–93. http://dx.doi.org/10.2307/1856595

Freyre, Gilberto. *The Masters and the Slaves: A Study in the Development of Brazilian Civilization*. New York: Knopf, 1946 [1933].

Genovese, Eugene. *Roll, Jordan, Roll: The World the Slaves Made*. New York: Random House, 1974.

Gould, Stephen Jay. *The Mismeasure of Man, Revised and Expanded Edition*. New York: Norton, 1996.

Gray, Lewis C. *History of Agriculture in the Southern United States to 1860*. Washington, DC: Carnegie Institute, 1933.

Greene, Jack P. and Philip D. Morgan, eds. *Atlantic History: A Critical Appraisal*. New York: Oxford University Press, 2009.

Hall, Gwendolyn Midlo. *Slavery and African Ethnicities in the Americas: Restoring the Links*. Chapel Hill: University of North Carolina Press, 2005.

Hannaford, Ivan. *Race: The History of an Idea in the West*. Baltimore: Johns Hopkins University Press for the Woodrow Wilson Center Press, 1996.

Harris, Marvin. *Patterns of Race in the Americas*. New York: Walker and Co., 1964.

Hawthorne, Walter. *From Africa to Brazil: Culture, Identity, and an Atlantic Slave Trade, 1600–1830*. New York: Cambridge University Press, 2010.

Heuman, Gad and Trevor Burnard, eds. *The Routledge History of Slavery*. New York: Routledge, 2011.

Heuman, Gad and James Walvin, eds. *The Slavery Reader*. London: Routledge, 2003.

Hine, Darlene Clark and Jacqueline McLeod, eds. *Comparative History of Black People in Diaspora*. Bloomington: University of Indiana Press, 1999.

Holt, Thomas C. and Elsa Barkley Brown, eds. *Major Problems in African American History*. Vol. I. Boston: Houghton-Mifflin, 2000.

Inkori, Joseph E. and Stanley Engerman, eds. *The African Slave Trade: Effects on Economies, Societies, and Peoples in Africa, the Americas and Europe*. Durham: Duke University Press, 1992.

Jablonski, Nina G. *Living Color: The Biological and Social Meaning of Skin Color*. Berkeley: University of California Press, 2012.

James, C.L.R. *The Black Jacobins: Toussaint L'Ouverture and the Saint Domingue Revolution*. London: Allison and Busby, 1980 [1938].

Jeffrey, Julie Roy. *The Great Silent Army of Abolitionism: Ordinary Women in the Antislavery Movement*. Chapel Hill: University of North Carolina Press, 1998.

Jordan, Winthrop D. *White over Black: American Attitudes toward the Negro, 1550–1812*. Chapel Hill: University of North Carolina Press, 1968.

Kadish, Doris Y., ed. *Slavery in the Caribbean Francophone World: Distant Voices, Forgotten Acts, Forged Identities*. Athens: University of Georgia Press, 2000.

King, Wilma. *Stolen Childhood: Slave Youth in Nineteenth Century America*. 2nd ed. Bloomington: Indiana University Press, 2011.

Klein, Herbert S. *The Atlantic Slave Trade*. Cambridge: Cambridge University Press, 1999.

Klein, Herbert S. and Francisco Vidal Luna. *Slavery in Brazil*. New York: Cambridge University Press, 2010.

Klein, Herbert S. and Ben Vinson III. *African Slavery in Latin America and the Caribbean*. 2nd ed. New York: Oxford University Press, 2007.

Knight, Franklin W. *The Caribbean, The Genesis of a Fragmented Nationalism*. 2nd ed. New York: Oxford University Press, 1990.

Knight, Franklin W. *Slave Society in Cuba in the Nineteenth Century*. Madison: University of Wisconsin Press, 1970.

Knight, Franklin W., ed. *The Slave Societies of the Caribbean*. Volume III of *General History of the Caribbean*. London: UNESCO, 1997.

Kolchin, Peter. *American Slavery, 1607–1877*. Rev. ed. New York: Hill and Wang, 2003.

Lindsay, Lisa A. *Captives as Commodities: The Transatlantic Slave Trade*. Upper Saddle River: Prentice Hall, 2008.

Linebaugh, Peter and Marcus Rediker. *The Many Headed Hydra: Sailors, Slaves, Commoners and the Hidden History of the Revolutionary Atlantic*. Boston: Beacon Press, 2000.

Litwack, Leon F. *Trouble in Mind: Black Southerners in the Age of Jim Crow*. New York: Knopf, 1998.

Litwack, Leon F. *Been in the Storm So Long: The Aftermath of Slavery*. New York: Knopf, 1979.

Lockhart, James N.D. and Stuart B. Schwartz. *Early Latin America: A History of Colonial Spanish America and Brazil*. Cambridge: Cambridge University Press, 1994.

Manzano, Juan Francisco. *The Autobiography of a Slave: A Bilingual Edition* [English-Portuguese], intro. Ivan A. Schulman, trans. Evelyn Picon Garfield. Detroit: Wayne State University Press, 1996.

Mattoso, Katia M. *To Be a Slave in Brazil*. New Brunswick: Rutgers University Press, 1986.

McAlister, Lyle N. *Spain and Portugal in the New World, 1492–1700*. Minneapolis: University of Minnesota Press, 1984.

Meinig, D.W. *The Shaping of America, Volume I: Atlantic America, 1492–1800*. New Haven: Yale University Press, 1986.

Midgley, Claire. *Women against Slavery: The British Campaigns, 1780–1870*. London: Routledge, 1992.

Miller, J.C. *Slavery and Slaving in World History: A Bibliography* (Volume I, 10,344 entries; Volume II, 3,897 entries). Armonk, NY: ME Sharpe, 1999.

Mintz, Steven, ed. *African American Voices: A Documentary Reader, 1619–1877*. 4th ed. Malden: Wiley-Blackwell, 2009.

Moitt, Bernard. *Women and Slavery in the French Antilles, 1635–1848*. Bloomington: Indiana University Press, 2001.

Morgan, Edmund. *American Slavery, American Freedom: The Ordeal of Colonial Virginia*. New York: Norton, 2003 [1975].

Morgan, Jennifer L. *Laboring Women: Reproduction and Gender in New World Slavery*. Philadelphia: University of Pennsylvania Press, 2004.

Morrissey, Marietta. *Slave Women in the New World: Gender Stratification in the Caribbean*. Lawrence: University Press of Kansas, 1989.

Mullen, Edward J., ed. *The Life and Poems of a Cuban Slave, Juan Francisco Manzana*. Hamden: Archon Books, 1981.

Myrdal, Gunnar. *An American Dilemma: The Negro Problem and Modern Democracy*. New York: Harper Brothers, 1944.

Norton, Marcy. *Sacred Gifts, Profane Pleasures: A History of Tobacco and Chocolate in the Atlantic World*. Ithaca: Cornell University Press, 2008.

Paquette, Robert L. and Mark M. Smith. *The Oxford Handbook of Slavery in the Americas*. Oxford: Oxford University Press, 2010.

Parker, Matthew. *The Sugar Barons: Family, Corruption, Empire and War in the West Indies*. New York: Walker and Company, 2011.

Parry, J.H. *The Age of Reconnaissance*. New York: New American Library, 1963.

Parry, J.H. *Establishment of the European Hegemony, 1415–1715: Trade and Exploration in the Age of the Renaissance*. New York: Harper, 1961.

Patterson, Orlando. *Rituals of Blood: Consequences of Slavery in Two American Centuries*. Washington, DC: Civitas/Counterpoint, 1998.

Patterson, Orlando. *Slavery and Social Death: A Comparative Study*. Cambridge, MA: Harvard University Press, 1982.

Peabody, Sue and Keila Grinberg. *Slavery, Freedom and the Law in the Atlantic World: A Brief History with Documents*. Boston: Bedford/St. Martin's, 2007.

Phillips, Ulrich B. *American Negro Slavery: A Survey of the Supply, Employment and Control of Negro Labor as Determined by the Plantation System*. Gloucester: P. Smith, 1959 [1918].

Rawick, George P. *From Sundown to Sunup: The Making of the Black Community*. Westport: Greenwood Publishing, 1972.

Reddock, R.E. "Women and Slavery in the Caribbean: A Feminist Perspective." *Latin American Perspectives* 12, 1 (1985): 63–80. http://dx.doi.org/10.1177/009 4582X8501200104

Rediker, Marcus B. *The Slave Ship: A Human History*. New York: Viking, 2007.

Russell-Wood, A.J.R. *Slavery and Freedom in Colonial Brazil*. Oxford: One World, 2002.

Schwartz, Stuart B. *Early Brazil: A Documentary Collection to 1700*. Cambridge: Cambridge University Press, 2010.

Schwartz, Stuart B. *Slaves, Peasants, and Rebels: Reconsidering Brazilian Slavery*. Urbana: University of Illinois Press, 1992.

Schwartz, Stuart B. *Sugar Plantations in the Formation of Brazilian Society*. Cambridge: Cambridge University Press, 1985.

Sheridan, Richard. *Sugar and Slavery: An Economic History of the British West Indies*. Baltimore: Johns Hopkins University Press, 1974.

Singleton, Theresa A., ed. *The Archaeology of Slavery and Plantation Life*. Orlando: Academic Press, 1985.

Skidmore, Thomas E. and Peter H. Smith. *Modern Latin America*. 5th ed. New York: Oxford University Press, 2001.

Stampp, Kenneth. *Peculiar Institution: Slavery in the Ante-bellum South*. New York: Knopf, 1956.

Sterling, Dorothy. *We Are Your Sisters: Black Women in the Nineteenth Century*. New York: Norton, 1984.

Tannenbaum, Frank. *Slave and Citizen*. New York: Knopf, 1946.

Thornton, John. *Africa and Africans in the Making of the New World, 1400–1800*. 2nd ed. Cambridge: Cambridge University Press, 1998.

Toplin, Brent. *Freedom and Prejudice: The Legacy of Slavery in the United States and Brazil*. Westport: Greenwood, 1981.

Toplin. Robert B. *Slavery and Race Relations in Latin America*. Westport: Greenwood, 1974.

Turley, David. *Slavery*. Malden: Blackwell, 2000.

Van Deburg, William L. *Slavery and Race in Popular American Culture*. Madison: University of Wisconsin Press, 1984.

Vaughan, Alden T. "The Origins Debate: Slavery and Racism in Seventeenth-Century Virginia." *Virginia Magazine of History and Biography* 89, 3 (1989): 311–54.

Wallerstein, Immanuel. *The Modern World System II: Mercantilism and the Consolidation of the European World Economy, 1600–1750*. New York: Academic Press, 1980.

Walvin, James. *Atlas of Slavery*. Harlow: Pearson Education, 2006.

Watson, Alan. *Slave Law in the Americas*. Athens: University of Georgia Press, 1989.

White, Deborah Gray. *Ar'nt I A Woman? Female Slaves in the Plantation South*. New York: Norton, 1985.

Williams, Eric. *Capitalism and Slavery*. Chapel Hill: University of North Carolina Press, 1994 [1944].

Woodward, C. Vann. *The Strange Career of Jim Crow*. 3rd rev. ed. New York: Oxford University Press, 1974 [1955].

Yellin, Jean Fagan. *Women and Sisters: The Antislavery Feminists in American Culture*. New Haven: Yale University Press, 1989.

Index